THE WINE BOOK

Jancis Robinson was born in 1950 and educated at Carlisle High School and St Anne's College, Oxford, where she took a degree in mathematics and philosophy and wrote a food and wine column (called 'Debauch') for the student magazine *Isis*. She spent three years organizing skiing holidays followed by a year in Provence learning about wine from the vineyards around her. Since 1975 she has been on the staff (she is now the editor) of the wine trade magazine *Wine and Spirit*; she also edits the *Sunday Times* Wine Club magazine and a monthly newsletter called *Drinker's Digest*.

THE WINE BOOK

A Straightforward Guide to
Better Buying and Drinking for Less Money

Jancis Robinson

Fontana Paperbacks

First published by Fontana Paperbacks 1979

Made and printed in Great Britain by
William Collins Sons & Co Ltd, Glasgow

To all my friends who have so nobly
shared their bottles with me

Contents

Introduction

This is not 'just another wine book'; it's meant to fill a gap which, incredible though it may seem, still exists in today's wealth of wine literature.

There are some wonderful books on wine for serious students of the subject, and a list of them appears on page 247. But it is by no means so easy to recommend books for people who want a concise, comprehensive guide that has the advantages of a manual and is actually fun to read. There is a tendency in wine guides to whisk the reader, within just a page or two of the preface, straight to the bleak January vineyard, or even to a few metres below it, where he is expected to receive instruction on the influence of geology on the vine – or perhaps to the laboratory where he is to study chemical equations. This book keeps him firmly by the fireside, glass in hand, asking him to step outside only when he's really interested enough to want to.

It is quite true that soil types play an important part in determining a wine's characteristics, and true that it is important to understand the theory of fermentation in any serious study, but there are all sorts of questions about wine that present themselves before that. 'Am I getting the most from this glass of wine in my hand?' 'Why am I not supposed to drink red wines with fish?' 'What sort of wines are particularly good value at the moment?' These are all questions that present themselves immediately to the wine drinker, which is why the main part of this book concentrates on all these practical aspects.

Part Two, the reference section, is no less important – it covers all the necessary basic facts on how wine is made and includes a directory of all the world's best known wines. It can be dipped into or read straight through, but it is the first part of the book which the reader may want to follow up.

This guide to enjoying wine is above all practical, in touch with the fact that wine drinking has changed a great deal over the last decade, as have the sorts of wines most commonly available in the shops. Wine making techniques have changed considerably – the most widespread perhaps being the speeding up of the whole process and the replacement of the traditional wooden cask with the much less *folklorique* stainless steel tank – and have had a considerable effect on the taste of wine.

The range of wines imported, and even made, in this country has broadened even more. In Britain we have long had a tradition for being more catholic in our wine buying than any other country, with centuries-old trading links with Bordeaux (for claret, its red wine), with Portugal (port), with Jerez in southern Spain (sherry) and with Champagne, for whose sparkling wines we have always been one of the most important customers. In more recent years we have imported wine from Australia, Cyprus and South Africa, as well as from the classic wine producing countries of Europe, and now we are seeing more and more wines from South and North America and from Eastern Europe so that the choice can at times seem overwhelming. Because the range in our shops is wider than in any other country, except perhaps for the United States, it makes sense to find out as much as possible about the wines on offer. The more expensive wine becomes, the more expensive are the mistakes in buying a bottle that turns out to be not what was expected.

The aim of this book is to help the wine drinker to avoid making mistakes, and to get as much pleasure as possible from his wine. There is so much pleasure to be had from a glass of even the most modest wine and this book tries to highlight this hedonistic aspect. Wine loving should be a practical, not theoretical, exercise and it is with this in mind that the first chapter is devoted to showing how to get the most from the glass in your hand. You should be able to at least double the pleasure it gives you by following the advice on wine drinking and serving given in Chapter One, none of which requires any detailed knowledge of wine geography, vinification methods or vine growing.

Chapter Two gives very practical advice on how to buy much better wines for less money. Most wine books have steered clear of being so specific in their recommendations, but with an ever-increasing range of wines available from an ever-widening choice of merchants, it seems only fair to tackle the problems that beset the British wine buyer in as much detail as possible. This section includes guidance on buying wine in shops, restaurants, by mail order, at auction and direct from the producer, and attempts to steer a course of common sense and realistic buying through the opportunities available.

The next stage in this 'backwards guide to wine', from mouth back to vine, is keeping, storing and cellaring wine. Again, a practical approach has been adopted with very specific recommendations on what is worth 'laying down' and what should be consumed as soon as possible. In Chapter Four is a brief outline of what wine does to your body rather than your mind or bank balance.

Chapters Five to Nine comprise the reference section, a comprehensive guide to how wine is made and to the wines made in each of the world's wine producing countries. The information is as detailed as possible in a guide of this size, which is almost certain to mean that the author has allowed errors to creep in and apologizes humbly in advance. The emphasis throughout is on value, and if that seems mean it should be seen in the light of the fact that good wine is made in all price brackets and can be glorious. Why waste money on the bad?

The author has been absurdly lucky in the opportunities she has had to sift through the bad and experience the great, for many of those in and around the wine trade have been extremely generous with their time, their knowledge and their corkscrews. But she also has the advantage, in terms of putting this book together, of coming relatively recently into the world of wine, and is still conscious of the quirks, the anecdotes and the peculiarities that fascinate the layman. This book tries to cover all of wine's more entertaining aspects, as well as providing a straightforward, realistic guide to just what a pleasure it can be.

Section I

A GUIDE TO SELECTING AND ENJOYING WINE

1. All about drinking wine

PART ONE: TASTING

Tasting v. drinking – Wine tasting for pleasure – Wine tasting in detail – Seeing – Smelling – Tasting – Assessing – Myth of the superpalate – Factors affecting wine tasting – Formal wine tasting – Opportunities to taste

TASTING V. DRINKING In most fields the practical is a lot more fun than the theory, and this is particularly true as far as wine is concerned. While boning up on exactly what sort of soil is most suitable for the Chardonnay grape, or memorizing the famous 1855 classification of the great châteaux of the Médoc can have advantages for the committed student of wine, the embryonic wine lover can get on quite happily without concerning himself with these details.

Wine is not a difficult subject. The most important part, actually drinking the stuff, is also the easiest. The rest follows naturally if the drinker allows himself to become interested in what he's drinking, which is why this book starts by looking at the all-important practical aspect of wine in the glass. The trouble is that most people, surprisingly enough, don't know how to get the most from what's in their glasses.

Wine drinking can be quite shockingly easy, but drinking without thinking is like hearing without listening. To merely gulp down a liquid that has involved a vineyard owner in at least three years' rearing of the vine before it will bear fruit, a winemaker in a year or more's careful nurturing of the fermented grape juice, and probably a wine broker's careful selection and bottling is like ignoring the work a great composer has put into his music by treating it as Muzak to talk by. A little bit of attention is repaid handsomely. And if a wine seems more of a Mantovani than a Mozart, then at least take notice so that you'll choose something more to your taste next time.

This plea for a moment's consideration when drinking wine is not for the benefit of the winemaker only, but also with the drinker in mind. In countries where wine is very cheap it is quite understandable that it should be regarded with no more reverence than the British accord a cup of tea. But in countries like Britain where duties on wine are so high, wine is an optional extra which deserves as much deliberate appreciation as any other luxury. The pleasure given by a wine can be enhanced immeasurably by thinking as well as drinking. If it's a good wine (and most wines have something to offer) then it's worth savouring. If it's a thoroughly bad wine, then it's worth noticing so as to avoid it in future.

In common parlance, 'wine tasting' is the term for this thoughtful drinking of wine, on this side of the Atlantic at least. Americans sometimes call it 'the sensory evaluation of organoleptic characteristics of wine', but it is much more fun than that long-windedness suggests. Actually tasting, rather than merely drinking, wine requires just a moment's concentration and a bit of background knowledge, and how rewarding it can be.

'Wine tasting' describes a wide range of activities. There are professional wine tastings every day in most major wine businesses at which white-coated laboratory workers 'in QC' (quality control) sniff and spit their way assiduously through a range of wines to make sure that theirs are up to scratch. Then there are professional tastings at which a company invites potential customers to come and taste their way through a range of the firm's wines in the hope of drumming up orders. There are tastings organized by wine clubs designed to make their members more knowledgeable. There are also competitions at which wines are assessed by accredited judges, and those at which wines are served 'blind' (label-less, in order to test the tasters' powers of identification). But the most important 'wine tastings' happen millions of times every evening when ordinary wine drinkers the world over open up a bottle and pour out their first glassful, for this is what wine is all about – giving pleasure to those who drink it sensibly.

If they merely fill the glass, take a mouthful and quickly swallow it they are missing out on all the fun, and they're denying the wine a chance to earn its keep by showing just what it has to offer, what makes it different from any other wine. They're also missing the pleasure of discussing a wine with fellow drinkers – not that a book like this would advocate a compulsory study session of ten minutes after any wine was first tasted in a social gathering, but wines are so very complex and so very variable that a great deal of pleasure can be had from discussion of their characteristics.

The great advantage wine tasting has over many other sorts of connoisseurship is that it's a game anyone can play, and it is often those who have had the least training who are the most perceptive. Many professional wine tasters know of countless occasions on which their rigorously formal comments 'light bouquet, medium sweet, short finish' were put to shame by the incisive 'tastes like fermented bubble gum' of a novice. 'The myth of the super-palate' is examined on page 34.

In blind tasting it is undoubtedly an advantage to have had a great deal of tasting experience on which to draw, but for wine tasting at home there is no need for a great bank of knowledge. Tasting itself prompts the taster to find out more in any case. This contrasts strongly and most attractively with the appreciation of, say, music or the visual arts in which a certain amount of theoretical knowledge is almost essential before one can play an important part in the practical game. Wine tasting is, above all, fun.

WINE TASTING FOR PLEASURE – AN OUTLINE Most people's 'wine tasting' takes place in relaxed surroundings – round the kitchen or the dining-room table – but that is no reason why they shouldn't try to maximize the pleasure they get from wine by finding out a bit more about how it acts on their physical senses. The next section deals with the subject in more detail and is meant as a guide to anyone who wants to take their wine tasting rather more seriously, but here are a few comments on wine tasting for pleasure.

There is a common fallacy that it is impossible to taste without swallowing. Swallowing is not an essential part of wine tasting at all, though it is necessary for those who like to 'metabolize their alcohol'. In fact, there are no taste buds in the throat and so it would be quite possible – though hardly likely – to be a teetotal wine expert. Man's tasting faculties are located at the pre-swallow stage, so that the teetotaller could experience all that a wine had to offer before meticulously spitting out each mouthful. He would probably be a superlative wine taster since his mind would never be clouded by the effects of alcohol, and indeed professional wine tasters make a point of spitting out every mouthful when they are tasting with a view to buying. It is usually wise to be sober when spending large amounts of one's employer's money.

The taste buds of course play an important part in assessing any food or drink, and wine is no exception. The human body has nearly 10,000 taste buds which are concentrated on the tongue, different parts of the tongue being particularly sensitive to different elements of taste. Wine tasters spend a great deal of time rolling wine contemplatively around in their mouths, because it is important to expose every part of the tongue to the wine.

Physiologists have identified four different taste components which are sensed most effectively by the taste buds in four different areas of the tongue. The tip of the tongue is good at measuring sweetness. The front edges detect saltiness, the very back edges pick up sourness or acidity, while the back of the tongue is most affected by bitterness. If all this sounds just a bit too fanciful or convenient, it is enough to think about the idea of drinking unsweetened lemon juice to note a distinct puckering of the back edges of the tongue, or to consider how and where on the tongue one tests a spoonful of soup to see how salty it is.

So sweetness, saltiness, acidity and bitterness are the four basic elements of flavour that taste buds alone can identify. Almost all wines have a trace of sweetness, and just how much will be assessed by the tip of the tongue. Not many wines are salty – though many detect this characteristic in Manzanilla sherry, from the front edges of the tongue. The acidity of wine is a most important element – imagine a mixture of alcohol and sugar and water with no shadow of tartness to liven it up. (For any who find it hard to grasp what acidity is, it is perhaps helpful to point out that lemons are high in acidity, bananas are not.) Bitterness is another component which is not often detectable in wine, though when it is, such as in some Italian reds, it is noticeable on the flat back bit of the tongue.

By relying on his taste buds alone, therefore, the taster is so far able to detect how sweet and how acid his wine is, and by swallowing it he will also be affected by how alcoholic it is. (See Chapter Four for the effects of alcohol on the body.)

But of course wine is very much more than just alcoholic sugarwater with a bit of acidity to give it bite – although it can be difficult to sense much more than this if it is just gulped and swallowed as it is by so many wine drinkers. The gulpers and swallowers might just as well be drinking a mixture of fruit juice and ethyl alcohol for all the benefit they are getting from wine. What gives each wine its own individual character are its deceptively evil-sounding 'esters and aldehydes', chemical compounds present in a particular and precise combination in each wine to form a small but very important three per cent of its volume. Another ninety per cent is made up of boring old water, with the remainder accounted for by alcohol, sugar and a wide variety of different acids.

These compounds cannot be appreciated by the taste buds alone; they need a more sensitive instrument, the nose. It follows, therefore, that to appreciate wine fully it is necessary to deflect attention from the throat to the nose, from the swallow to the smell. In wine tasting jargon, to 'nose' a wine means to smell it. *Always smell, or 'nose', a wine before drinking it.*

The most sensitive part of the human tasting mechanism is at the very top of the nostrils where vapours, such as those of the volatile esters and aldehydes, can be inhaled and absorbed by the cells there. The 'smell' is then whisked off by the olfactory system to the brain which receives messages very much more complex and subtle than the rather crude 'very sweet, quite acid' sort of signal that is all the taste buds are capable of relaying. Vapour can also reach this olfactory centre from the back of the mouth but it is via the nose that the passage is most effective, so 'nosing' is essential to get the most from a wine.

If all this smelling business sounds absurd, consider how much less 'taste' food seems to have to those suffering from a blocked-up nose, and take note of the fact that in controlled laboratory experiments, people whose noses are held apparently find it almost impossible to distinguish between turnips, apples and onions even after chewing them for some time. The sense of smell clearly plays a very important part in the process of tasting anything; think of the effect of good cooking smells on the appetite.

WINE TASTING IN DETAIL What follows is an outline of the classic way to taste wine 'properly', the approach that is used in professional wine tastings and one that can be adapted to suit amateur wine tasters who want to build up their knowledge of wine by the best method available, by drinking and enjoying it. Also included are comments on which bits of this sometimes rather contrived-seeming procedure can be safely transferred to the dining-room without bringing ridicule or loathing upon oneself.

In addition to the senses of taste and the all-important sense of smell, the sense of sight is also used in wine tasting. Though the sense of sight plays a secondary role, sight, smell and taste is the chronological sequence.

In addition to the pure sense of taste, there are also taste-cum-touch sensations. One of red wine's most notable features, tannin, is sensed by a puckering on the inside of the mouth, a sort of taste-cum-touch sensation. Tannin is a natural preservative that occurs in many red wines in varying degrees and leaves the mouth with the same sort of feeling as it has after swallowing some cold tea. Another of these taste-cum-touch sensations is experienced when tasting wines that are high in sulphur dioxide, a chemical used very commonly in winemaking which leaves a dried-out 'prickle' at the back of the throat. But this guide will concentrate on the vital aspects, what can be detected about a wine by the senses of sight, smell and taste.

Stage One: Seeing

The sense of sight in wine tasting is most useful for those who are trying to recognize an unidentified wine in those 'blind' tastings that are so terrifying and so exhilarating at the same time. In the normal course of events it is enough simply to check that the wine is not unhealthily cloudy (a haze, though not a deposit, usually indicates some malady in the wine) and that it is not sparkling if it is not meant to be (a wine that is slightly fizzy is either intended to be 'pétillant' or is going through an unintentional second fermentation in the bottle).

At the moment winemakers take great care that their 'commercial' wines, those that will be drunk within a year or so of bottling, are 'star-bright', crystal clear with no deposit in them. This they can do by constant racking or by filtration (see reference section on winemaking). It is commonly thought that consumers of wine are worried by small pieces of deposit floating in their wine and so there has been considerable investment in methods of 'clearing' wine. In fact these deposits are almost always harmless, a natural by-product of winemaking. They are white in white wines and dyed dark in reds. Some bottles carry warning labels pointing out that any crystals are harmless, as there are winemakers who are either unwilling or unable to filter or fine the crystals out of the wine. No one should be worried by a few small particles in the bottom of a bottle; they will usually be tasteless and the wine can always be poured off them into a decanter. Dead insects are worrying, however. They are indicative of a fairly cavalier attitude towards hygiene.

It is a possibility worth considering that there might be a swing in fashion along the lines of that towards 'real ale' to wine with deposit in it. The public may take it as a sign that the wine has not been over-treated – a sort of wholemeal wine.

There are four main elements to looking at wine:

1. *Clarity*. Make sure that the wine is not hazy; that if there are 'bits' floating in it, they are separate little bits of deposit, not just general murk. Bits of cork floating in a glass of wine do *not* mean the wine is 'corked' (see page 93 for what 'corked' does mean). They mean simply that a little bit of the cork has fallen into the glass and should be lifted out.

2. *Hue*. This can tell the 'blind' taster a great deal about the maturity and provenance of a mystery wine. The best way to assess the exact colour is to tilt the glass against a white background, preferably in strong natural light. There is little point in noting the intricacies of colour in private tasting, however, unless for your own interest's sake or in the unlikely event of your suspecting that a wine is not what it is claimed and this colour evidence vindicates your theory.

White wines go from watery-pale (sometimes with a greenish tinge) to dark tawny-gold with age. Reds go from purple to brownish-red, fading to a watery rim. Certain colours indicate certain geographical areas or grape varieties. This is the moment to get out the magnifying glass and deerstalker if taking part in a blind tasting.

White wines: Colour can vary from almost colourless to brown. Here are some clues –

Almost colourless – Soave, Muscadet, young Germans. Moselles have a slight greenish tinge, as can Chablis. Most Alsace wines.

Pale straw – Standard colour for the majority of whites. Classic young burgundies, white bordeaux, Frascati, Orvieto.

Yellow-gold – A darker colour indicates an older burgundy or very high class sweet German or white bordeaux. Spanish, Portuguese and some Italian and Austrian whites.

Gold – A good sign if this is an old classic. Can be a sign of oxidation, that flat sherry-like staleness resulting from over-exposure to air, in younger wines. A sniff should tell you which it is.

Deep gold – Some sauternes have still not reached their

peak even though they have got almost to an orange colour.

Brown – Unless it is a fortified wine like sherry or madeira, or a really exceptional sauternes, this wine's in trouble.

Red wines: Even more clues from colour here, but descriptions are more difficult. Wine tasters can find themselves quibbling over the exact difference between 'ruby', 'dark red' and 'crimson'.

Purple – Most red wines are purple when young. Depth of colour (see below) can give a clue as to quality and potential. Characteristic of young beaujolais.

Mulberry – If very deep-hued, this could be a Piedmont wine from the Nebbiolo grape, or a north Rhône from the Syrah.

Ruby – Wine on its way towards maturity.

Red – Most wines are ready to drink when their colour can accurately be described by this exasperatingly vague word.

Red-brown – An older wine. If it's still healthily bright then it should be fine, otherwise it may have oxidized.

Definitely brown – This may be very fine, very old and eminently drinkable, or it may be a fortified wine, or it may be vinegar.

Rosé wines: Colour varies tremendously according to the sort of grapes used, the way it was made and how old the wine is.

Pale purple – Could be an Anjou rosé, or a German rosé if it is even paler. If it is almost clear with a slight purplish tinge it may be a California 'blanc de noirs', white wine from red grapes. If the wine is much more intense, it could be a Spanish 'clarete'.

Definite blue tinge is usually a sign of a badly treated wine.

Orange – Common among Provence rosés. There is also a colour called *œil de perdrix* which seems to correspond to a pale orange noticed by those familiar with the eyes of partridges.

3. *Depth of colour*. This is another good indication of age and of where a wine comes from. Red wines tend to become paler with age, white wines become more deeply coloured. The best way to measure depth of colour is to look at the glass of wine from above, again against a white background if possible. (This, like testing colour against a white background in strong natural light, is another trick that is difficult to perform socially without drawing attention to oneself.)

In a fine red wine, made from a good year when the grapes were very ripe and vinified so as to extract as much colour as possible from them, the colour will be very intense and may not fade for several decades. It is certainly easy to think of vintages of first growths which were still rich in colour when fifty and more years old. Great intensity of colour may also indicate certain grape varieties such as the Nebbiolo, the Syrah, or the Cabernet Sauvignon in a ripe year.

A pale red wine may have been made in a 'wet' vintage when rain diluted the colour available, or it may have been made far away from the equator (the reds of Germany and Champagne tend to lack colour), or the winemaker was greedy about the amount of wine he tried to get out of his grapes.

In white wines there are fewer clues from intensity of colour, though it is an important factor in the ageing of great dessert wines which get deeper as they get older.

4. *Viscosity*. Water is not very viscous, golden syrup is. When a viscous wine is twirled round in a glass, it leaves much more noticeable 'tears' or 'legs' on the side of the glass afterwards than others. There has been much discussion of whether this is indicative of high alcohol or high glycerine content. What does seem clear is that it is some indication of how full-bodied a wine is, how much 'weight' or 'body' it has.

Stage Two: Smelling

With its smart name 'nosing', this is commonly accepted

among professionals as being the most telling part of the whole tasting operation – certainly the most revealing in terms of nuances of flavour since, as has been explained above, only the nose is sensitive enough to detect the more subtle aspects of a wine's characteristics. Some tasters even go as far as to say that the palate merely confirms what the nose has already guessed.

The best way to 'nose' a wine is to have it in a suitably shaped glass whose sides come in towards the rim, no more than half full so that the wine can be swilled around in the glass. This action will release those esters and aldehydes, the volatile elements that give the wine its character, by exposing maximum surface area of the wine to the atmosphere and they will collect in the top half of the glass. Hold the glass by the stem (so as not to alter the temperature of the wine), rotate it and take a concentrated but not desperate noseful that will carry the vapours up to the olfactory centre at the top of the nostrils. Scientific experiments have shown that there is a certain optimum level for the strength of the intake of breath needed to identify flavour characteristics, and that straining for a lungful won't make the tasting process any easier. It's that first thoughtful sniff that is the most telling.

It is fascinating to watch professional tasters proceed up a row of perhaps thirty glasses according each just one short, sharp sniff. They know from experience just how easy it is to become confused by continuing to worry over a smell. The first impression is the most important, which is why it is a waste to 'nose' a wine without concentrating – and this applies as much to the dining-room as to the tasting-room. The home-based wine taster will find that he is literally doubling his appreciation of a wine if he gives it a thoughtful sniff before drinking it, though be warned that the habit can become so ingrained in those who taste wine for a living that they provide constant entertainment for their nearest and dearest by 'nosing' every glass set in front of them, whether it is full of wine, orange juice or water.

When 'nosing' a wine the taster is looking at three main aspects:

1. *Cleanliness.* This is a very important quality; no winemaker can be proud of a wine that fails this test, and yet it is the most common fault of inexpensive wine today. Just one smell is enough to let the taster know whether he is repelled or attracted by a particular wine. If the nostrils are already crinkled by the time the nose leaves the glass then there must be something wrong. If there's a smell of wet wood, the wine has been kept in a wooden cask that was in poor condition. A metallic smell may mean there was a small hole by the stave so that metal deposit seeped in.

This may be rare, but a 'corked' or 'corky' wine is even rarer. Nothing to do with bits of cork floating on the surface, this condition, brought on by the exceptional presence of a cork weevil in a cellar or other deterioration of a cork, results in a rotten, musty smell in the wine. Any unpleasant chemical smells are usually a sign that the wine has been mis- or over-treated, although the smell of sulphur dioxide, the winemaker's Dettol, can be removed by swilling the wine around and releasing the gas to the air.

2. *Intensity.* The strength of 'the nose' or smell of a wine can be judged relatively easily. If it is necessary to stick the nose right into the glass before getting any sort of smell at all then the nose is light. If a wine's perfume can be smelt by the taster as soon as he enters the room in which it has been poured then it is intense. Of course the intensity of the smell varies with time. Some great wines go through stages, particularly early in life, when they are described as 'dumb', meaning that they will be much more forthcoming later on. Great wines also open up tremendously during the time they are in the glass, while more blowzy wines will exhibit their charms immediately and then fade rapidly. Sometimes when nosing a fine wine the taster is aware that there are many layers of complexity to the smell, and he has the feeling that he's smelling more than one obvious smell at a time. Some tasters talk about the 'dimensions' of a smell which may sound a bit pretentious but probably serves better than any other term.

3. *Character*. Here comes the difficult bit – how to describe a smell. With variations of colour, or pitch, or human speech, we have an accepted notation. We all agree what we mean by the word 'blue', or middle C, or the letter 'D'. Not so with variations in smell or taste. We have a few words such as 'sweet' and 'salty' that are more reliable than most, but other than that we are woefully short of words to describe flavours. We have to fall back on similarities: 'Smells like a cigar box', or 'reminds me of vanilla' and hope that other people have had the same cigar box-smelling and vanilla-sniffing experiences as we have had. While the smell of a particular wine may drive the taster wild with sensual pleasure, he may be completely unable to find the words to describe it, and indeed having the ability to come up with apposite descriptions of smells and tastes is an excellent qualification for a wine writer: the best ones are distinguished by the way they can conjure up strange but imaginative expressions to describe nuances of flavour. Having the ability to *remember* smells and associate them with others, on the other hand, is an excellent qualification for blind tastings.

What matters for the amateur wine taster is to develop the ability to identify smells, to assess them qualitatively and to retain them to associate with other smells in the future. A great help here are 'trigger words', words which the taster always associates with a particular smell. These will often be words which only he understands – the same smell may provoke a different response in another set of nostrils – but they will be a great help in future wine tasting. Wine tasting becomes fun when the taster has enough impressions stored in his 'smell memory' that he can say just by 'nosing' a wine 'that's a beaujolais', or 'that smells much richer than the '77 we tried last week'.

Any wine comes by its smell in two ways: firstly from the grape and the process of fermenting the grape juice into wine. This is called the 'aroma' of the wine, while the oft-ridiculed word 'bouquet' is used for that smell arising from the development of the wine in bottle.

One of the key factors in a wine's smell is the grape variety used in making the wine, to which there is a guide on pages 121–3. Many wines are made from one predominant grape variety, some of which have such obvious characteristics that they can be recognized after attentive 'nosing' of literally only a couple of samples.

Perhaps the easiest grape variety to identify is Gewürztraminer. This full, rich grape, whose name translated literally means 'spicy Traminer', is at its best in Alsace where it makes pungent dry white wines with a powerful aroma that reminds some of lychees, some of other scented fruit such as mangoes. Anyone who can work out their own trigger word for the smell of 'Gewürz' should be able to recognize it anywhere.

A good distinctive red grape variety is the Gamay that is responsible for the juicy-fruit wines of Beaujolais. One smell of the Gamay grape should be enough to imprint an unusual fruity, almost inky, sensation in the smell memory that will be accompanied by a slight mouthwatery feeling at the back edges of the tongue suggesting that the wine is going to be relatively high in acidity. 'Fresh and fruity' are the hallmarks of beaujolais tasting notes.

Two easy qualities to look for and contrast 'on the nose', as they say, are grapiness and fruitiness. There are certain grape varieties that happen to smell like grapes while most, surprisingly enough, do not – though they smell like other fruits (Gewürztraminer) or just generally fruity (Gamay). The grape variety Muscat and its variants such as Muscadelle and Moscato have a very 'grapey' smell, the sort of aroma that is obvious on the Muscat dessert wines of France and on Asti Spumante.

Some wines smell neither grapey nor fruity; their smells will be reminiscent of something quite different. Many associate good claret with the smell of cedarwood, for example, rioja with vanilla, the Riesling grape with flowers and honey, Condrieu with apricots. These are all well-known trigger words, and there are others that sound, though are not necessarily meant to be, a great deal less complimentary. 'Catspee' is a common reaction to the smell of many German wines; 'goaty' is a word used to describe the Dão wines of Portugal. For an excellent and thorough explanation of the terms commonly used in wine tasting, see Michael Broadbent's book *Wine Tasting* (Cassel and Christie's Wine Publications).

Stage Three: Tasting

This stage follows fairly naturally from the first two; the mouth is usually watering by the time a wine has been examined by eyes and nose – though of course the seeing and smelling stages take much less time to perform than to describe.

As has already been explained, it is vital to be greedy, to get a good mouthful of the wine so that all the sensitive parts of the mouth come into contact with it. And to really appreciate what the wine has to offer it is important to concentrate on the first mouthful rather than just rinsing the mouth in it, for it is first impressions that count. Inside the mouth, on different parts of the tongue, the taste buds get to work gauging the basic elements of sweetness and acidity, the interior of the mouth picks up the tannin content, the back of the throat may react to a high level of sulphur dioxide (which will probably also have been picked up by the nose) and more of the volatile esters and aldehydes are inhaled from the mouth up to the top of the nostrils so that the brain now has a 'cocktail' of all these elements to work on and can come up with a proper appreciation and assessment of the wine.

Some tasters believe that it encourages vaporization of the esters and aldehydes to draw in breath while the wine is in the mouth. This can result in some undignified sights and sounds in the tasting room and is definitely not recommended for the dining-room. Nor is the next vital element in a professional wine tasting – spitting. The reason that most professional wine tasters make a point of spitting out is that they will almost certainly be tasting at least another five wines that day – some of them taste up to a hundred wines in a day when they go on buying trips abroad. They might otherwise end up ordering thousands of cases of mediocre wine just because their five o'clock palate was none too fastidious.

In tasting wine these are the elements which should make an impression:

1. *Sweetness*. This is the sensation most easily felt by the taste buds at the tip of the tongue; the minute some wine is taken into the mouth it should be easy to detect whether it is bone dry, dry, medium dry, medium sweet, sweet or rich. Muscadet is a good example of a very dry white wine, red Loire wines or the more austere wines of the Médoc are very dry reds. We tend to overlook this factor in reds, worrying in our sugarphobe way only whether our whites are sufficiently dry, but in fact there is considerable variation in the sweetness or otherwise of red wines. Italian reds and claret tend to be drier, burgundy, Rhône reds sweeter, with port being the sweetest red wine of all – though it is a fortified, or 'strengthened' wine rather than a light ('table' in pre-EEC parlance) wine.

Some popular red branded wines, such as Britain's best-selling Hirondelle, are really quite sweet, and this doubtless accounts for their initial attraction for newcomers to wine. Most wine lovers follow a pattern of being drawn at first to sweetish wines, then moving determinedly towards wines that are drier, or they think are drier, as fashion dictates and then finally acknowledging that wines of all degrees of sweetness have their place, from the steely dryness of Chablis and Loire wines to the lusciousness of the great dessert wines of Bordeaux and Germany.

The great majority of wine falls into the 'dry' category, 'medium dry' being applicable to many German wines and 'medium sweet' to their richer counterparts. The great dessert wines of the world range over the 'sweet' and 'rich' descriptions. In commercial labelling there can be considerable confusion about the difference between 'medium dry' and 'medium sweet'.

2. *Acidity*. This is the PLJ puckering sensation felt on the

back edges of the tongue. If wine had no acidity it would taste very flat and lifeless. Wines from hot climates, such as those of North Africa, southern Spain and southern Italy, tend to suffer from a lack of acidity because the sun over-ripens the grapes unless they are specifically picked before they are fully ripe, or unless they are acidified by the addition of acid in chemical form. This should not have any serious effects on the taste of the wine if it is done carefully since acids that are naturally present in wine anyway are used.

Wine produced in particularly cool climates can be too high in acidity on the other hand, particularly in a year when there has not been enough sun to ripen the grapes sufficiently. This can be a problem in Europe's northernmost wine-producing regions, though wine can be chemically deacidified by the careful addition of chalk. In the ungenerous year of 1972 much of the wine produced in both France and Germany had to be chemically deacidified.

Acidity is more obvious in dry wines than sweet and indeed it can be difficult at first to distinguish between dryness and acidity in wines that seem very high in both. The key is to concentrate on the different parts of the tongue most sensitive to each element, the tip for dryness, back edges for acidity. Acidity is very important in sweet wines, since the sweeter the wine the more acidity is needed to counterbalance it. This is the key to distinguishing between a sweet wine of great quality and an inferior sweetie. If the mouth is left with a cloying sensation, then the wine did not have enough acidity, but the greatest sauternes and Beerenauslesen, however, rich they are, will have enough acidity to refresh the palate. Whereas tannin is the common preservative in red wines, acidity does the same job of keeping a wine lively while it is maturing for white wines.

Too much acidity for a wine's level of sweetness can be a fault and such a wine may be described as 'green', while the common and uncomplimentary terms for a wine that is not acid enough are 'flat' and 'flabby'. The ideal state is 'well balanced', a wine that has just the right balance between its sweetness and acidity and 'body'.

3. *Body*. This element in a wine, its 'weight in the mouth', is easier to experience than to describe, but with practice the mouth can sense how 'heavy' a wine is very easily. Wines that are full bodied are fortified wines like sherry and port, or rich dessert wines. Light-bodied wines have the weight only of a Moselle or a beaujolais. A red bordeaux is often lighter than a burgundy (though there is a tendency to make burgundy lighter nowadays), while some of the fullest non-fortified wines are Italian classic wines. There is a strong relationship between body and alcohol content – the higher the alcohol content, the 'heavier' the wine – though there's no necessary connection between body and sweetness. Asti Spumante, for instance, is sweet but light, whereas many red Italians are full but very dry.

4. *Tannin*. This is the preservative tasting like cold stewed tea that leaves the mouth puckered up in the taste-cum-touch sensation described already. It finds its way into red wine chiefly from the skins of the grape and will stop a wine from growing old while it is developing to maturity in the bottle. The level of tannin gradually declines so that in perfectly balanced wine it fades just in time to let the glorious flavour, the bouquet, of the wine unveil itself in its fully developed state. It would be unwise of a winemaker to make a great wine that would become fascinatingly complex in the next few decades without ensuring that there was some preservative in there too.

Most great clarets are built to last, though there is a tendency in modern winemaking everywhere to make wines that will mature faster, since today's interest rates and inflation make waiting around for a great wine to mature an expensive business. In great red wines, the winemaker allows the grape skins to stay in contact with the wine for a considerable time so that many potentially great wines are very high in tannin – and can taste almost repellent in infancy. Imagine taking a mouthful of cold stewed tea, lemon juice and extract of oak, for this is what the tannin, acidity and cask mixture can taste like.

Sometimes a shipper will hold a tasting of a vintage that looks as though it will be a classic just a few months after it has been gathered in and turned into wine. The spittoons will undoubtedly be full; the teeth of the tasters will be black and the insides of their mouths dried out by the harsh young tannic wines. The skill of tasting in this context lies in assessing what a wine will taste like in twenty and more years. This can be confusing, for experienced tasters may well rave over a wine that tastes extremely unattractive to the novice. They are usually talking about potential, not actuality.

Tannin comes not only from grape but also from the wood in which the wine has been stored. The newer the cask and the longer the wine has been stored in it, the more tannin it will absorb. There are wines in which the tannin is too high, usually because they've been kept in wood too long. The wine will be dried out and well past its best before the tannin has faded. This is a taste which seems not as unattractive to the Italians as to the British.

5. *Flavour*. This is closely related to the character of the smell, and as difficult to describe; yet it is its most important aspect. There are certain terms which have a more or less agreed definition, but they are no better than any others which may occur to the taster. Wines that have not enough acidity, for instance, are often described as 'flabby', while those that have too much acidity may be called 'green'. Again, see Michael Broadbent's book *Wine Tasting* for accepted vocabulary. This is the distinguishing mark of any wine and it is a wonder that the fermented juice of the grape can produce such a variety of different flavours.

6. *Length*. The length of time the taste of a wine lingers after it has left the mouth (front or back door) is a telling measure of the quality of a wine. A great wine will leave behind a marvellous reflection of itself, a sort of glow that can be savoured for several minutes while it keeps on making impressions on the brain. A lesser wine tends to make a

quick getaway and set the hand searching for the glass so as to repeat the experience and see what the wine really did taste of. This is why one bottle of very good wine can in some circumstances last as long as two of coarse everyday wine.

Tasters talk about the 'finish' of a wine. If it had a 'short finish', it lingered not, while wines with a 'long finish' left their mark.

Stage Four: Assessing

Strange that just one mouthful of wine could give rise to all the prescriptive comments given above. Reactions on the senses are always difficult to verbalize but, with wine, delightfully easy to experience. Putting together all these elements, the wine taster will have a good idea of the overall quality of the wine – and if he's tasting blind he may well have a suspicion as to its identity.

In the normal course of wine drinking at home it is enough to note how enjoyable a wine was; whether it was good value; whether it was ready to drink or could do with being left for a while before being drunk; whether further stocks should be laid in?

At professional wine tastings, on the other hand, notes are always taken, for if a detailed opinion of a wine is needed that is the only safe way of ensuring that an objective record of impressions is kept. There are even those who diligently keep a record of every single wine that they taste – not just in the course of work, but also at play.

Notes on wine tasting are usually presented in the sort of form shown opposite:

If trying to judge the relative merits of a range of wines, a useful exercise is to award them points in addition to making notes. This may smack of ice-skating competitions but if the range of wines is sufficiently narrow (there is little point in trying to assess a '76 hock against a '72 claret for instance) this does concentrate the mind wonderfully. Scores out of ten or twenty are usually easiest.

Wine	*Appearance*	*Nose*	*Palate*	*Conclusions*
Oberemmeler Scharzberg Riesling Spätlese 1971 (von Kesselstatt)	Pale straw, slight greenish tinge	Good quality Riesling nose with some age	Light-bodied with the acidity of a Moselle. Very well-balanced	Superior Moselle from an exceptionally good vintage. Will not get much better
Moulin-à-Vent, Domaine Charvet 1976 (Georges Duboeuf)	Healthy crimson with purple edge	Very powerful fruity nose	Still noticeable acidity and a bit of tannin. Concentrated Gamay flavour	An exceptional beaujolais – one that will keep and probably lose its strong Gamay character to taste more like a Côte d'Or wine
Ch. d'Angludet, Margaux 1975 London bottled	Very good deep purplish-red	Concentrated Cabernet Sauvignon with hint of wood	Noticeably high tannin. Dry with lots of fruit and long finish	Claret from a very concentrated vintage that will take many years to mature
Ch. Filhot 1973 Château bottled	Deep gold and high in viscosity	Heady, syrupy smell	Burnt caramel, some acidity but well-balanced, lively wine. Medium finish	A sauternes lacking the concentration and staying power of a great vintage. Not for keeping

THE MYTH OF THE SUPERPALATE It is commonly thought that wine tasting, like painting or composing, is a god-given gift, that there is a small elite of the human race that has been endowed with a sort of Superpalate that puts their tasting abilities far above those of ordinary mortals. It has been shown, however, that almost anyone can through hard work develop their palates so that they can compete on equal terms with the 'experts' (though very few people would ever admit to being a wine expert – the most modest are usually the most knowledgeable).

Developing into a good wine taster is a bit like becoming a good skier. There are a few, a very few, who are precluded from acquiring the skill because of some physical disability, but for most people it is simply a matter of training. The most difficult examination in the British wine trade is set every summer for aspiring 'Masters of Wine', of whom there are still only about 100 because the tests, both practical and theoretical, are so rigorous. In the practical examinations those that succeed in becoming 'MWs' may have to identify up to thirty wines served 'blind'. In the weeks leading up to the exam the candidates, like carefully nurtured athletes in pre-Olympic training, are coached with trials of up to forty anonymous wines each day. Sure enough most of them develop, through physical persistence, the ability to pick out the distinguishing characteristics of most wines. Similarly there are those who because their work requires them to taste wine every day, can often identify, as a party trick, the vintage and château of the wine in their host's decanter.

Frightening stuff and all a game in the sense that there are few practical uses in being able to identify unidentified wines, just as there are few directly practical uses to being a first-class chess player or solver of crossword puzzles. For the ordinary wine lover it is enough to develop tasting ability so that he is able to appreciate all the components of a wine, and to compare and contrast different wines. This exercise is particularly interesting if wines from the same place but different vintages are examined together (a so-called 'vertical tasting') or wines from the same vintage but different sources (a 'horizontal tasting') are tasted. Learning to taste wine rather than just drinking it dramatically increases the amount of pleasure it can give, and the value of its impact on life.

FACTORS AFFECTING WINE TASTING 'There are no great wines, only great bottles of wine' is by now a common saying in the wine trade. The wine taster's reaction to a particular wine can be affected by an enormous number of factors, including the state of a particular bottle but also ranging from the weather to how his fellow tasters are behaving.

It is important to be careful about what was in the mouth immediately before wine tasting. Toothpaste is a killer for the taste of any wine, and yet it is surprising how many people take care to brush their teeth before going out for the evening – even if they expect to savour a wine soon afterwards. The more pleasurable alternative is to brush teeth in ordinary water and if necessary use a mouthwash like Listerine which for some reason doesn't seem to affect the taste of wine adversely. Cough medicines, peppermints and most other confectionery can also spoil wine. Food and drink that is high in acidity affects the taste of wine – anything vinegary or with lots of lemon juice does wine no justice at all – and very strongly flavoured foods like curry can overwhelm most wines. See page 49 for more on food and wine combinations.

The order in which wines are tasted can also affect the wine taster's reactions. If a delicate German wine is tasted after a full-blooded Châteauneuf-du-Pape, for instance, the white will fade into insignificance by comparison. The generally accepted order is white before red, dry before sweet, lesser before greater. It is most flattering to ascend towards the greatest wine, making sure that quantities have not been so liberal on the way up that the taster forgets to look at the view when he's reached the top.

Wine can also vary considerably from bottle to bottle, even if the bottles have come from the same vat originally. A particular bottle may have been stored badly, left too close to the artificial strip lighting in a shop and become oxidized or perhaps one bottle has been corked badly. There is more variation between bottles of older wines because they have had longer to develop differences.

A wealth of psychological factors also play a part in how a taster reacts to a wine. Even the finest rioja will have its work cut out to impress someone prejudiced against Spanish-wine-full-stop if it is poured from a bottle so labelled, whereas the same wine poured from an unlabelled decanter might provoke quite a different reaction. Similarly there is the power of autosuggestion. It is seriously damaging to the mental health of any wine taster to hear the comments of anyone else before he's made up his mind independently about a particular wine. Like sheep we follow the lead of the first comment made if we are in the slightest doubt ourselves. And the taster's general frame of mind can affect the way he feels about tasting. There are those who claim never to be able to taste on a Sunday, or a Monday, or on the day they get their electricity bill.

And then there's the weather. How delicious a chilled, uncomplicated white can be on a sweltering hot summer's day. How mean and thin it can seem when tasted in mid-winter. A tasting of even superb reds can be ruined if the room is too hot and wines start to disintegrate. Proper cellars have the advantage of providing constant cool for professional serious tastings.

At such events smoking and any strong scents and after-shaves are frowned upon. Both can distract from the smell of the wine itself, though it would surely be churlish to insist on this professional rule's being kept by guests at home. Oddly enough wine tasting abilities do not seem to be seriously affected by whether the taster is a cigarette smoker. Many with fine palates are nicotine as well as alcohol enthusiasts.

A TYPICAL FORMAL TASTING This short description is intended for those who are invited to taste wine in formal or professional circumstances, to prevent them from putting their foot in the spittoon, so to speak.

Tasting wine abroad in the *caves* is the most exhilarating and the most demanding exercise. The *caviste* leads the way along rows of casks to extract a sample of cold, young wine from one of them. Spit it out on to the floor and tell him how good it's *going* to be.

Formal wine tastings back home are usually selling exercises of one sort or another and often take place in old cellars, difficult to run to earth under the pavements of narrow alleyways. The senses are thought to be in their best condition in mid-morning, so tastings can start as early as ten o'clock when the first of the worthy wine buyers arrives to find the wines laid out in long rows along trestle tables covered with white cloths, dotted with candles so that the colour of the wine can be seen properly. Tasting sheets, lists of the wines and their prices with a space for notes, are handed out to all comers who are expected to take notes in the prescribed form – though many resort to their own shorthand. Also on the table are pitchers of water for rinsing glasses and palates, and often plates of cheese and/or dry biscuits for those who want to sop up the wine, or forgot to have breakfast.

Each taster is given a suitable tasting glass, though if there are very few tasters and some expensive wines, one glass in front of each bottle may be shared by everyone. This is not for the cold-ridden or over-fastidious, but is perfectly healthy otherwise since alcohol is an antiseptic. The taster proceeds to the first wine that interests him (they are usually arranged in a sensible tasting order) and pours himself or is poured a tasting sample of wine, somewhere between a centimetre and an inch deep.

He then follows the prescribed tasting procedure, making notes all the while. Looking, twirling and 'nosing', and finally the swilling, gargling and spitting. It is worth noting that neatness and accuracy of a spit is a good measure of the professionalism and experience of the taster. Pamela Vandyke Price suggests practising in the bath. Spittoons can vary from a box filled with woodshavings to special waist-high funnels. The taster then finishes his notes and, with determined stride, empties the remains of his first wine into the empty bottles provided on the table and proceeds to the next wine.

It should be said that this self-restrained spitting is often followed by a rather more convivial session at which a glass or two of wine is actually *drunk*.

OPPORTUNITIES TO TASTE For those who want to get together with others interested in wine there are wine societies all over the country that combine education with fun. The magazine *Decanter* often carries letters from people advertising the existence of these tasting groups in various corners of Britain.

Most of the wine clubs listed on page 84 also run regular tastings, some of them strictly social, some strictly business and some very instructive. In addition to these clubs engaged in selling wine, there is the large International Wine and Food Society, 104 Pall Mall, London SW1 which is just what it says. Founded by Britain's doyen of gastronomy André Simon more than a century ago, the Society now has members all over the world and in this country specializes in putting on tastings, often highflown with prices to match. Membership is £7.50 a year.

In addition to these tasting opportunities there are also local authority evening classes on wine appreciation, always as good as the person conducting them. There is also the Wine and Spirit Education Trust, Five Kings House, Kennet Wharf Lane, Upper Thames Street, London EC4. The Trust's job is to run courses all over the country at different levels up to Master of Wine standard for members of the wine trade. They are not too strict in their definition of what constitutes 'being in the trade' and the courses are well worthwhile for anyone seriously interested in wine.

And then there are private tastings. Six friends can get to taste and compare six different wines in return for bringing just one bottle. A co-operative non-participant can even make these 'blind' tastings.

PART TWO: SERVING

Temperature – Opening the bottle – Decanting – Glasses – What to drink when – Leftovers

So much for how to get the most from the wine in your glass. Here is how to make sure that the wine in your glass is at its best.

TEMPERATURE The general rule that white wine should be served chilled and red wines at room temperature tends to be taken to extremes nowadays; restaurants serve white wines so cold and install them in ice buckets so glacial that their taste is iced into nothingness, and red wines are sometimes warmed to such an extent that they are on the threshold of a mull.

White wines and rosés do need a bit of chilling before they seem truly appetizing. Their lightness and fragrance calls for a temperature of about 45°F, rosés perhaps slightly warmer. A light chill, but not a freeze – unless the wine is so unpleasant that the only way to drink it is to numb the taste buds. The sweeter a wine is, the more it will need chilling, but a number of dry whites, particularly the better quality wines, need be only what is called 'cellar cool', i.e. the temperature of the ideal cellar, about 50°F.

The simplest way to chill a white wine is to put it in the fridge for an hour or so, taking care to put it upright should there be any sediment in the bottle. A quicker method is to use an ice bucket, or any container that will hold a wine bottle, some water and about a dozen ice cubes. This water and ice mixture is more effective than straight ice would be, incidentally. The only trouble with this method, which is also excellent for keeping wine cool once it has been opened and invaluable for drinking in the hot outdoors, is that the neck of the bottle is left unchilled. If the capsule, the metal or plastic seal over the cork, is kept on and there is no sediment, there is no harm in inverting the bottle in the ice bucket for a few minutes before the wine is opened so that the first few inches of wine are as cool as the rest. You can also, in moments of desperation, put wine in the freezer compartment of a fridge for fifteen minutes or so, but this is too severe and uneven for fine wines. There is nothing wrong with adding ice cubes to an ordinary wine, red or white, for a refreshing drink, though it would be foolish with anything better than every-day wine. The volatile elements of most red wines vaporize at a rather higher temperature than those of white, so it makes sense to serve reds warmer than whites if they are to give their all to the taster. Between 60°F and 65°F is the generally accepted optimum temperature – the temperature of a room not in a centrally-heated town house, but in a more spartan country house, the sort of rooms that were meant when the expression 'room temperature' was first prescribed. It is worth remembering that wine will warm up while it is in the glass, particularly in a well-heated house, so it is better to serve wine too cool than too hot. If it gets too hot, wine will start to become cloudy, may show distinct signs of turning to vinegar, and nothing can be done to save it except the swift addition of cinnamon, sugar and lemon peel.

Life is easy for those lucky enough to have a suitable cellar and a life that is organized enough for them to use it properly. White wines can be fetched as required and with red wine they merely make sure that it is brought up from the cellar the day or morning before it is needed and stood in a temperature of about 60°F so that it comes gently to the point of perfection. But few of us are so well-equipped and well-prepared. It is all too often the case that one finds oneself with a chill bottle of red wine bought at the off-licence on the corner and half an hour to get it to the right temperature.

The most important thing to remember is that the warming process should be as gradual as it can possibly be. Wine is not shock resistant. If the wine needs no decanting, put it in a warm but not hot place. A good rule to follow is not to put the bottle anywhere where one side of it might get hotter than another. Somewhere in the kitchen is usually ideal – though not too near the cooker – and mantelpieces can be good too. Most airing cupboards and the top of radiators will be too hot.

A more efficient method involves pouring the wine into a decanter (or old bottle) which has been rinsed out with tepid water and then standing this container in water that is just slightly warmer than the desired 60°F. If neither of these courses of action are possible because the bottle has to be transported to a friend's house, then the only alternative is to identify the warmest-thighed member of the party and leave the bottle in her charge for the rest of the journey.

In these circumstances, and when choosing wine for any occasion such as a picnic when the question of temperature may be beyond your control, there is a class of wines that are particularly suitable. Many light red wines such as beaujolais, Gamay de Touraine and other red Loires like Chinon and Bourgeuil, Valpolicella and Bardolino, and some of the lighter reds of the Midi and Provence, are delicious when served at the annoyingly typical off-licence shelf temperature that is too hot for white wines and too cool for most reds. The slight chill makes the best of their relatively high degree of acidity.

Fortified wines, being stronger, can stand up to a wider variation in temperature. Vermouth, dry sherry such as a fino or manzanilla, and white port are best chilled or even with ice – indeed the port shippers' favourite aperitif is dry white port with ice cubes and a twist of lemon rind. Room temperature is fine for most other fortified wines though one of the more commercial sweeter sherries won't be spoilt by the addition of ice cubes on a summer's day.

Sparkling wines should be served well chilled, the better ones slightly less so – and care should be taken not to shake them about. The warmer and more shaken up the bottle is, the more unnecessary fizz there will be.

OPENING THE BOTTLE There are two things which are the bane of the wine drinker's life – third-rate corks and thick plastic capsules. They can turn an evening into a struggle and put everyone into a very bad mood indeed. The cost of a decent lead capsule and good quality cork (the fewer markings on it the better) is minuscule, but when multiplied by the thousands of bottles sold by a shipper it must add up, for they make their appearance all too rarely now. Old bordeaux bottles were always graced by a cork a good two inches long protected by a metal seal that needed only the point of a corkscrew to unloosen it instead of the unseemly battle usually needed with the impenetrable plastic.

The strange thing is that only the top five per cent or so of wines need a cork and capsule at all. An ordinary screw cap would be quite adequate for most wine, since it remains in the bottle only a matter of months, sometimes weeks or even days. With wine becoming a mass-market commodity, *le cash flow* becomes all-important, and wine shippers now like to sit on their stocks for as short a time as possible. The cheaper wines will be bottled when an order comes through and dispatched immediately. Supermarket owners don't like to see bottles in their warehouses either, so they're put on the shelf straight away and if the housewives don't snap them up at once that line will be dropped from the store.

The point of using a cork as a stopper is that it can resist the effects of alcohol for long periods of time and allows very small amounts of air into the bottle which is thought to be the gradual process through which wine slowly develops and reaches maturity. But today the amount of maturing a supermarket wine is able to do in bottle is negligible. An ordinary screwcap would make no difference to the taste of the wine and would actually be easier to undo than all the cork-pulling business. But market research has apparently told the marketing men that we enjoy pulling corks. It is all part of the ceremony we associate with wine – that lovely Centre Court forehand pop that sets the gastric juices running, the psychological implications perhaps of the action. Wine without a cork still seems a bit of a cheat to most Britons somehow, so it will probably be some time before we can throw out our corkscrews.

The first thing to do when opening a conventionally

capsuled and corked bottle is to remove the capsule. The standard method is to cut it either with a knife or the point of a corkscrew round a line about quarter of an inch below the rim of the bottle. That way the capsule is still visible, it being polite to give one's guests some idea of the wine's identity, and there is no fear of contamination from the metal of the capsule. If the capsule is made of plastic, however, the whole business is usually much more difficult. There are people who incline to the view that those who encase their bottle necks in plastic should supply a free laser kit with every bottle.

Once the capsule has been cut the rim of the bottle should be wiped clean if it looks mouldy, as this may affect the taste of the wine too.

There are many different sorts of corkscrews, each with its own quirks and devotees. The best advice is to head for the most functional but not to economize. Good corkscrews seem to be one of those items often ignored by those equipping a house, like my friends who spent the first three years of their married life tussling with a small Swiss Army penknife and an average consumption of a dozen bottles a week. The most efficient corkscrew is a simple flat spiral screw with a sharp point on the end, but the screw must not be a googly. Good value corkscrews can be found in junk shops while cheap modern versions are usually rather on the puny side.

Another reliable sort is the metal double action one that works on the principle of leverage of its two arms, particularly good for recalcitrant corks. Their wooden counterparts are not usually so easy to handle as it is difficult to see exactly what is going on. An instrument popular in the United States is the 'butler's friend', so called because its two parallel prongs can be inserted either side of a cork, the cork extracted and then reinserted without any telltale marks. (The butler perhaps had a friend who supplied capsules.) Butler's friends can react badly with loose corks while the appliances which pump CO_2 into bottles by means of a needle inserted into the cork can be just too dramatic by a bottle.

A particularly stubborn cork can sometimes be moved by running the bottle neck under a hot tap, taking care not to wet the cork, so that the bottle expands. Failing all else, the cork can sometimes be pushed down into the wine with a clean chisel or similar instrument and the wine decanted, cork held down all the while, into a decanter or jug.

Sparkling wine calls for a different technique altogether. Take off the metal foil and undo the wires, making sure that the wine is not ready to push off the cork without your help. Then take the cork firmly in the right hand and, keeping it steady, *twist the bottle round* with the left hand, all the time holding the cork into the bottle so that when it starts to 'give', the cork can be eased very gently off with a sigh, not a pop. That way there is neither waste nor danger.

With still or sparkling wine, the more shrivelled the cork and the more deposit there is on it, the longer it has been in the bottle since the *dégorgement*, the removal of the deposit and final corking. If it is still springy and clean then the wine was corked or re-corked recently. Corks are a good way of telling where a wine was bottled. If it carries a number preceded by the letter W then it was bottled in the United Kingdom.

DECANTING The strange ritual of pouring wine from its original container to another strikes at the very heart of those who are put off by wine lore and wine snobbism (though it may be the saving grace of hosts who like to hide their wines' humble origins). The practice originated when wines of the day, old claret and port, threw a heavy sediment in the bottle. The traditional procedure was to descend to the cellar, having first checked the evening's menu with cook, to withdraw suitable bottles from a 'bin' of a particular wine, bottle stacked on bottle to rest, to uncork them and decant them against the light of a candle. The decanters of nice clear wine would be taken up to the dining-room to come to the right temperature and to 'breathe' before the evening's feast.

That was a century ago, but cellars, bins and candles just don't seem to fit into today's world somehow – not that there is the same need to decant most of the wine we drink today. As already explained, only a small proportion of the wines we drink today throw a deposit – fine bordeaux, older burgundy vintages and vintage port are the exception.

If it is necessary to decant a wine, fortified or light, off its sediment, make sure that the sediment is firmly collected on either the belly (if the bottle has been lying on its side) or the base (if it has been standing up) of the bottle and pour the wine slowly but steadily into a clean vessel against a strong light, though not necessarily a candle, so that the sediment can be seen clearly. The pouring should stop as soon as the dreggy bits at the end are reached. An alternative to this is to pour the wine through a funnel lined with a coffee filter, muslin, or similar material. This helps nicely with the second reason for decanting, aeration.

The process of ageing for a wine is closely linked to the action that air has on it. Over the years minute amounts of air will enter a bottle through the cork and react with the wine to soften and ripen it to maturity. This is the process of ageing 'discovered' by Pasteur in the last century. It follows, therefore, that if a wine can be exposed to greater amounts of air by pouring it from one vessel to another, there will be some simulation of this ageing process. This is why decanting a wine is so much more effective than merely removing the cork and allowing a wine to 'breathe', which exercise is virtually pointless except for any wines, some cheaper reds, which happen to have an unpleasant-smelling vapour between the cork and the wine.

Decanting is therefore a useful exercise for wines that need to be helped along the way to maturity, though can be dangerous for those on their last legs. The younger and harder the wine, the more the aeration given by decanting will benefit it. A more venerable wine may need decanting because of the sediment, but it is often safer just to stand the bottle upright and pour carefully.

White wines can benefit from aeration as well as red, but the decanter will have to be put into a cool place like the fridge or ice bucket. With white wines and the more mature reds it is often enough just to pour from a height above the glass so that the wine receives a certain amount of aeration then. Air will act on wine in the glass in any case – unless the glass is held by a very keen drinker indeed.

The exact shape of the decanter or any second vessel is not critical. A jug will do, and it may even improve young reds because it allows more of the wine to be exposed to the air. What is important is that the material does not taint the wine, which is why it should be glass, not metal, and always clean and free from any smells. The best way to keep a decanter or decanter-substitute clean is to wash it with hot water (but not detergent) immediately after use and to keep it filled up with clean water so that it gets neither dusty nor smelly.

Try leaving stained decanters full of vinegar or Steradent overnight for a day or two to lift off the grime, but rinse thoroughly at least five times afterwards.

This is a rough guide to how to deal with various sorts of wines in terms of temperature and decanting:

Most whites, and rosés: Chill, open just before serving but try pouring from a height to give them a little bit of air.

Whites with a sediment: Decant and put the decanter in an ice bucket half an hour before serving.

Young reds high in acidity: Chill for a quarter of an hour and open just before serving.

Cheaper medium- to full-bodied reds: Open and decant one to two hours before.

Better quality full-bodied reds: Open and decant up to four hours before.

Better quality medium-bodied reds up to fifteen years old: Open and decant two hours before, more for younger wines, less for older.

Very old reds: Open just before serving and pour carefully.

Baskets or wine cradles are much loved by fancy restaurants and again originated from the time when most wine had a sediment and they allowed a bottle minimum disruption between bin and table. They are little more than an affectation now, particularly considering the careless treatment that wine gets in many restaurants. They take up considerably more space on the usually cramped table than a straightforward bottle or decanter, and (is this why restaurateurs like them?) make it considerably more difficult for diners to judge how much wine they have left in the bottle.

GLASSES It is surprising how different wine can taste from different drinking vessels, though happily the best glasses are not necessarily the most expensive. Why is it that tea tastes best out of bone china, beer out of pewter, and wine out of thin glasses, while metal and pottery seem to have an adverse effect on the taste of wine? The reasons may be mainly psychological, but there is some sound physical back-up evidence too. Glass imparts no flavour to the wine at all, it does not affect its temperature in the way that metal goblets do, and it allows the drinker the pleasure of seeing its colour and clarity, both of which help in anticipation. To get the most from a wine it is important to drink it from a glass with a stem so that it can be held and twirled to release the flavour without affecting the temperature of the wine – this is particularly important with whites. Reds may need to be warmed by cupping the bowl of the glass with the hand. So that the wine can be swilled around to allow the released esters and aldehydes to vaporize, it is helpful if the glass goes in towards the rim, and if it is big enough so that when it is only a third to a half full this is still a generous measure. This stops the wine from spilling out when it is being rotated and the empty top half of the glass will 'collect' the flavour of the wine. For serious wine tasting coloured and cut glass is frowned upon since it makes it more difficult to examine the colour and clarity of the wine (which was the very reason why glasses were so fancy in the days when winemakers were less skilled).

The ideal glasses, therefore, are clear, uncut and with a bowl or tulip shape. Paris goblets, almost spherical bowls on two-inch stems that are available very cheaply from many chain-stores are quite adequate for wine tasting. The finer the quality of the glass the more pleasure it gives, but this is a nicety rather than an essential. Wine merchants Berry Bros & Rudd of St James's Street, London SW1 have traditionally imported excellent glasses that are made specially for them.

Despite what some glass manufacturers may suggest, there is no need at all to have a great battery of glasses, a set for hock (Rhine wine), another for burgundy and so on. The simple shape described above is quite adequate for all light still wine, for sparkling wine and, filled only one third full, could even be used for fortified wines and brandy. The champagne saucer, supposedly modelled on the shape of Marie Antoinette's breasts, has now been thoroughly discredited since it allows the bubbles of sparkling wines to dissipate too quickly and is also too easy to knock over. Nowadays the standard wine glass or a trumpet-shaped champagne *flûte* is usually used. For fortified wines, smaller versions of the wine glass can be used, bearing in mind that they are up to twice as strong as light wine. The traditional sherry *copita* with its tulip shape can be ideal for serious wine tasting since it concentrates the 'nose' of a wine in its deep narrow bowl.

The most important aspect of a wine glass other than its shape is that it should be completely clean. It is best not to use detergent as this can leave a taste and, if not rinsed off properly, will affect the sparkle of a sparkling wine. Care should be taken that glasses are dried hot with a cloth that imparts no smell or fluff, and that they are stored away from anything strong-smelling. Some wine producers rinse out each glass with wine before allowing them to be used for tasting. This may seem excessive, but it can be worth sniffing each glass before use.

Another recognized drinking vessel in the wine world is the tastevin, those silver saucers which dangle on sommelier's chests. They are meant to highlight the colour of a wine and are rarely used nowadays outside Burgundian cellars.

WHAT TO DRINK WHEN Some of the worst bits of wine pseudery are written and spoken about combinations of food and wine; there are some who maintain for instance that Ch. Malescot St Exupéry 1962 is the *only* thing to drink with veal kidneys Bercy, that anyone who suggests anything other than Quarts de Chaume with peaches must be mad. Far be it from the spirit of this book to be so blinkered and so dogmatic. It is a pity that the subject of what to drink with what perplexes so many people when in fact it matters remarkably little.

Of course it is great fun to try to match wines to food, to find particularly apt combinations, but to show just how arbitrary our supposed 'rules' about the subject are it is enough to consider habits in other countries. The French usually drink sweet wines *before* meals - sauternes is a common aperitif in the Bordeaux region, while the local red wine is often drunk with strawberries. The Portuguese like nothing better than a glass of red wine with their delicious Atlantic seafood, and the Germans choose to drink their wines with no food at all.

There are a few, very few, combinations of food and wine that do not work because the mixture brings out the worst in each, but other than these, there is a whole field of delicious and often unlikely partnerships to be explored by those who are prepared to experiment. Sauternes, the sweet white wines of Bordeaux, are usually thought of as an accompaniment to pudding, but can be delicious with many sorts of cheese, particularly strong blue cheeses like Roquefort, and the French, always game for a gastronomic treat, recommend it with foie gras.

When working out which foods to avoid, it is worth remembering the old port trade maxim 'buy on an apple, sell on cheese', meaning that the tartness of an apple makes wine seem worse, while the mellowness of most cheeses flatters the taste of wine. Most foods that are very high in any sort of acidity spoil a fine wine.

Here are a few combinations to avoid:

Full, tannic red wines with fish: A light red with some

acidity like the red vinhos verdes drunk in Portugal can be delicious with fish – indeed fish needs a bit of acidity to show at its best, hence all those recipes with lemons and capers – but most fish will taste a bit metallic if drunk with full, round red wines. Don't waste a good heavyweight red on a subtle fish dish as it will overpower the food.

Expensive wines with eggs, sharply dressed salads, highly spiced foods and strongly flavoured cheeses: This is just to save unnecessary waste of money. Eggs in most forms, unless they play a very minor role in a dish, tend to coat the mouth making it difficult to taste the nuances of flavour in a fine wine (besides, they perhaps belong too firmly to the breakfast table in our minds to go with wine?). Try a fino sherry or any inexpensive light wine. Sharply dressed salads also coat the mouth in acidity, making it difficult to taste well. If the salad is a side dish it is enough to take a mouthful of something innocuous like bread before going back to the wine if you want to enjoy it properly. If it is the main dish, a salade niçoise perhaps, choose a light red like valpolicella or a dry rosé, Provence being the most appropriate choice in this case. As for highly spiced foods like curries, beer or water are the most sensible choice, with a chilled fairly assertive white for those who can't bear to desert the grape. Provided the food is spicy but not inflammatory, a strongly flavoured dry white such as a Gewürztraminer can stand up to it. Otherwise, try a vouvray or a fuller-bodied Italian white like an Orvieto or Frascati. Chinese food is often rather sweet and jasmine tea is a delicious accompaniment. Or try a cabernet rosé d'Anjou or another medium dry wine. Strongly flavoured cheeses can completely overpower fine, elegant wines. Go for a very assertive red like a Rhône or heavyweight Spanish or Italian, or perhaps for a sweet wine.

Red wine and puddings: Red wine can be good with fruit, as witness the Bordelais predilection for claret and strawberries, and dishes like pears or peaches in red wine, but it does not usually make a good foil for any richer dish. With most puddings serve a sweet white wine from Bordeaux, Germany, the Loire or perhaps Hungary, or champagne of any degree of sweetness, or nothing at all. With chocolate it's difficult to find anything that tastes right. A glass of milk perhaps?

Apart from these inadvisable combinations, try anything once. Some sorts of red wine can be delicious with fish. And no thunderbolt from on high will strike those who want to drink white wine with meat, or anything else for that matter.

Here are some outline suggestions for the general categories of wine that are most useful for different sorts of occasion, either when entertaining or in more ordinary circumstances. A guideline for quantities the host should lay in is, very roughly and pretty generously, a bottle of wine a head. That way, late-night panics should be avoided with all but the thirstiest of guests.

Aperitifs: Wine can be a very satisfactory and economical alternative to spirits for pre-prandial drinking. Spirits tend to blunt the brain and the appetite whereas wine seems to leave the palate on edge ready for the food. Sherry and vermouth are easy to serve and bottles once opened will usually stay in good condition for at least a week. Fino and manzanilla, very dry sherries, chilled can make a delicious prelude to most meals, but there is nothing more warming than a good amontillado or nutty oloroso served at room temperature before lunch on a winter's day.

Light wines can make good aperitifs too. Champagne is the king, of course, whether it be a half bottle shared between two while dressing to go out, or a magnum to start off an evening's gathering of six or eight. There is no doubt that the bubbles and the elegance of it somehow console, cheer and enliven one's spirits. Less expensive sparkling wines can do almost the same job and some that are particularly good value are those from San Sadurni de Noya near Barcelona, and some sparkling saumurs and vouvrays from the Loire. Still wines can make a good start too, white wines being easier to drink without food and making a better prelude to a meal that may include a series of wines. Nothing too dry or too high in acidity for drinking on an empty stomach – a good German Qualitätswein or Kabinett would be fine; an Alsace Muscat makes a delicious aperitif as can a good white Mâcon.

Party wines: Much the same considerations apply as to aperitif drinking. A choice of a red and a white wine can make life simple for the host – champagne makes it even simpler, once the cheque has been written. Any of the whites described above and a light, fairly soft red would make a good pair of alternatives. Claret is difficult to drink without food because it is dry and tannic but beaujolais or one of the lighter reds from the southern Rhône or Provence could keep people going without food for an hour or two.

Wine cups and other mixtures have the advantage that their strength can be altered as the evening goes on. One of the most popular for entertaining is Buck's Fizz, the sparkling wine and orange juice mixture. For heartier drinkers, Sunday lunchtime perhaps, there's Black Velvet, sparkling wine and Guinness; for the more delicate, a glass of sparkling wine with a drop of pink raspberry liqueur in it.

Perhaps the best known white wine mixture is vin blanc cassis or kir, dry white wine, traditionally Bourgogne Aligoté in its native Dijon, laced with a little blackcurrant liqueur. More exotic mixtures can be concocted by steeping fruit in brandy and then adding wine, lemonade, soda, lemon juice, ice cubes and/or sugar.

Everyday wines: For an informal meal, the sort of wine that can be opened up any time without too much fuss and remorse, the shop shelves are crammed with alternatives. At the moment, best value is in some of the better quality vins de pays and VDQS wines of the south of France, the medium quality wines of Spain, Portugal and Italy, and the better made wines of Eastern Europe.

Wines to drink out of doors: These should be cheap, wines for drinking by the draught rather than the sip that are not too fussy about the temperature at which they're served. Rosés and light reds such as beaujolais, other wines from the Gamay grape, red Loire wines and some from north east Italy come into their own here as they are so versatile.

Dinner party wines: This is where prescription has to stop and experimentation and individual preference play the major part. Guests and food may be such that one wine seems quite enough – or it may be a very grand affair where two or even three wines are to be served with each course. If more than one wine is served, and it is always fun to try out a range, then it is usual to have a dry white wine with the first course, followed by a red with the main course if it is a meaty dish, or a grander white if it is lighter, with perhaps a sweet wine with the pudding or port after the meal. If this is a feast and cheese is being served too, it is often sensible to follow the French and have it between the main and sweet course so as to use up any red wine that is left, though some 'blue' cheeses can be delicious with a sweet white.

Suitable wines for first courses are dry sherry, dry Loire whites, Alsace, white burgundy (the classic first course wine), German wines no fuller than Spätlese quality, any other German-style wine such as Eastern European rieslings, white Rhônes, dry white bordeaux, dry whites from anywhere else.

Main course wines can be taken from any of the world's better quality wine producing areas. It can be fun to present a couple of wines for comparison in the form of a horizontal or vertical tasting as already described.

After-dinner wines: Port is the classic post-prandial wine, with a sweet madeira such as a bual or a malmsey in second place. Some people like to drink them with cheese, others with a fruit-and-nut sort of dessert, or they can be delicious on their own.

LEFTOVERS There are some wines which can be left opened for a week and more without suffering, others which need careful treatment if there are any leftovers. Full-bodied reds from Spain, Italy and the Rhône can go on improving after being opened for well over twenty-four hours. These are useful wines for everyday drinking where one is loath to have one's consumption ruled by the size of a wine bottle. Most fortified wines can safely be left opened for up to a fortnight, madeira being famous for its longevity. Of these heavier wines, finos, manzanillas and dry white vermouth fade fastest. They should be stoppered up and kept chilled, and the same general preservational rules apply to them as to light wines. Just as aeration can be a good thing because it speeds up the development of a young wine before it is drunk, it can also speed up the deterioration of wine that is already at its prime. So to keep an opened bottle of wine youthful, decant the remains into a smaller container so that it comes into contact with as little air as possible. It is wise to keep a stock of empty half bottles for this purpose, and to save stopper corks that come on sherry bottles, and wizened old champagne corks that are also good for re-use.

Leftover sparkling wines need not deteriorate before a couple of days or more if they are kept tightly stoppered with a resealing patent appliance. These cost little more than £1 at off-licences and ironmongers. Some even swear by the addition of a pinch of bicarbonate of soda to enliven sparkling wine that has lost its fizz.

2. Choosing and buying wine

In the shop – Bottle shapes – Bottle sizes – Labels – What to look out for – Where to buy – In the restaurant – Buying wine elsewhere – Good value wines

INTRODUCTION In a sense this is the most important chapter of the book, for it is the one that distinguishes it most from other guides to wine. Next to tasting, buying is the most important activity of the wine lover and the more specific the guidance he has to help him on what marketing men call 'the buying decision', the more likely he is to enjoy his wine. And this book is about enjoyment.

At the risk of producing a book that is aimed directly only at those living in Britain, that will inevitably include some personal prejudices and that will certainly not endure as a guide to wine for the twenty-first century, the author has tried to give as much practical information as possible. This includes comments on the big off-licence and supermarket chains and individual merchants, the best known branded wines, advice on reading labels and lists and on choosing and handling wine when eating out.

Wine is too exciting and varied for it to be sensible to stick to the cheapest on offer and it is far from the spirit of this book to stop its readers spending as much money as they can afford on wine, but it *is* the book's aim to make sure, by giving honest background information on wines and their pedigrees, that every penny is well spent. At the end of this chapter there is even a list of specific wines, divided into certain styles, that are particularly good value at the moment, including some of the world's more unusual wines that are just starting to make an impression on British wine buyers.

IN THE SHOP In Britain we are extremely lucky to have such a wide range of wine available, but it can lead to some very confusing choices. The average customer walking around in a wine shop often has that dazed and panic-stricken look as he scans the rows of bottles desperately looking for some recognizable feature before finally plumping for the bottle with the prettiest label. The aim of this guide is to help the reader buy better wine, for less money if possible, and to avoid expensive mistakes.

Of course the ideal way to buy wine is to get in sample bottles of anything that takes one's fancy and to place orders on the basis of tasting them in the comfort of our own homes. But few of us can afford to do that. We normally have to be fairly certain that we're going to enjoy every bottle that we buy, which is not too difficult to arrange provided we look carefully at all the clues provided, which may be sparse if we're choosing from a catalogue or wine list rather than getting the chance to see the bottle before we buy.

BOTTLE SHAPES The most obvious clue to what's in a bottle is its shape. There are certain classic shapes associated with certain classic regions, many of which have been adapted for use by producers in other areas. The principal shapes are shown below.

Wine is occasionally put into very fancy bottle shapes indeed, like the German bottles with monkeys climbing up them and the Barolos in bottles that look like old tree trunks. This is an indication of superior prices though not necessarily of superior quality.

In Spain and in the Rhône bottles are sometimes enmeshed in thin metal netting, a practice that supposedly originated to stop substitution of labels. Chianti bottles or *fiaschi* were traditionally encased in straw and made wonderful decorations for Italian restaurants, but these are dying out to be replaced by brown bordeaux bottles with no detrimental effects on the wine at all.

BOTTLE SIZES There is still great variation in the size of the 'standard' wine bottle, although at last legislation has been introduced that requires capacity to be stated on bottles for sale in most countries. Capacity in Europe can vary from 68cl for some German wines to the full 75cl, a variation

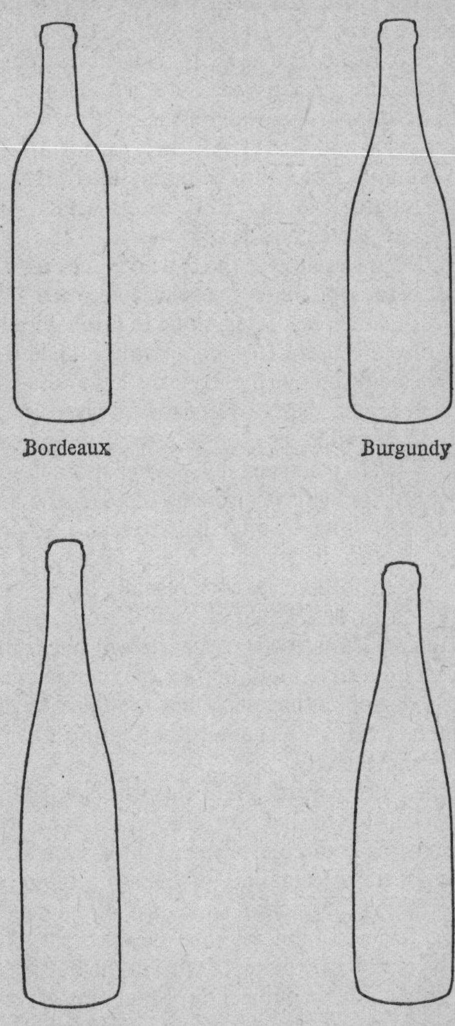
Bordeaux
Burgundy
Alsace
Germany

that represents more than 10 per cent. The most common sizes now are 70cl and 75cl. A 70cl bottle at £2 is the equivalent of a 75cl bottle at £2.14 so it is worth examining prices and contents carefully. The content given on the label is the *average* quantity of wine in the bottle. In the United States, Australia and South Africa it is normal for wine bottles to contain 75cl and it is highly likely that this will soon be mandatory in the EEC soon, which will make comparisons of value considerably easier.

Half bottles are useful for those who want only a modest amount of wine to share between two, perhaps as an aperitif, or for someone dining alone to drink with his meal. They can also be useful for comparative tasting without comparative bankruptcy, but they do have disadvantages. Firstly, there are so many overheads involved in getting a bottle, no matter what size, on to a shelf that a half bottle drinker is usually penalized by paying more for his half than he would for half an ordinary-sized bottle and many bottlers are unwilling to offer halves at all. Secondly, the maturation process in a half bottle is faster and brusquer than in a bigger bottle. The cork, usually being no smaller, lets in as much air as it would into a full bottle, which means that although a wine ripens earlier, it will not usually gain the same complexity. Half bottles of champagne can be particularly disappointing since they are filled by decanting half of the contents of a standard bottle into them and are inclined to go flat early.

Magnums – the word itself suggests something really rather special, as indeed are the wines that eventually emerge from these double bottle 1½-litre sizes after many years of maturing. Magnums of fine wines nearly always sell at a premium at auction since it is calculated that this is the size for optimum balance between air coming in through the cork and volume of wine in the bottle. The wine matures slowly but magnificently. Magnums are also commonly used now for cheaper wines, indeed the success of Italian wines in recent years has been largely dependent on the introduction of the 'big bottle' for parties and entertaining. There are two-litre sizes too, though these tend to be unwieldy. Be careful of assuming that the bigger the bottle the better value it offers for this is not invariably so. A mathematical brain or a pocket calculator are invaluable when wine buying, but here is a chart of equivalents which may be helpful:

Two litres	£4.00	£5.33	£6.67
Magnum (1½ litres)	£3.00	£4.00	£5.00
One litre	£2.00	£2.67	£3.33
One bottle (75cl)	£1.50	£2.00	£2.50

THE ALL-IMPORTANT LABEL The label is any bottle's most important clue to the wine inside; it provides a sort of 'passport' for the wine and repays careful study.

First find the country of origin. Every wine, no matter where it was bottled, should carry some indication of which country it came from. The only exception to this rule is that relatively new animal, EEC table wine. This is wine, usually of fairly commonplace quality, which is a blend of wines from more than one EEC country. (Blending of EEC and non-EEC wines is forbidden, presumably to keep us pure New Europeans.) Such wine should be labelled in the language of the country in which it is sold, 'wine from different EEC countries', for example, but some German bottlers have been known to bottle such blends with fancy Gothic script-bedecked labels calling them 'Tafelwein aus Ländern der EWG' in tiny letters. This means the same thing but the shopper can easily mistake it for a German wine. ('CEE' is French for EEC.)

Next try to narrow down what sort of quality the wine is. Again we have those who pace the corridors of power in Brussels to thank for the fact that this has to be clearly stated on wine labels nowadays. The EEC recognizes three basic sorts of wine:

1. *Table wine produced in the EEC*: This is the most basic level of wine produced and should be described as 'table wine', 'vin de table', 'Tafelwein', 'vino da tavola' or 'vino de pasto' on the label. Such wine is what most people call

'plonk' and is not usually allowed to claim any geographical characteristics.

2. *Better quality wine produced in a particular region in the EEC*: This should, in theory anyway, be wine of superior quality. The exact clues given to each sort of quality designation vary from country to country and are given below.

3. *Wine from outside the EEC*: This should be described simply as 'wine' on the label but if it is recognized as having a special quality designation, this will be stated instead.

Here is a country-by-country guide to terms denoting quality that may be found on wine labels.

FRANCE

APPELLATION CONTRÔLÉE DESIGNATION The French system has several gradations of quality starting at the top with Appellation Contrôlée which system has been taken as a model in wine regions all over the world, most of whom by now have instituted their own equivalents. The system was developed by one Baron Le Roy in Châteauneuf-du-Pape in the Thirties. Each wine-producing area in France has its own particular quirks (Burgundy especially) but in essence, the Appellation Contrôlée (AC) wines of France are her best, those wines which depend for their characteristics on the location of the vineyard. Each AC designates a specific geographical area, the vine varieties permitted for AC wine production, the maximum yields (amount of wine produced per area of vineyard) which may be altered from year to year, the methods by which the wine may be made, minimum alcoholic strength allowed and sometimes go into more detail than this. The appellations in most French wine producing regions are like sets of Russian dolls fitting one inside the other and in general the more specific the region designated by the appellation, the better quality the wine will be. In Bordeaux, for instance, a wine that carries the simple appellation Bordeaux can come from anywhere in the whole Bordeaux wine producing region.

An AC Médoc, on the other hand, will have to come from the Médoc region of Bordeaux; an AC Haut Médoc must come from the superior Haut Médoc area inside the Médoc, while a wine that is AC Pauillac must have been made in the commune of Pauillac in the Haut Médoc. This means that if a wine carries the simple AC Bordeaux it will almost certainly be from one of the fringe regions of Bordeaux (otherwise it would carry a higher appellation) or will be disqualified from a superior appellation because it is not up to scratch in some other respect. So it is fair to assume that in France that the bigger the geographical area designated by the AC, the less fine the wine will be.

Two common exceptions to this spring to mind. In Alsace there is just one appellation Alsace for most wines with Alsace Grand Cru designating superior vineyards and growth. And in Champagne the name champagne is regarded as enough – there is just one appellation and it is the only AC area in France which does not have to print the words Appellation Contrôlée on the label.

Champagne apart, the magic phrase to look out for when trying to identify a quality French wine is Appellation Contrôlée. This means that if everyone has obeyed the rules, and they now usually do, the wine comes from the particular region specified and satisfies all the other requirements laid down for that particular appellation. In general the French have been careful to award the AC only to those areas that are capable of producing wines of a certain minimum level of quality, and are constantly updating the list of ACs so as to reward those regions lower down the ranks that have been trying harder. In the past the system was open to considerable abuse and it was not until the 1973 vintage that the wines sold in Britain had to conform to AC regulations. Enforcement of the rules has been tightened up considerably. Tasting is compulsory now before a wine may call itself AC and all wines must be accompanied by documents to certify their authenticity.

VIN DELIMITÉ DE QUALITÉ SUPÉRIEURE The category below Appellation Contrôlée is VDQS which includes a number of interesting wines, perhaps not great, but usually well made. They have less well established reputations than AC wines, and the producers are usually keen to earn AC status eventually, so their quality can in general be relied upon.

VINS DE PAYS These, strictly speaking, are classified as table wines but are a cut above the generally very disappointing level of French table wine as their producers have a local reputation to make or lose. Most *vins de pays* are concentrated around the sweep of vineyards in the hinterland of the Mediterranean coast, with the Aude, Hérault and Gard departments usually being the most easily identifiable clue to geographical origin. The words '*vin de pays*' appear on the label together with the name of the '*pays*' of which this is a *vin*, but exact nomenclature is a problem as there are so many tiny areas each claiming a place on the label but unidentifiable to anyone without a Guide Michelin in his hand. The system was designed to reward those prepared to make good wine in these Midi areas where the extra effort is sometimes hardly worth it economically. Many of these robust, lively reds, sort of 'hot clarets', can be good value.

Other clues given on French wine labels are:

GEOGRAPHY AND TYPE

Côtes de X: This usually means that the wine will be superior to wine simply called 'X' since it is on the Côtes, the hillside, that the best vineyards are often sited.

Coteaux de X: Similar to Côtes de X.

X Villages: This again will usually be superior to wine labelled simply as 'X' for it signifies that it comes from one or more special villages in the region of X.

X supérieur: Not necessarily any better quality than X, but higher in alcoholic strength, by one per cent in most cases. Not always too significant. In many vintages of Beaujolais, for instance, almost all wine produced could be called 'Beaujolais supérieur' but no one bothers to label it as such.

Primeur: A wine vinified fast to be drunk within three or four months of the vintage. See beaujolais nouveau.

CLASSIFICATION

Cru classé: 'Classed growth' literally translated. Usually meaning that it comes from a vineyard that has been rated in an official classification, most famous of which is the 1855 classification of Médoc.

Grand Cru: Great growth, top notch vineyard, usually from the Côte d'Or or Chablis, or Château d'Yquem.

Premier cru: 'First growth' literally. Means it is top rank in red bordeaux (only five châteaux in Bordeaux have been awarded this accolade in the 1855 classification), second to 'grand cru' in white bordeaux and burgundy.

Deuxième, troisième, quatrième, cinquième cru: Second, third, fourth and fifth growths.

Cru bourgeois: Some excellent value Médoc claret officially just under fifth growth level with 'cru grand Bourgeois' being the better of them.

SWEETNESS (This is important to look out for in white wine, particularly from Bordeaux where whites can vary from bone dry to unctuous at a wink from the winemaker's wife. Jurançon wines vary a great deal too, and it is vital to look for some sweetness clue – usually on the neck – on bottles of sparkling wine):

Brut: Very dry.
Sec: Dry.
Demi sec, Moilleux: Medium sweet.
Doux or *Rich*: Sweet.

SPARKLE

Champagne: What it says, i.e. wine from the Champagne region made by the méthode champenoise.
Mousseux: Sparkling.
Crémant: Slightly less sparkling.
Pétillant: Slightly sparkling.
Perlant: Just fizzing.

BOTTLING

Mise (en bouteilles) à la propriété, mise le propriétaire, mise à la domaine: Bottled by the grower at the property.
Mise (en bouteilles) dans nos caves: This can mean at the cellars of any wine merchant specified on the label, usually a foreign merchant but it is even used by some British bottlers to describe thus bottling in their 'caves' under London Bridge or in the Home Counties.
Mise par le négociant: Bottled by the shipper who selected the wine.
Shipped and bottled by X: All his own work.
Shipped and bottled for X: Someone else has done the bottling.

ITALY

The Italian quality designation system is similar to the French Appellation Contrôlée system except that the Italians have been less discriminating in choosing which wines are to be given the DOC, the Denominazione di Origine Controllata. It would be fair to say that, with certain honourable exceptions, one could present the relative quality of the wines designated in the French and Italian systems crudely thus:

DOC ————————
Italian table wine ————————
AC ————————
VDQS & vin de pays ——————
French table wine————————

dreadful pleasant magnificent

There is considerable overlap between the quality of the worst of the Italians' DOC wines and the best of her non DOC. While the designations AC, VDQS and vins de pays can be taken as reliable though approximate guides to the quality of a French wine, the letters DOC on an Italian wine label offer no such guarantee.

The problem is that Italy's wine producers are a powerful lobby and many of them, even from relatively obscure regions producing even more obscure wines, have managed to win the DOC for themselves. There are now about 200 which cover too wide a variation in quality to be useful. One or two producers such as Corvo in Sicily who are producing quite good quality Italian wine have made the conscious decision not to encourage the granting of the DOC to Corvo wines. If they were granted the DOC, then any other producer in the area could capitalize on the reputation they have worked so hard to build.

If the letters DOC do not provide too certain a guarantee of quality, a new and superior category, Denominazione di Origine Controllata e Garantita (DOCG) may be more reliable. This requires stricter conditions to be met and the Italian government is showing itself very much more tight-fisted with the honour. So far suggested for DOCG are Barolo, Barbaresco, Brunello di Montalcino, Vino Nobile di Montepulciano and Chianti Classico. It may be that the letters DOCG will eventually denote the truly better quality wines of Italy.

Italian DOCs may be named after a place, grape variety, a combination of the two or straight fantasy as in Lacrima Christi.

A better indication of quality is often to look for certain key words on the label:

GEOGRAPHY AND QUALITY

Classico: This added to the name of a region means that the wine has come from the heartland of that region and is almost always superior in quality.

Riserva: Matured for longer than usual in wood, often a special selection of the vintage.

Vecchio: Also matured for a specified period, usually one year less than Riserva. Not a common description.

Superiore: Higher in alcohol and usually conforms to stricter specifications of winemaking than the run of the mill.

SWEETNESS
Orvieto particularly can vary considerably in how sweet it is.
Amarone: Bitter, very dry (and usually high in alcohol).
Secco: Dry.
Abboccato, Amabile: Medium dry to medium sweet.
Dolce: Sweet.

SPARKLING
Spumante: Sparkling.
Frizzante: Semi-sparkling.

BOTTLING
Most Italian wine other than that for the big brands like Hirondelle is imported in bottle into Britain.
Imbottigliato dal produttore: Bottled by the producer.

OTHER DESCRIPTIONS
The Italians are great ones for numbered bottles. This should be a sign of strict controls on the amount of wine produced and forms an important part of the controls in the Chianti Classico region, for instance.
Consorzio: Consortium of growers who impose their own, stricter than average, standards on production.
Cantina: Shipper, cellars.
Cantina Sociale: Wine growers' co-operative – very common in Italy, with a good reputation for fair to medium quality wines.
Tenuta: Wine estate, property.
Vendemmia: Vintage.

GERMANY

Germany's quality control system is quite different from that of the French and the Italians. The German Wine Law is based less on geography than on ripeness and, producing wine as far north as they do, it is perhaps not surprising that the Germans are so preoccupied with this aspect of their wines. The following are their categories of wine quality above Tafelwein level. It does not matter where the wine was made (though this will be stated on the label); to attain one of these levels of quality it is important only that the wine passes the necessary physical and chemical tests. As one would imagine therefore, the proportions of wine that qualify for each particular category vary tremendously from year to year according to how generous the weather has been – unlike the position in most other wine producing countries where quality is determined by location.

The level of quality immediately above Tafelwein is Qualitätswein bestimmter Anbaugebiete or, rather more comfortably, 'QbA' which means 'quality wine from one of Germany's eleven quality wine regions'. This represents well over 50 per cent of all wine produced in Germany in an average year (whereas Tafelwein may represent less than 10 per cent), and certainly the vast majority of German wine sold in this country is QbA – all that Liebfraumilch, Piesporter and Niersteiner.

The next level up is Qualitätswein mit Prädikat (QmP) and it is the sun that determines how much German wine gets which sort of Prädikat each year. Being ripe wines from northern climes, these wonders can cost dear. The Prädikats awarded, in ascending order, are Kabinett, Spätlese, Auslese, Beerenauslese and Trockenbeerenauslese of which further details are given in the reference section.

These quality 'predicates' are added to the geographical origin of the wine which will usually specify the name of the village plus the suffix 'er' and then the vineyard. A wine from the famous Doktor vineyard in Bernkastel, for example, is called Bernkasteler Doktor, and if it reaches Auslese quality the label will describe it as 'Bernkasteler Doktor Auslese'.

For a wine to get the seal of approval from Ze Cherman System, as a QbA or QmP wine, it must be awarded an Amtliche Prüfungsnummer (AP number) by the relevant wine testing station, one for each of Germany's eleven wine regions. The number of a German quality wine should be made up as follows:

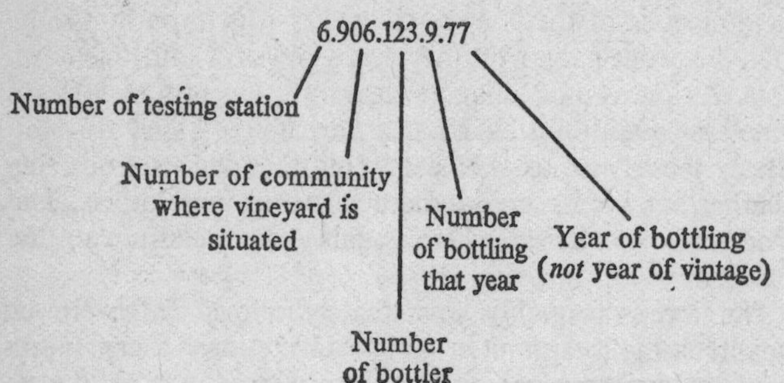

GEOGRAPHY
Gebiete: Wine producing region – Germany has eleven.
Bereich: Large sub-region within a Gebiete (30).
Grosslage: Collection of small vineyards under one, the most famous, vineyard name (150).
Einzellage: Single vineyard sites (2500), much more exclusive than a Grosslage, though difficult to tell apart just by looking at the label (see reference section for clues).

SWEETNESS
The official Prädikat system gives a good indication of the ripeness of QmP wines. There is also a current craze for making Trocken or Diabetiker wines that are much drier than most German wines.

SPARKLE
Schaumwein: Sparkling wine, usually made from imported still wine.
Sekt and *QbA Sekt*: Better quality sparkling winethat has been aged for nine months. Only Sekt for which a region inside Germany is specified must be made only from German wine. Plain 'German Sekt' is often made from wine imported from another EEC country into Germany.

BOTTLING
This is an important aspect of a German wine label. Most estate-bottled wines can be taken to be of the best quality.
Erzeugerabfüllung: Bottled by the grower.

SPAIN

Spain is still in the process of putting her wine quality designation system in order and at the moment has different systems for each region run by their own *consejos* or other administrative bodies.

The words to look out for are Denominacion de Origen which is their equivalent of the Italian DOC and works well in Rioja, the most important quality wine producing region. The name of the region should be prominently shown by the DO sign, though each region has its own peculiarities. Rioja has its own deckle-edged seal while Penedes puts a paper seal over the neck of every bottle.

QUALITY
Reserva: Wine of superior quality aged for longer than usual, sometimes too long for older vintages. This will usually be followed by the number of years it was kept in wood, *año*, or the vintage *cosecha* or *vendimia*.
Vino de mesa, vino de pasto: Table wine.

SWEETNESS
Seco: Dry.
Abocado, Dulce: Sweet.

SPARKLING
Espumoso: Sparkling.

COLOUR
This can be important for reds and rosés because the Spanish have an intermediate stage between the two (*tinto* and *rosado* respectively) which they call *clarete*. White in Spanish is *blanco*, a fact that can be useful when buying Spanish wine

in one of those hessian-covered bottles.

BOTTLING
Being bottled in Spain almost defines her better quality wines. Any Spanish wine bottled in Britain should carry the name and address of a British merchant.

MORE CLUES FROM THE LABEL So far we have looked at the most general clues available from the labels of wines from various countries. From those already discussed it should be possible to work out the approximate style and quality of the wine but it is possible to find out more specific information.

If the wine is from a particular region, does it come from a single vineyard – in which case it will probably be very special – or is it a blend of different wines? In Bordeaux, with only one or two 'Domaine' and 'Clos' exceptions, all the best wines are called Château Something, but then many of her more ordinary wines blended up to provide a merchant with a cheaper alternative to the prestigious classed growths are also given a fancy-sounding château name. The reference section explains how to do one's best in negotiating the Girondin minefield of appellations. The reference section also helps with Burgundy, an even more complicated area. The key to finding a single vineyard wine from Burgundy is to look for the name of a commune, Aloxe Corton, for example, followed by a name of a vineyard such as Les Perrières. A wine coming from this single vineyard would be labelled Aloxe Corton Les Perrières. In Germany, as has already been explained, it can be difficult to distinguish between an Einzellage and a Grosslage, a single vineyard and a collection of vineyards that are now trading under the name of the best known in that collection. For help in solving all those problems three books are invaluable: *The Wines of Bordeaux* by Edmund Penning-Rowsell (Penguin), *Burgundy Vines and Wines* by John Arlott and Christopher Fielden (Quartet and Davis-Poynter) and *German Wine Atlas* (Davis-Poynter and Mitchell Beazley).

If the label gives no more indication as to geography, it may give some indication of the grape variety or grape varieties. A description of grape variety characteristics is given in the reference section too.

The wine may alternatively be sold under a brand name. Brands are now established as firmly in the wine market as in the soap powder market and there can be few wine drinkers who have never drunk a branded wine. They account for well over half of all wine drunk in Britain and can be a useful stepping stone to acquiring a taste for more interesting and subtle wines. Most branded wines are sold in such enormous quantities that their owners' chief preoccupation is in maintaining a consistent style. They buy in vast amounts of suitable wine and blend it all up, thereby smoothing out the individual characteristics of each batch. This means that most branded wines can be relied upon to be never very bad, but never very good. And in those that are advertised heavily, you always have the uneasy feeling that by buying your bottle you are subsidizing the encouragement of others to do the same.

Here is a selection of the best known brands of wine with some highly subjective comments on them:

Mateus rosé: The world's best known branded wine. Made in Portugal to fulfil a marketing man's dream – neither sweet nor dry, white nor red, neither still nor sparkling. It is a bland wine which is artificially carbonated, but has a lovely picture on the label.

Blue Nun: Another international brand, Sichel's best-selling Liebfraumilch. Heavily advertised and in competition with Langenbach's Crown of Crowns and Deinhard's Hanns Christof.

Mouton Cadet: Highly successful branded AC bordeaux which relies heavily on the cachet of the Rothschild name. Varies considerably from vintage to vintage and has attracted imitators such as La Cour Pavillon, Pontet Latour, Harvey's No 1 Claret and many more.

Hirondelle: Britain's best-selling range of branded wines in red, white and rosé from north-east Italy, sweet white from

elsewhere. All versions are relatively sweet and innocuous.
Nicolas: Range of French table wine. The gutsy Vieux Ceps red has its followers.
Don Cortez and *Corrida*: Range of blended table wines from Spain.
Justina: The same from Portugal.
Piat: Trying to make a brand out of beaujolais and the white wines of the Mâcon area.
Lutomer Laski Riesling: For many, this *is* Yugoslavian wine, medium dry whites in the style of a spicey German wine. Cloberg from up the road is similar, as are Pecs Riesling from Hungary and the rather racier Schluck from Austria.
Bull's Blood: Hearty full-bodied red from Hungary.

Place names, grape varieties and brand names apart, another clue to the likely quality of a wine is in the name of the shipper or supplier. All EEC wines should state the name of the producer on the label and all wines imported from outside the EEC should carry the name of the importer. This is designed to protect the consumer so that if he has a complaint he knows who to complain to.

Wine is originally produced by a vineyard owner, which may be one man and half an acre that he looks after at week-ends, or a multinational group whose thousands of acres of vineyard are but one of their many interests. The wine may then be made and bottled by the vineyard owner who may sell it privately from his cellar door or he may sell it to wine brokers (called rather charmingly *courtiers* in France), to local wine merchants (*négociants*) or direct to merchants in an importing country. He may sell grapes, to be vinified by a larger concern; he may sell finished wine in bulk to be blended with other wines by a *négociant*; or he may sell his own wine in bottle which will probably then carry his name on the label. The phrase 'mise en bouteille dans nos caves', therefore, can cover a multitude of caves.

Long and bitter is the controversy over the merits of domaine or château bottling, and, for cheaper wines, the merits of foreign bottling as opposed to British bottling. It should be possible to tell from the label where a wine was bottled. If it was bottled at the property (mise à la propriété etc), this *may* mean no more than that a mobile bottling plant with standards of hygiene and sophistication none too high arrived at the *chai* (the above-ground premises where wine is made and stored) one morning and the wine was bottled there with an eye only to the extra francs that can be earned by the magic phrase 'Mise en bouteille à la propriété'. This is not necessarily a sign of superior quality therefore, although it should be a guarantee of authenticity and cannot be bettered on properties which have a meticulous maître-de-chai and sophisticated bottling equipment.

The wine may alternatively have been bottled abroad by the *négociant*. A big company is more likely to have modern bottling equipment though it is more likely to be interested in blending too, which is an art in itself. Or the wine may be imported in bulk and blended and bottled in this country. This is certainly the case for most of the mass market brands over whose quality the brand owners like to have complete control. The degree of care taken in transportation and eventual bottling is the key here. Most wine moved in bulk now travels in huge stainless steel containers and is piped carefully from one container to another, when it eventually reaches the large bottling halls owned by British bottlers involved in these more everyday wines.

Certain British firms have built up reputations over the years for their bottlings of first class French wines, bordeaux and burgundy particularly. Among them are Avery's and Harvey's of Bristol, Berry Bros & Rudd and Justerini & Brooks of London. Many of them continue with this practice today although wine producing countries are increasingly insisting on bottling fine wines themselves.

The best, though very time-consuming way to navigate a way through the names of overseas suppliers and importers is to get to know the individual merchants and their reputations from personal experience. It is sadly impossible to give an exhaustive list in a guide of this size, and reputations change almost from year to year, but see 'Where to buy' for more specific advice. Various area-by-area guidelines are also given in the reference section of this book and Hugh Johnson's *Pocket Wine Book*, revised annually, can be useful on individual merchants abroad for those prepared to read between its excellent lines.

VINTAGE AND AGE EEC rules no longer allow ordinary table wine labels to be graced with a vintage date, but in a better quality wine, after its quality designation and provenance, this is the most important clue as to how a wine is going to taste and whether it is worth the price asked for it. How common it is to see bottles of 'off vintages' of well known classed growths being offered for sale in out-of-the-way places at prices which show that the vendor is hoping his customers left their vintage charts at home!

As explained in the reference section, the weather of each particular year plays an enormous part in determining the characteristics of each vintage – a bottle of good bordeaux made in a good year can fetch several times as much at auction as one of a poor year – but simply knowing the rating of a vintage on a vintage chart is not enough to know how the wine will taste. For the 1964 vintage in Bordeaux, for example, the vintage charts usually give a rating of six or seven out of ten, but the quality of each individual wine is totally dependent on whether the grapes were harvested before or after the start of the solid fortnight of rain that constituted, quite literally, a watershed of quality that year. A good sunny summer was followed by this disaster in the middle of the vintage with the result that the early pickers produced full, firm wines, while those who hung on hoping for a bit more sunshine found their wines hopelessly diluted by the downpour.

And then another factor to be borne in mind by those tempted to use vintage charts is that the wines of a particular vintage are continually evolving. What looked like a very attractive vintage in its second or third year may suddenly show signs of falling apart in its fifth, so vintage charts must be constantly revised. No, vintage charts can only point out the most general of trends. The trick is to get to know individual winemakers who are able to beat bad weather, or to follow the 'unfashionable' vintages, those good vintages which are overshadowed by superlative ones, or by a more conveniently fashionable one that precedes them.

The finer the wine, the more variation there will be between vintages. Suitable everyday wine can be made from most vintages, but the finest grapes are most at the mercy of the weather. If a fine wine bears no vintage year, it is a safe assumption that it is a blend from more than one year.

The vintage date of course indicates not only what sort of characteristics to expect from the wine as a result of that year's weather, but also the age of the wine. There is a common fallacy that all wine improves with age. This is certainly true of most of the world's greatest red wines, classed growths of Bordeaux and the meatier red burgundies and Rhônes. Many of Italy's nobler reds and their counterparts in Spain need some time to come round too, but it is far from the case with the majority of wine sold today. Most white wine, indeed all but the most expensive white burgundy, the late-picked German and the sweet white wines of the Loire and Bordeaux, are at their best within one to three years of the vintage – and many whites from Australia, South Africa and South America can happily be drunk during the year of the vintage, which takes place in February and March in the southern hemisphere. Many everyday reds should be drunk relatively young too, for few of these wines are built to last. Beaujolais is perhaps the classic red for quick consumption, particularly the much-vaunted beaujolais nouveau which can taste decidedly stale even by Easter. Most of the red wines selling in the low to mid price range are probably at their best two to three years after the vintage. For this reason, there is little point in buying mediocre wine and cellaring it for years, although most wine benefits from a few months' rest after bottling. In the guide to storing wine (Chapter Three) recommendations on how long to store various types of wine are given.

WHAT TO LOOK OUT FOR Quite apart from careful study of such clues given by the label and the bottle shape, there are other ways in which you can find out more about a wine and make sure that the bottle you choose will give maximum pleasure.

'Own brands': Many sellers of wine like to offer their 'own brand' of a certain wine. Barnetti Valpolicella for example is the version of this common Italian red offered as the house version of the Augustus Barnett chain, and all of Marks & Spencer's wines are labelled as their own selection. If you want to find out more about exactly which supplier the wine comes from you will have to read the small print, and it is often helpful to look at the capsule. You will sometimes spot a capsule on a 'buyer's own brand' that is identical to that on a similar wine carrying a different label just a few inches along the shelf. By choosing wisely and not being put off wine with a chainstore label on it, you can sometimes get better value as the 'own brands' are sold cheaper than well known brands which have marketing costs built into their price.

Choosing the right bottle: Take care when choosing a particular bottle from the shelf that it is not in a position where it has obviously been exposed to heat or strong light, either natural or artificial, as this can oxidize a wine and affect its colour. Of course it is impossible to know by what route a bottle has reached its present position on a shelf, but if you have the choice it is always wise to go for one that is stored horizontally if the batch looks as though it has been there for some time. This keeps the cork moist and prevents the wine from oxidation. In older wines, check that there is as small a gap between the bottom of the cork and the surface of the wine as possible as this 'ullage' (from the French *ouillage*) can also cause wine to deteriorate fast by letting too much air act on it.

Special offers: These are always worth looking at. Wines described as 'bin ends' are usually just that – odd bottles at the end of a lot that need to be cleared away as quickly as possible, which usually means that they will be sold at keen prices. If a fine wine merchant is selling off odd bottles of superior wines, inspect them carefully for they may be in dubious condition. Inspect the level of wine in the bottle particularly and bear in mind that it is difficult to re-sell any bottles whose labels have been badly damaged – though these can be excellent value for one's own consumption. Also make sure that the cork is still firmly covered by the capsule. If the wine looks as though it stands every chance of being in good condition, then snap it up.

'Special offers', other than the usual loss-leader exercise with which every sort of shopper is bombarded, may be at the other end of the scale of quality. Parcels of very cheap wine are occasionally offered around the trade – it may be bankrupt stock or wine that is very cheap for some other reason. It is usually bought eventually and offered as a 'specialité de la maison'. If it really is very cheap it may be worth trying a bottle but it is impossible to recommend such wines in general. The lower the quality of the wine, the more idiosyncratic its style and the more difficult it is to predict who will like it. A test bottle that is loathed can always be mulled or used for cooking. Those who decide the wine is a great bargain would be ill advised to lay in more than they can drink in a month or so since wines of this sort may well be unstable and go out of condition quickly.

Some confusing wines: While most of those in the wine trade are considerably more upright than the popular press would like to make out, there are certain sorts of labelling that can lead to confusion, though steps are being taken to prevent this in most instances. The labelling of EEC blends to make them look like German wines with 'Tafelwein aus Ländern der EWG' writ small has already been mentioned. Also misleading are the attempts of some Burgundy *négociants* who try to present wine that is classified only as table wine as though it were fully fledged burgundy. This they do by giving it a fancy name, playing down the 'vin de table' bit and playing up on the label the town in which they have their headquarters, usually somewhere that sounds impressive such as Beaune or Nuits-St-Georges.

Some of them, knowing that this is not allowed, are even going as far as to use lesser known appellations that could easily be confused with Burgundy appellations such as Fitou in the Midi and again capitalizing on their Burgundy addresses.

Not that Bordeaux is totally without its confusions. Château Latour is one of the four Médoc châteaux allowed to class itself as *premier cru* and is one of the world's greatest wines. Since 'tours' or towers are by no means uncommon in the Bordeaux region, it is hardly surprising that there should be a great number, nearly 100, of other châteaux whose name somehow incorporates the word Latour or La Tour, some trying more obviously than others to ride on the back of the 'real' Château Latour's reputation. Only a label saying 'Grand Vin de Château Latour' on a very plain label with a little turret on and the appellation Pauillac is the world-famous Château Latour, which is substantially British-owned incidentally. With so many different properties in the region there are a number of other 'near misses' in terms of names. Be suspicious of anything that is wildly below market price, and remember that, as explained in the reference section, Château Tire-jambe may be used as a brand name for any old blend of AC bordeaux so long as it comes from a certain area.

Awards and medals: Some labels are adorned with decorations and awards, some such as the lovely Marques de Riscal rioja bottle, to attractive effect. Rarely do these awards mean very much. The most prestigious prizes are to be won at the two big French wine fairs at Mâcon and Paris and Tastevin approval in Burgundy is also much valued.

WHERE TO BUY We now have more choice in where we buy our wine than ever before. Supermarkets, wine clubs, mail order outfits, cash and carry depots, department stores have all joined the ranks of the traditional wine merchant who, in many instances, has been squeezed out of business by the low margins at which most of these alternative wine sellers are able to operate.

Sometimes we have no choice as to where we buy our wine. We need a bottle now and the only place we can get to is the corner shop that stocks only rock bottom Spanish wine and a range of overpriced brands. Every wine buying method has its advantages and disadvantages but it is possible to give some general advice and specific recommendations of which this is one: try not to get into the position where you are forced to go to the corner shop. The more you are able to buy at a time, the better prices you will pay, and you'll have a store of wine to fall back on that will save you from paying over the odds.

THE BIGGER OFF-LICENCE CHAINS In this category are all the brewery-owned chains and their less beer-dominated counterparts such as Augustus Barnett and Oddbins. Allied Breweries own Victoria Wine, Peter Dominic and Westminster Wine belong to the same Grand Met group as Truman Watney Mann; Courage own Arthur Cooper, both members of the Imperial group; Whitbread own Threshers and Mackies; Bass own Galleon; Greenall Whitley have Drew; and outside the brewers Cadbury Schweppes own André Simon; and Lonrho, through Holts, own Sakers and Ashe & Nephew. Augustus Barnett is owned by the giant Spanish banks-and-booze company Rumasa.

Each have their own house brands and specialities which are given in more detail below.

Augustus Barnett: Since being taken over by Rumasa, Augustus Barnett have, hardly surprisingly, offered good value for sherry and Spanish light wines, particularly the riojas of Paternina and Bodegas Franco Espanolas, and have some interesting cheaper Spanish wines. They have always offered a range that puts to shame most of their competitors; their list includes some very fine wines and prices are keen, though not as good as they were. Their only disadvantage is that they offer none of the extras at their very basic, almost sordid, shops. No delivery, no case discounts, no fridges. Knowledge and charm is rare in their staff. However, they are one of the few companies brave enough to print a price list and stick to it so if you don't find much help from behind the counter, at least you can study the list at leisure back home.

Oddbins: Started selling bin ends by a man who ended up doing the same thing in a warehouse in Wapping, Oddbins' strength is in buying eclectically. As for Augustus Barnett, prices of cheap to medium-priced wines are best here. Some of their German wines are good value; their more expensive claret can be less so. Good range and the overall level of knowledge in their staff is good. They go in for the languid student type rather than the honest Irishman favoured by A. Barnett.

Victoria Wine: The biggest retail chain in the country has in the past suffered from having a more restricted choice than many of its competitors. There is a 'specials' list from which more interesting bottles may be ordered, but this requires determination and planning on the part of the shopper. Their 'own brands' include Nicolas, Don Cortez, Goldener Oktober, the Grants of St James's range of generic wines (from different regions). Harvey's sherries and madeira and Cockburn's ports are all from a sister company so they usually have good prices for these lines. Range improving.

Peter Dominic: This is a similar operation but with rather more extras such as the associated Wine Mine mail order club, occasional free literature and a wide, adventurous range of wines. They list a good selection of Italian wines including the excellent Rubesco Torgiano and Fontanafredda Piedmontese wines, a few better quality wines from Spain and even a Chilean Cabernet. Their own brands include Justina, Carafino, Les Grands Vignobles ranges of generics and they also have strong links with Piat and Château Loudenne, de Pez and Giscours. Fair prices at about the same level as Victoria Wine's. Westminster

Wine is owned by the same company, is open later at night and therefore tends to charge higher prices.

Arthur Cooper or *Saccone and Speed*: Not always a very inspiring choice but they have good links with Kressman of Bordeaux, Lanson champagne, Riccadonna vermouth, Cloberg Yugoslav and Rocamar branded Spaniards and several rioja producers.

Threshers: Sister company to Stowells of Chelsea whose range of generics they sell together with brands like Corrida and Langenbach German wines.

Galleon: Bass Charrington don't really seem all that interested in fine wine in these retail shops though they have good links with all from the Baron Philippe de Rothschild stable. Should have good prices for Mateus, Hirondelle, Mouton Cadet and a range of Italians that includes Ruffino, Bolla, Corvo and Gancia.

Davisons: This family-owned chain around London is worth investigating as they do a high proportion of their own bottling and have good prices for mature stocks of wines from the classic areas, especially Bordeaux.

SUPERMARKETS AND GROCERY CHAINS Sad to say, this group rarely offer interesting wines, choosing instead to confine themselves to the well-known brands and the odd range of 'own brand' generics whose quality is often disappointing. Cullens with their Gourmet and Goblet stores is a notable exception and the 'high class grocers' like Fortnum and Mason and Harrods also have very good wine departments that put them firmly into the traditional wine merchant category.

There are three further exceptions to the generally disappointing level of interest in wine in the grocery trade: Marks & Spencer, Waitrose and Sainsbury.

Sainsbury's claim to sell one in every forty bottles of

light wine bought in this country, which is not bad going for a chain that is far from national. They have an interesting range of wines at keen prices and are particularly good on German wines. Marks & Spencer have a carefully put together range of their own branded wines, though those with good eyesight can always discover exactly where they're from by studying the bottom of the helpfully designed label. Few startlingly low prices but the same dependable level of quality as one expects from St Michael's meat pies and underpants. Upmarket grocery chain Waitrose has, as one would expect, an upmarket wine list – very adventurous and can be excellent value.

TRADITIONAL WINE MERCHANTS In the early seventies it looked as though this was about to become an extinct species, but a few have managed to hang on and there are now signs of a 'new wave' of independent wine merchants (see below). These are the sort of merchants, long established family firms, who offer a high degree of personal service, discounts for purchases of a case of a dozen bottles, often delivery and tasting facilities and good literature. They usually carry a fine range of bordeaux, burgundy, German wines and vintage port and are able to talk knowledgeably about them. These are the merchants from whom Oxford colleges and City institutions buy, the buyer usually well primed by a tasting and lunch in the boardroom.

For spirits and the well known brands, these merchants can rarely compete with the supermarkets and the big off-licence chains whose buying power gets them mammoth discounts on such items. Wine buyers are realizing the advantages of the traditional merchant, however. In addition to those listed above, they usually have a good range of older vintages of the more classic wines, often at prices that have not been updated to keep pace with what it will cost to replace them. Their livelihood is strongly linked to their reputations so they can afford even less than most to sell sub-standard wine. Establish a rapport with any of them, better still with one of their staff in particular, and you should be sure of good advice and perhaps a glass of sherry when you call in to order. They will lend out glasses, invite you to their tastings, offer cellaring service and so on.

Most areas are served by one of these merchants. Many of them are now owned by large groups but they seem to be left to get on with their own business. Here are some of the best known:

Adnams of Southwold, Suffolk: Part of the local brewery, very good prices.
Avery's of Bristol: Highly original family firm with international reputation.
Berry Bros & Rudd, London SW1: Their shop is a treat in itself, 'a step back in history', as they say. Uninformative wine list but their own bottlings of a wide range of wines.
Christopher's, London SW1: Three centuries old.
Corney & Barrow, London EC2: Traditional City merchant. Good literature, highish prices.
Dolamore, London W2, Oxford and Cambridge: Traditional university supplier.
Ellis Son & Vidler, Hastings: Especially good on madeira.
Harvey's, London, Bristol and Portsmouth: Now owned by Allied Breweries. Fine wines.
Hedges & Butler, London W1: Fine wine arm of Bass with some very good buys.
Justerini & Brooks, London SW1: Fine wine arm of Grand Met. Prices have risen sharply recently.
Lay & Wheeler, Colchester: Good range, complicated pricing system.
O. W. Loeb, London SW1: Excellent German and Rhône wines.
Arthur Purchase, Chichester.
Quellyn Roberts, Chester.
Tanners of Shrewsbury: Lively family firm.
Youdell of Kendal: Their own sherry is some of the finest.

MAIL ORDER AND THE 'NEW WAVE' WINE MERCHANTS While most of the traditional merchants listed above offer some sort of mail order service in addition to having retail operations, there has been an encouraging emergence recently of a new breed of wine merchants, often concentrating on mail order. Many of them are ex-employees of larger companies who want a bit more freedom, some began as amateurs rather than wine professionals and continue with other occupations, and some have decided to specialize in one particular sort of wine. There is inevitable overlap between this category and that of traditional wine merchants.

For those living in any part of the country that is badly served by wine merchants, then mail order must be the most sensible way to buy wine. The mail order merchants have relatively low overheads, sometimes keeping the wine in bonded warehouses until orders arrive so they start from a fairly low base before costing in delivery. Comparison between different merchants' catalogues is made more difficult by the fact that not all of them include VAT in their prices, and only a few of them include delivery.

The disadvantage of mail order is that the buyer normally has to commit himself to a minimum order of twelve mixed bottles, and he can study only the catalogue rather than the label before buying. There is wide variation in the quality of the literature and information provided but opposite is a guide to some of the better mail order, 'new wave' all-round merchants, and those that have a particular speciality.

WINE CLUBS When is a wine club not a wine club? When there is no membership fee. The Malmaison Wine Club, for instance, is classified as a straight mail order operation despite the excellent wine tastings it holds, since anyone who buys wine from them automatically becomes a 'member'. In this section we look only at clubs which charge a fee:

The Wine Society or, to give it its full title, the International Exhibition Co-operative Wine Society, is the doyen of the wine clubs. Founded at a meeting held at the Albert Hall in 1874, its advantages are that it offers an enormous range of wines and pursues a policy of buying fine wine conscientiously in order to lay it down and sell only when it is ready for drinking. It is not cheap but the literature and graphics are excellent – a Wine Society label has the prestige

Les Amis du vin, 51 Chiltern Street, London W1: See under Wine Clubs below

Bacchus Wine Company, Kensington Church Street, London W8

Bonhote Foster, Long Melford, Suffolk: Particularly good for regional wines of France

Bordeaux Direct, New Aquitaine House, Caversham Road, Reading: Also good for lesser known French wines

David Burns, Lymington, Lyndhurst and Bournemouth

Caves de la Madelaine, 301 Fulham Road, London SW10

Richard Granger, Newcastle-upon-Tyne

Hawkins & Nurick, Langham in Rutland, and a London office

Hicks & Don, PO Box 7, Westbury, Wilts: Good quality wines chosen by a team of two Masters of Wine

Richard Kihl, 164 Regent's Park Road, London NW1

Laymont & Shaw, Truro, Cornwall: Excellent range of Spanish wines

Laytons, Gough Square, London EC4: Particularly good for burgundy and opening offers

Lorne House Vintners, Cranleigh, Surrey: Unusual wines from around Europe

Andrew Low Fine Wines, Dunwich, Suffolk: Makes a speciality of old and rare wines

Malmaison Wine Club, St Pancras Chambers, London NW1: Excellent value mail order wines from British Rail

La Reserve: Shops around London offering fine wines and helpful service

Geoffrey Roberts Associates, 98 Cheyne Walk, London SW10: Specialists in high quality California and Australian wines

Sherston Wine Co, Sherston, Wilts: Wide range of riojas

Stapylton Fletcher, Hillgate Farm, Colts Hill, Paddock Wood, Kent

Stonehaven Wines, Headley Down, Hants: Italian specialists

Yapp Bros, Mere, Wilts: Very good Rhônes and Loire wines

Yorkshire Fine Wines, Leeds 1

that a Sainsbury's one will never have. Admittance: £5 for a lifetime's 'share'. Gunnels Wood Road, Stevenage, Herts.

There is also the *Direct Sunday Times Wine Club* in which the author, who edits their quarterly magazine, must declare an interest. Membership fee is £3 a year and the Club's main advantages are its president Hugh Johnson, its selection of off-the-beaten-track wines, some jolly tastings and trips abroad – and the magazine of course. New Aquitaine House, Paddock Road, Caversham, Reading, Berks.

The Wine Mine Club is run in parallel with Peter Dominic, although they add to the PD list the odd special offer. Membership is £2.16 a year and they also organize tastings and wine tours. Vintner House, River Way, Harlow, Essex.

Les Amis du Vin is a 'new wave' wine merchant that has its own 'Le Club' and is connected with the American organization of the same name. Good range of unusual wines and excellent tastings and lectures. 51 Chiltern Street, London W1. £3.50 (or purchase of two cases of wine) a year.

BUYING AT AUCTION For very fine wines, the saleroom is the territory of the wine broker and the American millionaire. Those buying at auction are usually professionals who are fully aware of current market values, so when prices are rising it usually makes more sense for the amateur to buy from a traditional merchant who may have fixed his prices six months before. If prices are falling the converse, of course, is the case. There are also end-of-bin sales, particularly at Christie's South Kensington branch. There can be some bargains at this sort of sale but be careful about the condition of the wines, and take full advantage of any pre-sale tasting facilities – an exercise that can be an education in itself. Since the bigger the lot, the lower the unit price, it can make sense to buy in a consortium of friends. Make exact calculations about exactly how much VAT, duty, delivery charge and commission is payable before raising your hand. Christie's and Sotheby's are the top-flight auctioneers.

OTHER WAYS OF BUYING There are now a number of discount warehouses at which customers may taste wines and buy them by the case. They can keep overheads low, but do insist on trying everything before buying. General cash-and-carry depots, rather than those which specialize in wine, do not offer any great wine bargains in the writer's experience.

Be wary of buying from one-off newspaper advertisements. Always get some references for the 'company' before committing pen to cheque book as this is one of the Fraud Squad's oldest chestnuts.

People often think that the cheapest way to buy wine is to hop over the Channel, bring back a barrel or two and bottle it here. Nice idea but impractical and fraught with danger for anyone who has no bottling expertise. The wine can go out of condition easily and wooden casks themselves are very expensive. Do you have access to a high speed bottling line, bulk discounts on corks, bottles and labels? And you'll have to pay duty on the wine. Forget it. If you do buy wine abroad, buy it in a bottle. The current duty-free allowance for an EEC country is eight bottles a person, provided that person has no duty-free spirits.

GOOD VALUE IN GENERAL These are some general guidelines on what is better-than-average value at the moment:

Dry reds, claret style: Bordeaux of 'overshadowed' vintages such as '71 and '74, Bergerac, Côtes de Buzet, Côtes du Roussillon, Corbières, most vins de pays, claret-style riojas, north east Italian Cabernets Merlots, Chianti Classico, Rubesco Torgiano, Spanna, Gattinara, Cabernet Sauvignon from Bulgaria, Chile, South Africa.

Richer reds, burgundy style: (See page 170 for less expensive alternatives to the famous names in Burgundy) Rhône reds, burgundy-style riojas, Penedes, Yugoslavian Pinot Noir, some Argentine wines, South African Pinotage, Australian Shiraz.

Light, fruity reds, beaujolais style: Côtes de Ventoux, Coteaux du Tricastin, Gamay de l'Ardèche, Gamay de Touraine, Côtes du Forez.

Dry whites: This is the most difficult type of wine for which to find alternatives to the now increasingly expensive Burgundy and Loire regions. Try one of the Mâcon villages, one of the Pouilly villages other than Fuissé (not Fumé either), Sauvignon de Touraine, much dry white bordeaux, Côtes-du-Rhône, the whites of the Gard département, Vinho Verde, white rioja, Soave, north east Italian Pinots, Verdicchio, South African Steen and Chenin Blanc.

Medium dry white, German style: Many German wines themselves are still good value but alternatives are Austrian wines, Yugoslavian, Italian and Hungarian Rieslings.

Sweet whites: Sweet white bordeaux and Loire bargains still to be had, also richer Austrians as an alternative to sweeter white German wines.

Sparkling wines: Spanish sparkling wines from San Sadurni de Noya, some northern Italian dry wines plus Moscato Spumante as an alternative to the sweeter Asti Spumante.

Fortified wines: Most sherry is remarkably good value, montilla can be similar and even cheaper. Vermouth is cheap.

CHOOSING In choosing a wine from a restaurant or hotel wine list, very much the same considerations apply as in choosing wine from a wine shop, except that there are rather fewer clues to work on. That vital clue, the label, is available for inspection in only the most enterprising of wine lists. Most of them are maddeningly short on information. On some there is indication of neither shipper nor vintage, just the litany 'Beaujolais, Nuits-St-Georges, Côtes-du-Rhône, Valpolicella', and that degree of accuracy in spelling is exceptional. In cases like this you are quite justified in demanding more information, though you may well feel churlish about insisting on your rights on a busy Saturday night.

The most dubious wines on carelessly compiled lists, often a selection from the list of just one merchant, are the better known burgundies – Nuits-St-Georges, Beaune, Pommard, Volnay for red, Chablis and Pouilly Fuissé for white. Genuine versions of these wines are now heading for the £5 to £10 a bottle bracket in the shops, so be wary of cheap versions, and check to see that they are at least described as Appellation Contrôlée (though this alone is no *guarantee* of quality).

In most restaurants, the more you pay for a wine, the worse bargain you're getting because it is standard catering practice to add a set percentage, usually about 150 per cent, to the cost price of each wine in order to calculate its price on the wine list. This means that if diner A chooses a bottle that originally cost £2, he will have to pay £5 for it, while diner B's bottle which originally cost £8 will be marked up to a whacking £20. So whereas A pays an extra £3 for his bottle, B has to pay £12 extra. The answer then is to go for the cheapest bottle you feel is appropriate to the occasion. If a wine list shows every sign of being compiled by someone who cares about wine, then by all means try the house wines: it will probably be available by the glass for tasting first and may well be very good indeed.

READING THE WINE LIST Next to wine waiters, wine lists can be the most terrifying part of dining out. That heavily padded tome, the most expensive champagnes on the first page, the affordable wines hidden at the foot of the last. The wine waiter or sommelier looks on superciliously as the desperate diner riffles through trying to give the appearance that he knows each wine intimately and that it is only by chance that evening he decides to try that interesting-sounding country wine from La Mancha.

Do not panic. The average wine waiter, sadly, almost certainly knows much less than the average wine drinker. A highly skilled one will offer advice in a friendly way, otherwise he is probably trying to disguise his ignorance beneath a mask of contempt. The greatest wine authorities in the world would expect to be given some time in which to study a wine list, so insist on having a few minutes with the list on your own. Any good list should be divided into table wine and the different wine producing regions, with reds separated from whites, sweet whites from dry whites (this is particularly important for bordeaux) and champagne from other sparkling wines.

The information given on the wine list should include:

Name of the wine: Again, the more specific the better.
Its quality designation: By law this should be shown on wine lists as well as on labels. German wines described simply as 'Quality wines' will almost certainly be just QbA, unless a particular Prädikat is specified. In the claret section Château X AC Bordeaux, for example, is likely to be inferior to Chateaux Y AC Pauillac Cru Classé (see reference section).
Producer/négociant/importer: This information should be given too. There can be a world of difference between different shippers' versions of the same wine.
Vintage: This, as in choosing in a shop, is a vital factor. Be wary of lists that sport the careless '71/72'. A restaurateur who assumes two vintages of such differing quality are interchangeable is hardly likely to take much interest in other aspects of his wine cellar – and it is fairly safe to

assume that the worse vintage will appear. Do ask which vintage they really mean in cases like this, as it is only when customers show that they care about wine they get that the catering trade will do anything to improve the wines they offer.

From here on the same considerations apply as when choosing in a shop and when choosing the order of wines and what will go with what, the same considerations apply as when dining at home.

When confronted with a particularly terse list, the following may be of help:

1. Bordeaux is in general more reliable than burgundies whose shippers are not specified, provided one recognizes a château name.
2. If shippers *are* specified in Burgundy, widely available and always reliable are the 'two Louis', Latour and Jadot, with Georges Duboeuf beaujolais and Mâconnais wines usually coming well up to scratch.
3. Alsace is a good bet since their compulsory Alsace-bottling makes disappointments so rare, and even the worst wine list will surely list the grape variety of their Alsace wines.

RESTAURANT WINE LORE Having chosen your wine, you are well advised to work out exactly how many bottles you are going to need so that they can be opened and if necessary decanted (though this luxury is still largely reserved for the very swishest restaurants) in advance. The waiter should return to show you each bottle ordered. Do look to make sure he's got it right, particularly the vintage and the shipper, and check that the capsule is untouched. It has been known for bottles rejected by one diner to be palmed off on another. Carafe wine will simply be brought to the table, and wine lists must state exactly how much wine is in each carafe.

The waiter then cuts the capsule and takes out the cork prior to the Great Tasting Ritual. This practice of pouring the host the first sample of the wine has its advocates. It evolved from the time when the risk of being served a bad bottle of wine was considerably higher than it is now for all but the oldest and finest of wines. The idea is that the host should make sure that the wine is in good condition (*not* whether he likes it or not) before it is offered to his guests. This is all well and good except that today this performance can so often cause embarrassment and make an uncomfortable hiatus in what should be a relaxed social occasion. One wonders whether it wouldn't be better to dispense altogether with the ritual for all but the rarest of wines.

If a wine does happen to be in bad condition, which happens mercifully rarely with the sort of wine that makes up the bulk of restaurant orders, then it would surely not be disastrous if it had already been poured into each glass on the table rather than just the host's? If it's bad then the waiter can always keep a sample to send back to the merchant who supplied it and bring on clean glasses. This would seem sensible for everyday wines, and even the most ill-trained of wine waiters should be able to identify great wine lovers ordering very special bottles when the tasting ritual really is appropriate. In most restaurants the tasting ritual is made even more farcical by the fact that the wine waiter performs it only with the first bottle ordered. If the host asks for a second bottle of the same wine he will very rarely be given the chance to taste it separately, it will merely be used to top up the glasses – although in theory it stands quite as high a chance of being out of condition as the first one. The whole thing seems very illogical.

Since few restaurateurs share this view, most diners *are* expected to take part in the tasting ritual, which is really quite simple so long as it is kept in proportion. It starts to get out of proportion when over-zealous wine waiters pull the cork, sniff it and stick it under the host's nose so that he can have a whiff too. If the cork really stinks then so will the wine and the wine waiter should immediately do something about it rather than sharing the experience with his customer. Another bit of embarrassing ritual.

The next stage is to pour a tasting sample, centimetre to

an inch depth, into the glass of the host who should then just follow the usual tasting procedure outlined in Chapter One. Take a quick look to see that the wine is not murky, don't bother too much about any small bits of cork in the glass, swill the wine around and 'nose' it. (This should impress the wine waiter.) Your nose should be enough to tell whether the wine is clean and in good condition, though you may want to taste the wine too. If it really does smell dirty, stale, or in any other way repulsive, then the chances are that you have one of those rare bottles that are faulty and you should ask the wine waiter whether he would like to take the wine away, taste it himself and come back with his opinion and (you hope) another bottle. This is a good move since it prevents a dispute at the table spoiling the fun and allows the waiter to get a second opinion if necessary. Of course if there are any great wine lovers in the party, it is wise to get their opinion too at this stage. You are quite within your rights to send back a bottle that is clearly 'off', though it is unfair on everyone to send it back just because you don't happen to like it.

This is the stage at which you should note the temperature of the wine, particularly white wine, and specify whether you think the wine should be kept in an ice bucket or not.

In Australia there are a healthy number of restaurants where you can bring your own wine, some 'BYO's being very interested in wine indeed. This is sadly uncommon in Britain where it is always worth trying to take along your own bottle for special occasions, if you want to. The restaurateur will set his own corkage charge and you should always discuss this in advance. Even the fiercest levy rarely leaves you worse off than choosing a similar wine from the restaurant list.

BUYING WINE ELSEWHERE

Pubs: One word of advice – don't. Most pubs sell wine in poor condition and this is one of those vicious circles. The fewer of the pub's customers drink wine, the longer it takes to finish a bottle, the more disgusting the wine left in the bottle becomes, the fewer customers want to drink wine, and so on. So far, there are no regulations covering the size of 'a glass' either, so all in all the wine lover gets a bad deal in most pubs. A light, dry sherry on the rocks is sometimes the only solution for the wine lover.

Wine bars: Can be wonderful. Good for tasting practice and comparing different wines without buying a whole bottle. If buying by the glass be wary of bottles that have obviously been open a long time though. Wide variation in the range and quality of wines offered.

Travelling:
Trains: Those in charge of buying wine for British Rail (and British Transport Hotels) really do care about the quality as well as the price. Their shops on main-line stations can often offer excellent value, specially 'bin ends', and are much better than the prices and range offered 'aboard'.
Planes: Airlines seem to believe in cold storage for everything and that includes their red wine, so it is usually more sensible to order white, though airlines' own brands of wine can be pretty disappointing. The quarter bottles of champagne served on aeroplanes are usually greatly inferior to the wine sold under the same label in standard bottles. Make sure they're opened in front of you and not topped up with the first class passengers' leftovers. These quarter bottles make good containers for your own wine leftovers at home.
Ships: If you can afford a cruise, you probably don't need any advice on wine.

3. Storing wine

Is it worth it? – What to lay down and for how long – Ideal storage conditions

IS IT WORTH IT? Long gone are the days when being a wine lover was synonymous with maintaining a vast cellar, which is a reflection of the cost of money and the ways of modern architects nowadays. Most houses in the UK now don't even have a cellar – indeed in very modern houses it can be difficult to find any part of it where the temperature ever falls to the ideal cellar temperature in the low fifties, let alone a spot that is free from vibration, strong light and smells. And yet so much fine wine is sold today long before it is ready to drink that it would be to commit infanticide to pull the cork before sitting on it for a while.

Fine wine is fine because it is so complex. During their ripening the grapes absorb a marvellous range of elements from the soil which, when the wine is young, are raw, undeveloped and still not knitted together. When the wine is young it will have the 'aroma' of the grape but will not yet have the subtle 'bouquet' that comes only when the wine has lain in bottle for some years. During this time air enters the bottle in minute amounts via the cork, combines with the wine and welds the elements in it together.

In ordinary, less subtle wine, on the other hand, most of the flavour will already be coming into its own by the time it has been bottled and the wine may be best as soon as it is bottled. Many cheaper wines now are heated up before bottling, specifically so that they will *not* change in the short term in any case. The chances are that your supermarket wine was bottled only a couple of weeks before you bought it, although some bottlers make a point of warehousing their wines for a few months before dispatching them to the shelves.

So does it make sense to buy wine ahead? If you are the sort who has been drinking wine at the average rate of a bottle a night for the last twenty years and yet have never managed to keep a spare unopened bottle in the house overnight, then the answer is clearly 'no'. But for people with just a fraction of self-restraint, then the answer is a resounding 'yes'. (The way to stop yourself filching from your own cellar is to make it as inaccessible a place as possible, as explained below.)

There are so many advantages. If you have a selection of wines to choose from in your 'cellar', whether it be vaults of well stocked bins under the house or a couple of cases in the broom cupboard, it can be very satisfying to choose just the right bottle for the food you're going to eat or the friends you're going to entertain. And you should never be left in the exasperating position of running out of wine, or being forced to buy it expensively and disastrously at the local pub. Whatever wines you buy in advance of consuming them, from finest claret to the most modest wine, it makes sense to buy in quantity. Almost all merchants give discounts on wine bought by the case of a dozen bottles, twenty-four halves or six magnums, and may well not mind if this is a mixed case.

And then there is the more general question of economics, or more precisely for most of us, the question of finance. If wine prices are rising faster than the bank rate, then it must make sense to buy as much wine as the bank manager will allow. Obviously the faster a wine rises in price the better economic sense it makes to buy in advance, though to take gambles of this sort requires a combination of clairvoyance and careful study of price trends in auction prices. Joining the mailing list of Christie's and Sotheby's can help a great deal here.

While it would be unwise to invest in more fast-maturing, everyday wines than one could drink in six months or so, it makes a great deal of sense to buy fine wines early in their lifetime and 'lay them down' to mature. The earlier you buy from a vintage that looks certain to be a good one, the more of a bargain you are likely to have, and you will be certain of your supply. Good wines of good vintages come on the market about eighteen months or two years after the vintage and then have a habit of disappearing into thin air only to reappear in the salerooms fifteen years later tagged by handsome reserve prices. Most of the traditional wine merchants and many of the 'new wave' lot make special 'opening offers' of good wines of most vintages. You may have to wait a while until you actually get to see the wine, but since you'll have to wait considerably longer for it to mature, this is no great hardship and allows you more of that valuable commodity, cellar space. And when you do have a case or two of a maturing wine in your cellar, you will be able to follow its development by judicious sampling of single bottles over the years. This itself is a fascinating exercise and helps you to drink most of the wine when it is absolutely at its best.

You will also be completely sure that the wine is what it claims to be, and need have no worries that the wine has been mishandled for you can guarantee correct temperature, humidity and so on yourself. The deposit that forms during the wine's development will be disturbed only when you carry the bottle from cellar to dining-room.

As for buying wine solely for investment, this always seems a bit sad, like buying a beautiful picture only to put in a safe until you need to raise some cash. Investing in fine wines usually does make commercial sense, and if only by investing in a case of first growth claret can you afford to drink a bottle of it, then perhaps it is justifiable.

Once you have bought your wines for investment, you will have to sit on them until they are mature to realize your investment satisfactorily. This normally means selling the wine through an auction house. Since there are certain fixed costs involved in selling any wine, it makes sense to sell only fine wine, so head for the most expensive wine you can afford. At the time of writing vintage port, classed growth red and white bordeaux and burgundy of single vineyard status are all safe bets – but then who is to know what catastrophe will render these poor investments?

WHAT TO LAY DOWN AND FOR HOW LONG In times of high interest rates it is a happy man who convinces himself that he likes his wines best when they are young. The French have got nearer to a sensible solution to the current problem of affording wine at its best than we have for they regularly drink wine of vintages that most Britons consider are still in their infancy. Winemakers themselves are helping to a certain extent too by making wines that mature faster by fermenting the grapes faster, allowing grape skins to come into contact with the must for a shorter time and reducing the harsh tannin content that can make young wines so hard to enjoy. This may mean that the resulting wine will lose a bit of its potential complexity, but makes a very much more commercial proposition. There are those who maintain that while the quality of the world's worst wine is getting better all the time, the quality of the best wine is gradually lowering. It is still true, however, that the world's greatest wines need time to show how great they are. Below is a guide to what they are and how long they should remain in your cellar.

Vintage port is the classic wine to lay down and needs time to be even pleasant, let alone great. The magnificent tradition of laying down a 'pipe' (about 750 bottles) of port for one's newly born godchild's 21st birthday gives some idea of port's stamina. This intensely concentrated wine tastes fiery, hard and almost metallic when young and in a good ripe vintage it can be decades before it is worth even trying.

Vintages to drink now: 1960, 1958 and any pre 1955.
Those to keep: 1977 1975, 1970, 1967, 1966, 1963, 1955 and some 1945s.

The finest *claret* too may need decades to mature. First growths particularly and those châteaux with a high proportion of Cabernet in the vineyard (Edmund Penning-Rowsell's book in Bordeaux gives the *encepagement* of most important châteaux) need twenty years and more to soften them, particularly in good, ripe vintages, while less concentrated wines from a much more 'forward' vintage such as 1973 were coming into their own within three or four years of the vintage. Generally speaking, the wines from the 'right bank' of the river, the St Emilions and Pomerols, mature faster than the Médocs and Graves from the rive gauche, and the cheaper blended wines that cost considerably less than the classed growths may be ready even before this. The recommendations given below are for a cru classé of the Médoc.

Vintages to drink now: 1974, 1973, 1971, 1967, 1964, 1962, and anything pre-1960.
Vintages to keep: 1978, 1976, 1975, 1970, 1966, 1961.

Fine *red burgundy* is well worth investing in if you can afford it, but only above the level of a single vineyard from a reputable grower. It is a sensible thing to buy early for your own consumption, if you can afford to, particularly as you will be able to enjoy it before your claret of the same vintage. All but the very best will be ready within ten years of the vintage, depending of course on the individual vintage characteristics.

Vintages to drink now: 1973, 1972, 1971, 1970, 1969, 1966, 1961.
Vintages to keep: 1978, 1976, some 1971s.

Sweet white bordeaux is recovering from a period of being out of fashion in most major wine buying countries and if you are a lover of sauternes it would be wise to assure yourself of something to drink through the Eighties before prices take off. The great sauternes will keep for decades, a 1900 Suduiraut was still lively when tasted nearly eighty years later. Do not be alarmed by the toffee colour in very old sauternes, this is not necessarily a sign that the wine is out of condition.

Vintages to drink now: 1971, 1970, 1969, 1967, 1962, 1961.
Vintages to keep: 1978, 1976, 1975.

The great *German sweet wines* are also worth keeping and can often develop similar characteristics to old Sauternes, the major difference being that they keep the 'nose' of the grape variety, usually Riesling. The seventies were blessed by outstanding vintages in 1976, 1975 and 1971, some of whose wines of Auslese quality and above will last until the turn of the century.

Vintages to drink now: 1977, 1973, 1970.
Vintages to keep: 1976, 1975, 1971.

White burgundy of good quality deserves maturing to give it a lovely richness that comes only with age – though many of the lesser appellations and the wines of the Mâcon area are best drunk young. Expect the wines to gain in colour.

Vintages to drink now: 1973, 1971, 1970, 1969.
Vintages to keep: 1978, 1976, 1975, 1974.

These are all the wines that it is traditional to lay down, and those which appear regularly in the salerooms. In addition to these are all sorts of less 'classic' wines that will repay keeping for some years after the vintage before they are drunk, most of them reds. Wines from the northern Rhône and the meatiest sort of Châteauneuf-du-Pape need almost a decade before they are showing their best, and the powerful wines of Piedmont, Barolos and Barbarescos, need at least this until they are soft enough to enjoy. Good chianti will also probably need about seven years' ageing but most other Italian wines commonly available in this country are ready to drink within a few years of the vintage.

In the past, riojas tended to be released for sale only when they were ready to drink, but the increasing popularity of these wines is bringing about a change here. Most good rioja will need about seven years before it reaches a state of maturity, while its Portuguese counterpart Dão often needs even longer.

It is rarely a good idea to sit on stocks of beaujolais; and nouveaux of any sort should be drunk as soon as possible. The exceptions to this are Beaujolais village wines from an exceptionally ripe vintage like 1976, particularly from Moulin-à-Vent, the village whose wines become curiously like more northerly burgundy with age. Other French reds worth ageing are the more concentrated wines of the south west such as superior Côtes du Roussillon, Corbières and Cahors, noted for the longevity of its 'black' (tannic) wines in olden days. There are a few wines from classic European grape varieties, notably the Cabernet, being exported from producers such as the Bulgarians now and these wines cry out to be stored away for a decade or so. Further afield, but for similar reasons, the thick, better quality reds of Chile, Argentina, South Africa, Australia and particularly those of California will become very much more interesting with several years' cellar age.

As for white wine, there are a few names other than classic white burgundy and the dessert wines of Bordeaux and Germany that deserve a place in any spacious cellar. The Loire valley produces some very underrated dessert wines too and these, like their counterparts further south in Sauternes, need time to show their greatness. Some of them are remarkably long-lived. Also well worth at least a decade's bottle age are Alsace's answer to Germany's sweet wines, Vendange Tardive wines and the odd Reserve Exceptionelle made only in specially good years. Some of Rioja's better quality Spanish whites age into the style of a fine old white burgundy and can provide an alternative for a fraction of the cost. The same happens to Portuguese whites of a similar style, though while they continue to export very little other than vinho verde this advice must remain theoretical. It is difficult to think of any Italian whites that improve with age, but the richer Austrians repay waiting handsomely. All Chardonnays repay keeping.

Most people would advise against giving sparkling wines any precious cellar space and this is certainly true of most of the non-champagnes and of the non vintage champagnes from famous houses which should be sold only when they are ready to drink. There are two exceptions however. One reason why less well-known champagnes are often so relatively inexpensive is that their producers sell them as soon as they are legally allowed to do so rather than letting them rest and acquire enough bottle age to take the sharp edge off. It can make sense, therefore, to put a few bottles of 'buyer's own brand' champagne away for a year or so. And if you have a quite understandable penchant for old champagne (one of the many things the French find impossible to understand about British wine buyers) then your only chance of laying your hands on some is probably to put some good vintage champagne away in your own cellar. Otherwise, buy champagne hand-to-mouth – unless a friend in Rheims tips you off that champagne prices are about to rise.

Most other wines need not be laid down for more than the optional few months to rest them. Light dry whites like Muscadet, Sancerre, Pouillys of all sorts, Mâcon of all villages, anything labelled Sauvignon, all but the very best dry white bordeaux, most Alsace, German QbAs and most Kabinetts, white Rhône, Italian Soave, Verdicchio, Frascati, Orvieto, most white from the Iberian peninsula, most Eastern European whites (except Tokay), and all but Chardonnays from the world's newer wine producers should be drunk as young as possible, from the best vintage of the previous three years say. Lightweight reds, most beaujolais, most southern Rhône, all but the finest red Bourgeuil in the Loire, vins de pays and most VDQS, Valpolicella, Bardolino, anything remotely 'fresh and fruity' should again be gobbled up while it can still be described as such.

Most fortified wines other than vintage port need be bought only as you need them. The only exception to this is fine madeira and very superior sherries, not the mass market ones that have been sweetened up for current consumption, but fine true amontillados and olorosos that will become beautiful fortified and fortifying wines.

IDEAL STORAGE CONDITIONS The essential attributes of an ideal place to store wine, a place that can be called, however inappropriately, 'a cellar', are that its temperature should vary by no more than a few degrees throughout the year and that the wine should be protected from strong light and vibration. Nor should it be too easily accessible: the 'cellar' that consists of a wine rack in the dining-room, keeping the wine nicely at ideal drinking temperature, is easy to empty.

The exact process of ageing in a wine is still not crystal clear to scientists and winemakers, but it seems that the higher the temperature the faster the wine matures, the lower it is the longer it will take for the wine to reach its peak. One might think, therefore, that all wine should be packed away in the fridge so that it would mature ever so subtly to reach a level of complexity never before encountered in a wine. But of course the wine's natural deterioration would make this ploy a disaster. The preserving effects of the tannin or acidity would give up the struggle long before the wine had got anywhere near ripeness, and the wine's owner would presumably be well into his dotage. Through experimentation it has been found that the ideal temperature at which to age wine is between 45° and 55°, with whites at the bottom end of the range (and therefore the bottom end of the wine rack – hot air rising and all that) and the reds at the top.

It has also been shown that the constancy of temperature may well be more important than the temperature itself. Whatever the actual temperature it is important to avoid sudden changes as this will give the wine a jolt and interfere with the gentle maturing process. The cellars of some restaurants whose wine lists have won the finest of reputations are a revelation. Shirtsleeve stuff, for the wines are kept at constant ready-to-serve chambré temperature.

The cellar space should be sufficiently free from vibration that the bottles and sediment are not jolted (what all those rich San Francisco wine lovers will do when the next quake comes, I dare not think) and the wine should not be exposed to strong light for any period of time since this can spoil the wine by affecting its colour and occasionally causing oxidation. Wine such as Sauternes is particularly vulnerable to light. Don't treat the cellar like a dark room though; a few hours with the door open will hardly cause irreparable damage.

It is often very difficult to find anywhere in modern houses that can offer a few dozen bottles these conditions. Old air raid shelters are fine, but few houses are built with air raid shelters nowadays either. At least the British climate helps. Texans, Floridans, Australians and South Africans have to have cellars built specially. In Britain it is enough to find somewhere free from draughts at a fairly constant temperature. There are a few possibilities here, even without having recourse to miles of subterranean passages. The bottoms of rarely used cupboards are often good, particularly if the cupboards are fitted and therefore won't shake every time the doors are opened. A well-insulated attic or cupboard under the stairs can do at a pinch, particularly if fitted with special vibration-minimizing wine racks, or an old fireplace excavated with doors added. If there really is nowhere in your house that is suitable, most serious wine merchants can offer cellaring facilities for not much more than £1 a case a year, but this has disadvantages for anyone who gets pleasure from the sight as well as the thought of their wine collection. If you buy a very large quantity of wine straight from a foreign merchant you may be able to store it in the bonded warehouse of a merchant, thereby avoiding paying duty on it until you want to drink it.

Supposing you do find a suitable resting place for your wine, install a wine rack that will take as many bottles as possible – its material and construction will not have any great effect on the wine. It is important only that you are able to store any wine you keep for more than a year in a horizontal position so that the cork is kept from drying out to a state of not fulfilling its function as a closure. Store reds above whites and remember that the smaller the bottle the faster it will mature – a good reason for leaving halves on the bottom shelf perhaps? A rack of some sort is well worthwhile since the alternative cardboard cases are easily collapsible, particularly in a cellar where there is any humidity.

Too little humidity can cause corks to dry out prematurely and hastens the development of the wine, but too much can have serious effects on the labels. Try spraying the labels with some fixative before cellaring the bottles.

Care should be taken that there are no strong smells that could affect the wine in your cellar. Don't put your precious bottles in the same place as you keep the weed-killer.

If you have more than a few dozen wines in your cellar it is wise and can be fun to keep a record of what you've got and how it was when last tasted – you can even go so far as to call it your cellarbook and hope that you do as well out of it as Mr Saintsbury did.* Keep your notes in columns under the headings: detailed description of wine, quantity bought, price paid, when bought, where bought, when tasted, tasting notes and comments. This way, even with quite a modest wine, you can compare a series of impressions of different bottles of the same wine tried at intervals over a few years.

* George Saintsbury's 'Notes on a Cellar Book' is a classic record of wine drinking published in 1920.

4. Wine and health

There is something intrinsically healthy and natural about the whole concept of wine, wine as defined by the usual wine trade definition:

> Wine is the alcoholic beverage obtained from the fermentation of the juice of freshly-gathered grapes, the fermentation taking place in the district of origin according to local tradition and practice.

Despite its apparent longwindedness, this definition sums up a delightfully simple process requiring no extraneous chemicals or physical techniques whatsoever, for all that is necessary to make wine is contained in one simple package – the grape itself. Inside the ripened grape is sugar which when the skins are broken ferments under the action of yeast on the outside of the skin to produce alcohol, swelled by the water content of the grape, enlivened by its acidity and flavoured by a wealth of elements absorbed from the soil in which it was grown.

All so simple that men have been making wine for centuries – certainly since the tenth century BC, according to archaeologists. The advent of the sealed container started a new era for wine by allowing it to develop to maturity, and now modern winemakers are able to make the production of good wine a certainty rather than a possibility.

It is only very recently that wine has slipped from the status of medicinal to simply pleasurable. Ancient texts are dotted with references to wine as a cure, prophylactic and antiseptic, many patent remedies in the last century had a wine base and wine was still being prescribed as a restorative for the wounded of the First World War.

There has never been a shortage of people who claim beneficial properties for particular wines and in the most recent publication on the subject, *Wine – the best medicine*, a French doctor E. A. Maury manages to prescribe a (French) wine for almost every known ailment. While it may be a little optimistic to expect a couple of glasses of red Graves a day to cure anaemia, or a daily dose of Sancerre to relieve gallstones, it is certain that wine is an important aid to digestion. By playing on the taste buds and the olfactory system it excites the appetite and prepares the body for an intake of food. And it is worth pointing out here that moderate wine drinkers are noted for their longevity.

Wine is also a good killer of harmful bacteria. The addition of wine to water of dubious origin has been recommended throughout the ages and is still practised today in countries without a reliable water supply. Alcohol itself is an antiseptic and the particular solution in which it occurs in wine seems to be optimal in terms of washing out the body without washing out the brain.

For there is no doubt that one of the attractions of this liquid, nicely balanced between sweet and acid, subtly flavoured, is in one of its components, a particular chemical compound $C_2H_5.OH$, ethyl alcohol. Without deadening the senses in the way that spirits can, or bloating the stomach in the way that beer and cider do, wine manages to provide alcohol in just the right dose to stimulate the intellect and relax the body. Alcohol is a drug in the same way that caffeine in coffee is, or nicotine in cigarettes. It can be a very beneficial drug, becoming harmful only when taken in excess – unlike nicotine which has a cumulative effect. It is difficult to stipulate what constitutes 'excess', since it varies according to body weight and the drinker's attitude, but moderate wine drinking is surely one of the most pleasant ways to regulate alcoholic intake.

Roughly speaking, light wine is three times as strong, volume for volume, as beer and one third as strong as spirits, though wines themselves vary tremendously in strength, which is important to understand when monitoring consumption. Light wine varies in strength from about 8 per cent in lightweight Moselles (i.e. there are eight centilitres of pure alcohol in every litre of the wine) to the rather manlier 16 per cent of some of the more full-bodied Italian reds. (Percentage alcoholic strength for wines is often expressed as degrees on the label.) The average light wine sold in this country is probably between 10 and 11 per cent, while fortified or 'heavy' wines vary from just under 18 per cent for most sherries and vermouths (sometimes as little as 15 per cent for lighter sherries and Montilla) to 21 per cent for full-bodied fortified wines such as port. With practice it is possible to gauge the alcoholic strength of a wine even if it is not given on the label. As explained in Chapter One it is a matter of tasting the wine's 'weight'.

Spirits like gin, whisky, brandy and rum are 40 per cent alcohol (40° Gay Lussac as used commonly to describe wine's strength, 70° British proof, 80° US proof), vodka about 37 per cent and liqueurs can vary from much less than this in fruit brandies to very much more for liqueurs like Chartreuse. This means that a standard 1/6 gill measure of most spirits contains about the same amount of alcohol as an eighth of a standard bottle of wine, rather less than a glassful. Since it takes the body about ninety minutes to completely assimilate this amount of alcohol, little and often is very much more beneficial than mammoth doses of alcohol in any form.

Unlike spirits, wine is rich in nutrients and minerals, containing not only carbohydrate but also protein, a range of vitamins and is an important source of minerals including potassium, magnesium, calcium, sodium and iron. These trace elements vary considerably from wine to wine depending on the mineral composition of the soil in which the grapes were grown. The origin of the Graves-for-anaemia prescription, for instance, is that there is a high proportion of iron in the soil of the Graves region.

A litre of wine contains between 600 and 1000 calories, a bottle between 450 and 600 and a glass between 75 and 100 calories depending on the strength and sweetness of the wine. A half pint of beer contains about 150 calories while a 1/6 gill measure of spirits contains about 70, and with a mixer could make up to 170 calories.

Both alcohol content and sweetness contribute to making a wine high in calories. Light, dry wines such as Muscadet and Chablis are some of the least fattening, while heavy sweet wines such as port and the richer sherries are some of the highest in calories. It is a myth that white wine is less fattening than red. Some of the least fattening wines are red, provided they are light and dry like beaujolais, the Loire reds of Chinon and Bourgeuil, and some Italian reds. Most of the apparently innocuous German whites on the other hand are fairly high in sugar, and Beerenauslesen and Trockenbeerenauslesen are loaded high with calories, though it is a rich man who can afford to put on weight by indulging his passion for these rarities.

Section II

A WINE DIRECTORY

5. How wine is made

Climate – Soil – Situation of the vineyard – Vines and grapes – The vineyard year – Secrets of the winery

The magic of wine is its variety, how the juice of a single fruit, the grape, can through fermentation and nurturing be persuaded to produce liquids as different as Muscadet and Sauternes, Médoc and Sekt. This is because so many factors play a part in affecting the final taste of a wine – the weather of a particular year, the sort of soil in and below the vineyard, its exact siting, the variety of grapes planted, their age, the way they are tended (viticulture) and the way they are made into wine (vinification). To realize how important each of these factors is, it is enough to consider what happens when one or more of them are changed.

There is a winemaker who was given the freedom to search the world to find a place that would most exactly duplicate the conditions in Bordeaux. He has now settled in California's Napa Valley and is making wine as close to the Bordeaux model as possible – same grape, same wood, same techniques of viticulture and vinification. The only differences are slight variations in soil and climate. This is enough, however, to produce a style of wine that is quite, quite distinct from claret. His wines have a definite California nose to them.

Then there are those who have planted different parts of the same vineyard with different grape varieties. The wine from the different plots will be totally different. And the wine produced by the same vine variety in the same vineyard will vary very noticeably with how long the vine has been planted there. Any new vineyard goes through tremendous evolution of taste in the wine it produces over the years as the vines grow older.

CLIMATE If climate did not play an important part in wine production then the Eskimos and Bantus would doubtless be involved in winemaking. As it is, wine can be made satisfactorily from grapes grown only in two bands round the earth, roughly between 33°N and 50°N in the northern hemisphere (that's between Casablanca and Frankfurt) and between 23°S and 40°S in the southern hemisphere, from about São Paulo to Melbourne. The upper limit on distance from the equator is imposed by the fact that grapes need a minimum amount of sunshine, an average of about six hours a day from May to September, in order to ripen them. The mean, green grapes that vines in the north of England usually manage to produce would never contain enough sugar to make them worth fermenting. But vines also need a fairly cool winter during which they can lie dormant and gather their strength for the next summer's growth, so it is difficult to produce wine of any great quality from vines grown too near the equator.

There are those who try to defy the restrictions of climatology. There has been a steady increase in English vine growers, presumably encouraged by their mediaeval counterparts, who are doing their best to make wine considerably to the north of the 50°N limit – with a fair degree of success provided that they choose their vineyard site and grape varieties carefully. On the other hand, the Mexicans grow grapes very much closer to the equator than suggested by the limits suggested above. Vines may be planted at high altitudes where the temperatures are lower, and they may be grown in a climate so hot that the vines have to do without a winter holiday and two mediocre crops rather than one good crop are harvested each year or grapes may be picked very early and fermented at specially low temperatures.

The world's wine production is concentrated round the Mediterranean, towards the southern tips of Australia, South America and South Africa, on the west coast of North America and around Lake Ontario in the east. In many other areas within the two bands of latitude, inland climates or very high attitudes mean that winters are too severe for the vine to survive, but it is interesting and exciting to speculate about potential wine-producing regions that are yet to be exploited. Japan is already developing her wine production but there is no reason to doubt that parts of China could produce excellent wine. It is also thought that much of Australia has great potential for vinegrowing.

The first requirement in wine production then is that the vineyard should be planted where it stands a chance of getting the sort of weather it needs: an average annual temperature not far off 15°C (58°F), cool winters, warm sunny summers with enough rain to make the grapes juicy. Each year's weather may bring hazards, however, and each wine producing area has its own most-feared meteorological disaster.

Frost can be a great enemy of the vine and is a particular worry in northerly vineyards such as those by the Moselle which are not tempered by proximity to the sea. In mid-winter when the vines are pruned back to only a few inches of stump above the ground, they can withstand frost quite well. It is only when the temperature falls below −15°C (5°F) that the roots give up the struggle, split and die. Spring frost is much more dangerous as it can kill off an entire year's crop if it strikes when there are already tender young shoots on the vine.

At the time when the vine flowers, strong winds can seriously reduce the potential size of the crop, while a summer that is too dry will probably be followed by a vintage of shrivelled, thick-skinned grapes. Hailstorms at vintage time are disastrous as they split the grapeskins while still in the vineyard, exposing them to the risk of rot and spoilage. This is a great worry for Burgundian vignerons, some of whom have even been known to finance their own anti-hail airforce. Rain at vintage time is also regarded as a great misfortune and has the effect of producing weak, watery wines.

As well as each region's having its own particular climate, each tiny strip of vineyard has its own particular characteristics, as every gardener will recognize. It is important therefore that a vineyard is sited not only in a good climate, but in a good 'micro-climate'. See the section on situation of the vineyard below.

SOIL Vines are not unlike journalists: the worse the conditions in which they have to work, the better the end-product from most of them. Vines often flourish best in ground that is too poor to interest the farmer in any other crop. The vineyards of the Médoc where some of the world's greatest wines are produced are made up of a mass of pebbles on gravelly soil. The key to the quality of the wine produced in these vineyards is that they are well-drained, forcing the vine to search many metres below ground level to get moisture, embryonic wine, thereby absorbing a wide variety and high concentration of different trace elements that will eventually be responsible for great complexity and subtlety in the resultant flavour of the wine.

A vine planted in rich, fertile soil doesn't have to struggle at all. Life is easy, the wine has no need for deep roots, it can find enough water only a few feet below the surface, and providing the nitrogen content of the soil is sufficiently high, the vine will produce a high yield of unexciting wine with no trouble at all. Much of the wine produced in 'New World' wine regions is already of a very high standard. It will be fascinating to see what happens when the nether regions of their wine producing zones are explored.

There are certain classic combinations of wine and soil types and, knowing them, it is tempting to search for the 'taste of the soil' in the wine. Here are some of the best known:

Moselle and Rheingau	Slate
Champagne	Chalk
Médoc	Well-drained gravel
South Rhône	Large flat stones
Douro (port)	Schist
Jerez (sherry)	Chalk
Madeira	Volcanic deposit

SITING OF THE VINEYARD Of course there is immense variation in soil types even within very small areas and this is at least part of the explanation for the way in which wine produced from contiguous plots can taste quite different. What is vital to determine the taste of a wine are not only the characteristics of the region in which a vineyard is sited, but those of its own little patch on earth.

The perfect vineyard should not be too high, otherwise it could be open to the danger of strong winds; nor should it be in a damp, frost-ridden valley floor. It should not be too close to a plantation of trees as these tend to produce excess moisture, though it is not *always* a bad thing for vines to be close to a source of moisture – the grapes grown in vineyards on the steep sides of the Moselle and Rhine benefit considerably from the extra sunlight reflected off the river's surface.

A slightly sloping site is usually ideal as it maximizes exposure to the sunshine that is all-important in vineyards in northern Europe, while in wine regions closer to the equator particularly cool micro-climates are sought out for vineyards. Whether vines are planted parallel or at right-angles to prevailing winds can also be important, affecting the amount of heat that is retained in the vineyard.

And then there are other factors that would make a particular site undesirable as a vineyard site – being down-wind of some strong-smelling industrial development, for instance, or somewhere particularly prey to hungry birds. A vigneron's lot may not always be such a happy one.

VINES AND GRAPES Once the prospective wine producer has chosen his site, choice of grape variety is probably the single most important factor in determining the taste of a wine. The reason that the fermented juice of the grape should give rise to as much pleasure and variety as it does compared with other fruit wines is because the vine is such a remarkable plant. It is important therefore to choose the right sort of grape variety for any particular set of climatological and soil conditions.

In the far north of Europe's classic wine producing area, in Germany's more northerly sites where every minute of sunshine counts, any vine that is frost resistant and a late ripener is obviously at a premium, which is why the elegant Riesling is so popular with those who make superlative wines in good years. While in the Médoc where the soil conditions and climate are likely to produce a complex wine that will take some time to develop, growers choose Cabernet Sauvignon, a long-lasting grape with a long life and a thick skin which preserves colour and tannin and discourages rot.

It is fascinating to examine what happens when grape varieties are taken from one wine producing region to another. By now the classic Cabernet has been tried in all the serious wine producing regions of the world, to good effect in many of them; the native grape of the northern Rhône valley, Syrah, is now Australia's staple red in the form of Shiraz; South Africa is working hard on the Loire valley's Chenin Blanc; Californians have been wowed by Chardonnay, the white grape of Burgundy. It is noticeable that some grapes make much better travellers than others. While globe-trotting Cabernet Sauvignon has been planted successfully from Chile via Tuscany to Coonawarra, Burgundy's classic red wine grape Pinot Noir is a distinctly queasy traveller in unfamiliar wine regions, though it performs well in nearby Champagne.

The great wines of the world are great because the climate/soil/grape combination is already perfect even before the winemaker sets to work. Other wines may be less than exciting because they are made from the wrong sort of grapes. There is still enormous room for experimentation with established grape varieties in unfamiliar terrain. The Penedes firm Torres, for example, have produced remarkable results with classic French grapes planted in northern Spain, and the remarkable Sassicaia of central Italy is an example of what the great claret grape Cabernet Sauvignon can do in chianti country.

Also exciting is the constant development of new grape varieties, and here the German institute at Geisenheim and the University of California at Davis are pioneers in trying to find varieties that will produce good wines in worthwhile quantity in different sets of soil and climatological conditions. There has also been much work on clones of different vine varieties here.

Most of the world's greatest wines are produced in very

small quantities while vines with very high yields tend to make wines of much less subtlety. In France, for instance, the amount of wine produced per area, the yield or *rendement*, can be as little as thirty hectolitres per hectare (about half a bottle of wine per vine) for a top property while it can easily top 100 hectolitres per hectare in the Midi. For some time it was thought that this was a necessary inverse relationship, but work with some new varieties indicates what the accountants had hoped all along – that it is possible to combine quantity with quality. So while it is unlikely that any of these researchers will persuade the owners of Château Latour to replant with Ruby Cabernet in the near future, we should be seeing more of these new varieties being used for the production of medium quality wine in the next decade or so. The Germans are already well on the way to replanting some vineyards with varieties that have been specially developed for particular conditions.

THE VINE FAMILY Vines belong to the same botanical family as the Virginia creeper, and show the same inclination to clamber skywards given anything to clamber up, as witness all those vine-shaded doorways in southern Europe. Without a stake, vines grow wild in untamed bushes, but these are not usually suitable for wine producing.

The vine genus is called *vitis* and the particular species that produces the wine drunk in most parts of the world is *vitis vinifera*, 'wine-bearing vine'. There are many hundreds of different varieties of *vitis vinifera* – some known to be more closely related than others, while quite how others of them fit into the world's *vitis vinifera* family is not yet known. The Cabernet Sauvignon of Bordeaux and the Cabernet Franc of the Loire, for instance, are close relatives, and the Trebbiano which makes Orvieto and Frascati in Italy reappears as the Ugni Blanc in the south of France and further north as the St Emilion grape that makes base wines used in the production of cognac. But there are mysteries still, such as where California's native grape the Zinfandel came from. It sounds as though it has a colourful history.

On pp. 121–3 is a guide to some of the more important grape varieties.

CHARACTERISTICS OF CLASSIC RED GRAPE VARIETIES

Cabernet Sauvignon: Long-lasting, tough when young, blackcurrant aroma, at its best in Bordeaux but produces excellent wines in California, Australia and many other areas.

Cabernet Franc: Second grape of Bordeaux, lesser cousin of Cabernet Sauvignon, also used for red Loires, with an aroma often reminiscent of raspberries.

Merlot: Produces soft fruity wines. Used to soften Cabernet in Bordeaux, most important grape in St Emilion and Pomerol. Commonly grown in north eastern Italy.

Pinot Noir: Classic red burgundy grape and an important ingredient in Champagne where it is vinified off the skins so as to produce a white wine. Not too successful elsewhere, so far. Sweet and scented.

Gamay: The 'fresh and fruity' grape at its best in Beaujolais. Elsewhere its lightness and acidity are not usually so attractive.

Syrah: Classic grape of northern Rhône for Hermitage etc., and grown extensively in Australia as Shiraz. Easily recognizable by its intense mulberry colour and thick, almost 'gamey' smell.

Grenache: Useful medium weight slightly sweet grape widely planted in southern France and in Rioja where it is known as Garnacha. Good rosés.

Portugieser: No known connection with Portugal. Makes light, slightly inky reds in Germany and Austria.

Nebbiolo: Very dark purplish red, name comes from *nebbia*, the fog that can swirl round the vineyards of Piedmont. Dry, full bodied wine with a smell that evokes descriptions ranging from 'violets' to 'truffles'. Needs time to develop (both smell and vocabulary).

Sangiovese: Predominant grape in chianti and many other wines in central Italy. Can be hard when young, often mixed with white grapes to soften it.

Kadarka: Produces rich deep wine, notably Bull's Blood.

Principal vine varieties by region

Area	*Varieties for red wine*	*Varieties for white wine*
France		
Bordeaux	Cabernet Sauvignon	Sauvignon (dry)
	Cabernet Franc	Sémillon (sweet)
	Merlot	
Burgundy	Pinot Noir	Chardonnay
	Gamay (lesser wines)	Aligoté (lesser wines)
Beaujolais	Gamay	
Rhône North	Syrah	Viognier Roussanne, Marsanne
South	Mixture including Syrah, Grenache, Mourvèdre, Cinsaut	
Loire Nantais		Muscadet
		Gros Plant (lesser wines)
Anjou-Saumur	Cabernet (rosé) Groslot, Gamay	Chenin Blanc

Area	*Varieties for red wine*	*Varieties for white wine*
Touraine	Cabernet Franc	Chenin Blanc
Sancerre/Pouilly Fumé		Sauvignon
Alsace	Pinot Noir	Riesling, Gerwürztraminer, Muscat, Pinot Gris (Tokay), Pinot Blanc, Sylvaner
Champagne		Pinot Noir, Pinot Meunier (vinified to produce white wine) Chardonnay
Germany	Portugieser	Riesling, Müller-Thurgau, Silvaner, and many new varieties
Italy	Nebbiolo (Piedmont) Sangiovese (Tuscany)	Trebbiano

Spain, Portugal	Mixture of mainly local varieties	Mixture of mainly local varieties
Yugoslavia		Laski Riesling
Hungary	Kadarka	Furmint
California	Cabernet Sauvignon Zinfandel	Chardonnay, Chenin Blanc, Johannisberg Riesling, Fumé Blanc
Australia	Shiraz (Syrah) Cabernet Sauvignon	'Riesling' (Semillon)
South Africa	Pinotage (Pinot Noir x Cinsaut)	'Steen' (Chenin Blanc)

Zinfandel: Spicey, fruity grape indigenous to California and yet to be grown widely elsewhere. Responsible for a wide range of different styles of wine.
Carignan: Very widely planted in the Midi where it produces flat blending wine in great quantity.

CHARACTERISTICS OF CLASSIC WHITE GRAPE VARIETIES

Sauvignon (*Blanc*): Widely planted in Bordeaux, Loire and elsewhere in western France, as well as in California where it is often called Fumé Blanc (it is the grape of Pouilly Fumé and Sancerre). Steely dry wines high in acidity.
Sémillon: Its thin skins and high sugar content make it ideal for producing almost oily, sweet wines, notably in Sauternes where it is happy to be prey to 'noble rot'. Planted widely in Australia where it is sometimes erroneously called Riesling.
Chardonnay: Classic white burgundy grape, also important in Champagne and doing well in California. Ages well to deep yellow, full, dry wines with a 'smokey' smell.
Aligoté: Burgundy's everyday white grape. Thin, acid wines.
Viognier: Important only for Condrieu and Château Grillet in northern Rhône were it produces very individual dry wines with the scent of apricots.
Muscadet: Makes dry wines, sometimes bitingly high in acidity, round the mouth of the Loire.
Gros Plant: Even tarter than Muscadet, grown in the same area.
Chenin Blanc: Classic white grape of the middle Loire producing wines, particularly Vouvray and Saumur, that cover the full range from bone dry to luscious. Smells like straw to some, summer flowers to others.
Riesling: True Riesling is widely planted in Alsace (usually quite dry) and in Germany (sometimes very sweet) where it is regarded as the king of grape varieties. Makes elegant, racy wines capable of maturing into perfection. Many other grapes are called Riesling – Welschriesling, Italian Riesling, Laski Riesling, Olasz Riesling, Wälschriesling are not this 'real' Riesling at all and produce greatly

inferior wines. When true Riesling is planted outside Germany and Alsace it is usually identifiable as 'Rhine Riesling', or a similar local translation.

Gewürztraminer: Very distinctive spicey, pungent aroma reminding some of lychees. At its best in the full, dry wines of Alsace. Also grown in Germany, Austria, California, north Italy and elsewhere.

Muscat: Widely grown all over the world. Called Muscadelle, Moscato, Moscatel etc. Produces wines that, unusually, actually smell and taste like grapes. Responsible for fine dry wines in Alsace, sweet light wines in Spain, spumantes in northern Italy and dessert wines in southern France.

Pinot Gris: Full bodied, sometimes sluggish. Produces its finest wines in Alsace as Tokay (nothing to do with the great Hungarian wine of the same name) and some good Rülanders in Germany.

Pinot Blanc: Thought to be close though lesser relative of the Chardonnay.

Sylvaner: Fairly ordinary light wines, neutral and sometimes lacking acidity. Known as Silvaner in Germany.

Müller-Thurgau: Most successful newish grape variety developed by a Swiss scientist of the same name. It is now the most widely planted grape in Germany having replaced the Riesling and Silvaner in many areas because it is an early ripener, a high yielder and is not too fussy about where it is planted. Good sub-Riesling characteristics for the first few years but does not age well. Quite common in England and gaining popularity in Austria. Much discussion as to whether it is a Riesling x Silvaner cross or a Riesling x Riesling.

Trebbiano: Planted widely in Italy producing fairly full flavoured whites. Also encountered as Ugni Blanc in the Midi and St Emilion in the Cognac region.

Furmint: Rich white grape responsible for Tokay and other wines in Hungary. Grown elsewhere in what was Austro-Hungary.

Chasselas: Undistinguished grape grown in parts of France,

Switzerland (where it is called Fendant or Dorin) and Germany (Gutedel). On the decline. More successful in the fruit basket than the bottle.

GRAFTING Other important species of the *vitis* genus are *vitis labrusca, vitis rupestris* and *vitis riparia*, which grow wild in North America and in certain areas, notably in Upper New York State and in Ontario, are cultivated for wine production. These wines have a distinctive taste that can strike those accustomed to European wines as unpleasant. Their musky, sherbety smell is often described as 'foxy' by those who were not weaned on them. These vines are usually higher yielding than their *vitis vinifera* cousins and many of the grapes they produce are eaten as table grapes. It would certainly be difficult to produce wines with the finesse of Europe's finest wines from these North American vines, but all who enjoy European *vitis vinifera* wines are heavily dependent on them. Almost all the wine produced in the world's better quality wine regions is made from *vitis vinifera* vines grafted on to American rootstocks.

In the late nineteenth century *phylloxera vastatrix*, a tiny little insect native to America, crossed the Atlantic, probably on the underside of some interesting specimen brought over by an enthusiastic botanist. This louse, which had hardly been noticed in America since American vines are not remotely bothered by it, was to devastate European wine production. Finding the roots of European vines both irresistible and non-resistant, the phylloxera louse gobbles them up greedily and then, leaving the now rootless vine to die, passes on to devour the next.

It is difficult now to realize what immense damage was caused by this louse. Phylloxera eventually spread to almost every vineyard in France, and then to most of the rest of Europe, decimating wine production and costing France alone an estimated £400 million, according to Edmund Penning-Rowsell. Frantic, near-destitute vine growers tried all manner of chemicals to fight the phylloxera. Some even tried flooding the vineyards, but the louse munched on imperturbably. And if diseased vines were pulled up and new vines planted, these too would be attacked.

Eventually a solution was found and this started a practice that still has to be followed today if phylloxera is not to strike once again. The European vines were grafted on to American rootstock which is resistant to the ravages of phylloxera and today almost every vine in the world that has *vitis vinifera* characteristics and produces *vitis vinifera* wines is grown from grafts on to rootstock of one of the American species. There are commercial nurseries that specialize in growing American roots which are in demand from vine growers all over the world.

There are just a few exceptions to this – Bollinger's Vieilles Vignes and Noval Nacional are, respectively, champagne and port produced from ungrafted pre-phylloxera vines. And since the phylloxera louse likes eating in sand no more than most people like picnicing on windy beaches, vines planted in sand as at Colares on the coast by Lisbon and in the Camargue need not be grafted. This is also true of Chile where vineyards are have somehow been protected from phylloxera by a combination of mountains and desert.

'Pre-phylloxera' wine, wine made in the days before phylloxera struck, is now an expensive rarity and those who can afford to buy it usually reckon they are entitled to boast of its superiority to any wine produced from grafted vines, but there is no real true comparison that will show whether grafting has affected wine for the worse.

There are also hybrids, crosses between American and European vines, that are immune to phylloxera. These vines, often called 'direct producers', tend to produce mediocre wine in great quantity. They are gradually being grubbed up in the vineyards of the Midi to be replaced with grafted *vitis vinifera* varieties which produce much better quality wines. Seyval Blanc is a hybrid popular with English vine growers as it is hardy and does not have a 'foxy' taste.

AGE OF THE VINE Wine produced by a three-year-old vine tastes quite different from that made from a thirty-year-old vine planted next to it. By the time a vine is three years old it will be producing grapes from which wine can be made, but it will be a relatively immature, unsubtle wine. The root system of the vine will still be concentrated not far below ground level and the mix of minerals it is able to pick up from the soil will be much more restricted than what can be taken to the grapes by the deeper, more complex root system of a vine that has had thirty years in which to develop. The amount of wine produced by a single vine also improves as the vine gets older to reach an optimum quality/quantity balance at about fifteen years old. As it gets older, the vine produces less and less so that it is not earning its keep. By the time it is thirty it will usually be grubbed up to be replaced by a new vine.

THE VINEYARD YEAR The vineyard year starts in autumn just after the vines, by now turning red and gold, have been stripped of their grapes. The vintage can start as early as mid-August in North Africa and southern Europe and continues until late November in northern Europe with special grapes sometimes being left on the vine for special dessert wines. In the southern hemisphere the vintage takes place in February and March, and all other vineyard activities will take place six months or so earlier than described here.

After the vintage the leafy shoots are trimmed, and the land is churned up so that the soil is aerated and earth may be banked up against the vines in order to protect them from winter frosts. In some steeply sloping vineyards such as in Germany and the northern Rhône valley, earth that eroded during the growing season will painstakingly be carried back up the slope to provide a bit of topsoil.

Pruning is the only major activity in the vineyards during the winter months. This highly skilled process may start before Christmas and should be over before the sap starts to rise at the end of March. With just a few snips of his secateurs a trained vineyard pruner can determine the shape of each vine for the next vintage and influences the quantity and quality of the wine that will eventually be produced. If vines were not pruned they would expend too much of their energy sending out shoots in all directions and producing luxuriant foliage when the vigneron wants it to concentrate on producing good grapes. The object of the pruner is firstly to control by judicious snipping the number of shoots the vine will produce that year, and secondly to train the vine in the shape that is best for the climate and terrain of the vineyard.

In the steep vineyards of the Moselle, for instance, each vine is trained up a single post to save space and to raise the growth from ground level where frost can present the greatest danger, while in the southern Rhône the vines are left to grow in low bushes so that they absorb heat reflected from the flat stones in the vineyard. Further south than this, heat can be a problem and in Italy and the Vinho Verde area of Portugal the vines are trained high above the ground in trellises so that they don't get too hot – and another crop can be grown in the shade underneath. As mechanical harvesting becomes more common, vines are increasingly being planted on the Lenz-Moser system, named after the Austrian who pioneered this system of planting vines in widely-spaced rows so that machines can work in between.

The team of pruners is often trailed by an old metal burner, the dead shoots being hurled into this Heath Robinson apparatus that keeps up a continual streamer of smoke like a pennant in the winter vineyard. There are few sadder sights than a vineyard that has just been pruned. All that is left above the surface are rows of stubborn black stumps. It seems incredible that they are even alive, let alone capable of producing luxuriant green foliage within just a few months.

During the pruning, cuttings are taken for grafting on to American rootstock if needed. They will be planted out in the indoor nursery and nurtured there so that there will be a stock of new vines to replace those that are getting too old to be commercially viable producers.

During the winter months vineyard maintenance will be carried out too – fences mended, posts fixed, ditches dug. All this time the vine is 'resting', like an actor out of work except that the vine is certain of a big part come the summer.

By the middle of March the sap starts to rise, the vineyard may be ploughed again, perhaps fertilized if necessary though it is important not to over-fertilize, and any banked-up soil will be pulled away from the roots to allow them the benefit of any spring rainfall.

In April the successfully grafted cuttings which have already spent a year in the nursery will be planted out. The older vines start to put out their first shoots and these are tied up on the lower wires suspended between stakes in the vineyard according to the best method of training.

In May the attention of vignerons in northern vineyards is concentrated on the thermometer, for frost presents the greatest danger now that the tender young shoots have emerged. Most frost-fighting measures are time-consuming and expensive. In some vineyards little burners are lit in the hopes of counteracting sub-zero temperatures. In more sophisticated vineyards the vines may be sprayed with water. This covers the vines with a layer of ice and protects them from the ravages of frost.

At about this time the vines receive the first of many sprayings against the pests and diseases that plague them throughout the summer. In an average year each vineyard may be sprayed five times with various chemicals to keep the grapes healthy, but in damp years when the grapes are particularly susceptible to rot and disease, there may be as many as twenty different sprayings. This will be done either by men with backpacks or, increasingly, by helicopter. The vineyards of Champagne, for instance, have vivid markers to show which owners have paid their sub to the local helicopter service.

The all-important flowering of the vine takes place in June and it is important that it should happen in a settled period of warm weather. If the weather is unsettled the flowering will be uneven and has the effect of producing bunches whose grapes are at different stages of ripeness and health at vintage time. There should be no strong winds at this time either as these could blow away the pollen and stop the bees from getting on with the essential pollination.

Some growers even go so far as to plant brightly coloured flowers at the end of each row of vines in the hopes of attracting bees who might not otherwise succumb to the more modest charms of the vine blossom.

The vine may be thinned and only the best shoots tied up on wires to expose them to the all-important sunshine. In a northern European vineyard grapes must be given the maximum chance of ripening so that their sugar content, and therefore their potential alcohol, is as high as possible.

By July tiny grapes should already be visible and the vines may be given a 'summer prune' to stop the vine wasting any of its precious energy on new shoots, and in some cases to expose the grapes to more sunlight. The vineyard should be weeded at this point so that the minerals and moisture in the soil are concentrated on the vines.

During August the grapes ripen, the red, black and blue varieties start to change colour. At this point the acidity in the grapes is decreasing and the sugar content is increasing – unripe grapes can be very tart indeed while ripe ones are luscious enough to eat. Sugar can be produced in the grapes only if there is sufficient sunlight for it is when sunlight acts on the chlorophyll in the green leaves of the vine that the carbon dioxide in the air and water drawn from the soil by the roots will react together to form sugar. This process, photosynthesis, is illustrated in this simplified chemical equation which represents what is actually a complicated series of reactions:

$$\begin{array}{ccccccccc} 6CO_2 & \rightarrow + & 6H_2O & = & C_6H_{12}O_6 & + & 6O_2 \\ \text{carbon dioxide} & + & \text{water} & = & \text{sugar} & + & \text{oxygen} \end{array}$$

And while the roots are feeling way below the surface for water, they are also drawing up a wide range of mineral elements. Minerals of which the vine makes regular use during its development are nitrogen, potassium, lime, magnesium and phosphorus, all of which play their part in the resultant character of the wine. In theory it would be possible to influence the sort of wine made by judicious addition of these chemicals to the soil, but this would be a very expensive process and one in which it would be difficult to get the balance exactly right.

By the end of August the grapes should be ripening nicely. The spraying against rot, mildew and pests has to stop and the vineyard owner returning from his August holiday may dread that his entire crop has been wiped out by some dreadful blight. Now is the time for crossed fingers and preparation for the vintage. The equipment in the winery will be overhauled and cleaned. The *vendangeoirs*, the hostels that house the pickers, will be opened up and the nail biting begins.

There is no decision more crucial and none more difficult in the vineyard year than that of when to pick. In temperate zones if the grapes are picked early the grapes will be less ripe and have less capacity to produce alcohol, sugar and flavour. If the vigneron hangs on hoping for more sunshine, however, the crop may be spoilt by rain or hail. In hotter areas, it may be important to pick before the grapes are fully ripe so that there is still some acidity left but it can be difficult to judge when the sugar-acid balance is optimum. In some areas the vintage date is determined each year by the local authorities.

Once started, the vintage usually lasts two or three weeks depending on the condition of the grapes and staff levels in the vineyards. Pickers may be hired in troupes of itinerant professionals who regularly travel northwards from wine region to wine region throughout the autumn. It has been common practice in France to employ Spanish pickers, usually the same families have links with particular producers and work there year after year. Increasing wage levels in Spain and the advent of mechanical harvesters may change this. On smaller properties the vigneron may manage to get all the work done by dragooning his family. It is noticeable though that on properties of any size and quality there is a marked reluctance to employ students who are not seriously committed to learning about wine. Jolly japes in the dorm have obviously taken their toll.

For all the picture postcard scenes of happy harvest home at vintage time this is back-breaking work, starting in the cold mists of the early morning and continuing until sunset, for most vineyard owners, once having taken the decision to pick, are anxious to get the grapes safely in as soon as possible. The pickers may have to go through a vineyard more than once if the grapes are at different stages of ripeness. This becomes crucial in Germany where the level of rot and sugar in the grapes is all-important for the Prädikat it will be awarded and hence the price it will fetch.

SECRETS OF THE WINERY It is all too possible to produce poor wine from all the right ingredients – perfect vineyard, fine summer, healthy grapes – if they are given to a careless winemaker. Conversely, and happily, the number of winemakers who are capable of turning mediocre grapes into quite decent wine is increasing fast with better understanding of the techniques involved in vinification.

FERMENTATION The essential part of vinification, the frontier between grape juice and wine, is fermentation. With the yeast enzyme acting as a catalyst, sugar is converted into alcohol, thereby turning sweet grape juice into a rather drier alcoholic liquid. For those who like to see that all the molecules add up, this is the chemical equation for the process of fermentation:

$$\underset{\text{sugar}}{C_6H_{12}O_6} \xrightarrow{\text{yeast enzymes}} \underset{\text{ethyl alcohol}}{2C_2H_5{\cdot}OH} + \underset{\text{carbon dioxide}}{2CO_2}$$

This, broadly speaking, is what happens when anything ferments, whether it be a home-made apple wine, or a pot of jam in the back of the cupboard that starts to fizz ominously (the fizz is the carbon dioxide being given off). Provided there is the right sort of yeast about, any spare sugar is fermentable, hence some of the unlikely-sounding recipes in home wine-making manuals.

COMPOSITION OF THE GRAPE The reason that grapes are the traditional raw material for wine, is that they are self-sufficient; they contain all the essential elements for fermentation. A ripe grape, provided it is crushed slightly, is quite capable of fermenting on its own – though modern winemakers can improve on this solo performance if given half a chance. The grape is made up as shown below:

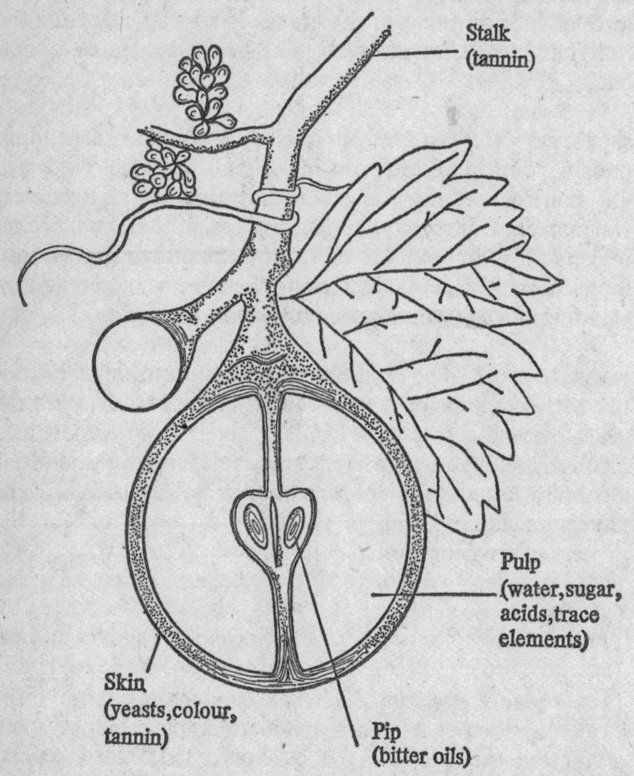

Pulp: This is the interesting part of the grape, or rather up to 30 per cent of it is interesting, the rest is just water. The sugar, all-important for fermentation, makes up the majority of the remainder of the pulp, but there is another element that is vital if the wine is to taste at all interesting, and that is acidity. A wine without any acidity would taste flat, like alcoholic sugar water, although wines that are too high in acidity can taste mean and tart. The range of different acids present in grape pulp and indeed in the resultant wine is enormous and the total amount is a function of how much sun the grapes have been exposed to – the more sunshine, the lower the acidity. In addition all the trace elements that have been picked up from the soil are in the pulp. The colour of this pulp, incidentally, is the same in almost all black grapes as in white varieties, a translucent greenish yellow, the colour of white wine – which is why it is possible to make white wines like champagne from black grapes.

Skin: This provides the second vital element for fermentation in the 'grape package', the 'bloom' on grape skins, the white dust, harbouring thousands of yeasts. In any established vineyard the air is thick with tiny organisms, wine yeasts that will promote fermentation, as well as wild yeasts that are less helpful in producing good wine. In addition to this the skin contains colouring matter and the preservative tannin, both of which are important elements in red wine.

Pips: As grape eaters know, pips are horribly bitter if chewed, and the winemaker is careful not to crush them when making wine.

Stalk: This can be another source of tannin, though most winemakers nowadays destalk the grapes before vinifying them.

It should not be very difficult, therefore, to get a grape to ferment. Provided it is crushed slightly, the skin should break, and the process of fermentation should start.

This is the outline of the process, but it has become much more sophisticated than this, for too much is left to chance when nature gets on with things unaided. Wine yeasts on the grapeskin act on the sugar in the pulp producing alcohol and giving off carbon dioxide. They work away on this mixture of skin, pulp and pips so that it bubbles away, getting hotter and hotter and burping carbon dioxide until it has either used up all the sugar in the mixture, now known as must, or the alcohol content reaches 15 or 16 per cent at which point it overpowers most yeasts. Alcoholic grape juice will be produced and this, once the grape solids have been strained out, can be called wine. If left to its own devices the wine then becomes prey to oxygen and bacteria, particularly acetobacter which eventually attack the wine and turn it into vinegar, just as any glass of wine, left open to the atmosphere for a day or so, becomes thin and vinegary. The word vinegar itself comes from *vin aigre*, 'sour wine'.

MODERN WINEMAKING In the modern winery, the technique of fermentation has been adapted so as to leave as little as possible to chance. This is not one of those miserable 'advances of modern science' in which all is reduced to the lowest common denominator; the average level of quality in wine today is higher than it has ever been.

The winemaker wants total control over what is happening so he will often, for instance, kill off all the yeasts that are found on the skin of the grape and instead add a strain of yeast that has been specially cultivated to be most suitable for the particular sort of wine he wants to make. Makers of Australian and South African sherry, for instance, use a special yeast strain found in *flor* in Jerez, while Epernay yeasts are used all over the world for sparkling wine production since they are particularly good for concentrating the deposit left in sparkling wines after their second fermentation. The winemaker may take steps to control the temperature at which his grapes ferment, or the point at which the fermentation stops. He now has a great deal of control over fermentation. The grapes are brought into the winery as quickly as possible since pressure in the baskets in which they are collected can split the grapes and start an uncontrolled fermentation, and a busy winery may receive grapes day and night during the vintage. They usually arrive on the back of a lorry whose load will be weighed and sugar content tested. If the grapes are being brought in by a grower who is selling his grapes to the winery or co-operative, he looks on anxiously as his grapes are assessed, for his bank balance depends heavily on exactly what readings are obtained. Payment tends to be made on the basis of sugar content since this determines how much alcohol will be produced, but in some areas there is a trend to give bonuses for other quality factors in the grapes.

RED WINES After weighing, the grapes are emptied into a hopper which leads to the *fouloir*, a large version of the domestic mincer where the grapes are crushed and in most districts the stalks are 'sieved' out, unless there is a need for their extra tannin and acidity. The mixture, almost must, is then pumped to the sterilized fermentation vat, usually made of stainless steel or other inert substances. It is at this point that the winemaker administers his first dose of sulphur.

Sulphur dioxide is to the winemaker as antiseptic to the surgeon. So long as it is used only in moderate amounts it reduces substantially the risk of contamination of the wine, either from oxygen or bacteria, and helps to control the fermentation. There have been winemakers, particularly makers of the cheaper sweet white wines, who have been heavy-handed with their SO_2 ladles and their wines have that struck match smell when first tasted. If any wine does seem too high in sulphur when first tasted, this will disappear if the wine is swilled about in a glass for a while.

The year's first fermentation may be difficult to start as the atmosphere in the cellar is not yet thick with yeasts and the must may have to be heated before it starts to ferment. Fermentation is a delicate process and is sensitive to many factors, one of the most important of which is heat. The cooler the must, the more difficult it is to start the fermentation, the slower the fermentation process will be but the more subtle will be the end-result. A hot, fast fermentation is a bit like boiling rather than simmering. The interesting volatile elements can disappear in a cloud of steam. The ideal temperature for red wine fermentation is about 25°C. For this reason, fermentation vats in modern wineries are fitted with ways of monitoring and controlling temperature, either by means of jackets into which heated or cooled water can be pumped or by sprays of water, these operations sometimes supervised by a computer.

Pressure can also affect fermentation. In areas of high pressure such as South Africa fermentation is slowed down and the flavour of the wine can seem more intense. And with grapes that have a particularly high sugar content it can be difficult to get the fermentation to start.

In some years there has not been enough sun to push the wines' sugar content up to the level at which it will make a wine with enough alcohol to make it interesting and durable. There is a very simple way round this problem which is to add sugar to the must before it ferments. Because this sugar is converted into alcohol it does not make the wine sweeter, just stronger. In most wine regions in France and Germany winemakers are allowed to add enough sugar to raise the potential alcoholic strength by a few degrees, always specified precisely for each region depending on its climate. It is rarely necessary further south, however. The process is called chaptalization after Chaptal, the French minister who saw that by promulgating its use he could solve at a stroke the nation's twin problems of gluts of sugar beet and poor wine at the beginning of the last century. From 1980 adding water at the same time as the sugar, as some German winemakers have done to reduce excessive acidity, is forbidden by law. Grape sugar may be used increasingly in preference to beet or cane sugar.

Once started, perhaps by warming the must if necessary, the fermentation is very vigorous for the first few days and then gradually subsides into a gentle exhaling of CO_2. With red wines the winemaker has to decide how long to leave the must in contact with the skins which are his chief source of colouring matter and the important preservative tannin. In Bordeaux some wines which are made to last for decades may be kept on the skins for up to three weeks with alcohol drawing colour from the skins to emerge from the fermenting vat almost black, and so high in tannin that they taste like stewed tea concentrate.

There is a trend in most wine areas to reduce the amount of time that the wine spends on the skins so that mature wines come sooner and therefore cheaper, which makes sense for low to medium quality wines or wines which depend more on the grape than on ageing for their characteristics. It would be a great tragedy, however, if it meant an end to the truly great wines of the world that have earned their reputations through the finesse and character they can achieve only with great age.

This trend has been taken to an extreme in a method of vinification that has been developed since the Second World War, *macération carbonique*. In carbonic maceration, sometimes called 'whole grape fermentation', which is slowly gaining popularity in the Rhône, the Midi and even to a cautious extent in Bordeaux, whole bunches of grapes, stalks and all, are thrown into a vat into which carbon dioxide is pumped and the vat is sealed. Exactly the same sort of fermentation of sugar into alcohol then takes place, but instead of being encouraged by yeasts on the skin, the presence of carbon dioxide and the absence of oxygen encourages enzymes inside the grape itself to start the fermentation. Just as in traditional fermentation, the alcohol draws colouring matter from the skins. The major difference is that no tannin is extracted and the lack of oxygen concentrates the flavour of the grape so that the resulting wine is much more intensely fruity. In practice, because of the way that the grapes at the bottom of the vat are crushed by the weight of those at the top and therefore undergo the traditional sort of fermentation, so-called carbonic maceration wines are a mixture of the product of fermentation by both the newer and the traditional methods. But the resulting wine is distinguished by its intensity of flavour and its fruitiness. Such wines are made for early drinking and are perhaps more vigorous than subtle, but suggest exciting new possibilities for more widespread use.

A similar though not, as is commonly thought, identical technique is widespread in the Beaujolais region. Here bunches are fermented whole, but the vat is left open and any carbon dioxide in the vat is purely the result of the gas given off as a by-product of a traditional sort of fermentation. It is a less 'pure' form of carbonic maceration but the wine shows some of the same characteristics.

Another advantage of carbonic maceration in cooler zones is that it automatically converts a high proportion of one of the harshest acids, malic acid (the sort that is found commonly associated with apples) into the much gentler lactic acid (the milk sort of acid). One of the northern winemaker's great preoccupations is to encourage this conversion process, called malolactic fermentation, to reduce overall acidity and to get it over with as soon as possible, certainly long before the wine is bottled. There are few things customers like less in their bottle of red wine than the little bubbles given off in a second fermentation. The malolactic fermentation will take place only above a certain temperature so it can be encouraged by warming the cellars. Otherwise the winemaker will have to wait for the warmth of spring. In hotter zones, the malolactic fermentation may be actively discouraged so as to retain as much acidity to liven up the wine as possible.

Once all the sugar in the grapes has been fermented out, as it normally is in red wines, the newly fermented wine, *vin de goutte*, is run off the mass of skins, pips and spent yeast cells into vats or casks where it will settle. The liquid is then pressed out of the remaining mixture, and this harsh tannic wine, *vin de presse*, may be added to give extra body and staying power to the *vin de goutte*, or it may be kept separate and given to the poor old workers. In some areas, the *marc*, the thick purple cake of compressed wine detritus that is left after the *vin de presse* has been extracted, is moistened, fermented and then distilled to produce *eau-de-vie-de-marc* in France, *grappa* in Italy, *aguardiente* in Spain and *bagaceira* in Portugal. In other areas it is used more prosaically as fertilizer.

The new wine meanwhile is settling down after its fermentation and it is important to let the particles of solid matter left in the liquid settle on the bottom of the cask. Because these can taint the wine, it is carefully pumped or 'racked' off into new sterilized containers, traditionally wooden casks.

The sort of wood used in making the cask, its size, shape and age are all factors which influence the final taste of the wine, as of course does the length of time the wine is kept there.

Each wine area has its own favourite sort of wood, usually some type of oak. It is tempting to think that this is dictated merely by tradition but inquisitive winemakers have found by experiment that the choice of wood is an important element in the final flavour of the wine. This results in some strange trade patterns. Wine producers in northern Spain have traditionally insisted on American oak for maturing rioja, while their counterparts in California go to great lengths to import casks from Europe. The size of the cask is important too; the smaller the cask the faster the maturation process because more air per volume of wine enters the cask and acts on it, to mature it. This explains why Barolo aged in the vast 5000 litre casks takes so long to mature, compared to claret which is traditionally kept in Bordeaux *barriques* holding only 225 litres. The exact shape of a cask can also affect how much air is let in. And the newer it is the more tannin there is to be transmitted to the wine. The winemaker has to prevent oxidation, too *much* oxygen spoiling the wine, by making sure that casks are kept topped up – evaporation makes this a weekly job.

Wine was originally put into wooden casks because they were the only sort of containers for any sort of quantity available. Now that we have all sorts of containers – vats, tanks and vacuum packs, including those made of completely inert materials – there is considerable experimentation with different sorts of storage and ageing. Most white and many red wines never see wood from grape to bottle and even for full-bodied reds there is a general tendency to allow wine to mature in bottle more and in barrel less. Most reds now stay no longer than two years in wood, some are stored only long enough for them to throw all their deposits after fermentation before they are 'fined', perhaps filtered, and then bottled.

Fining and filtering are both methods of clearing the wine, making sure that it is crystal clear to look at and doesn't harbour any solids that might start off chemical reactions in the wine once it is bottled. Fining involves adding a substance, usually bentonite but sometimes something as exotic as egg white or even oxblood, that will attract solids to it and cause them to fall to the bottom of the container so that the wine can be racked off them. All wines should be fined a few months after fermentation so that they are stable and most wines nowadays are filtered at least once before bottling.

ROSÉ WINES Rosés are often regarded with a fair degree of contempt, which is a pity since there are a number of charming wines that fit into this category, from the scented Cabernet d'Anjou to the crisp, dry rosés of Provence. Rosés are also very versatile wines, good for a wide range of foods and occasions. The rosé stigma may have developed because there are a number of poor rosés on the market, indeed some of them are made by simply mixing red and white wine and that is unlikely to produce a very harmonious end-result. Rosés can also be made by fermenting a mixture of black and white grapes together on their skins, but the classic method is to proceed as for red wine except that the wine is racked off the skins after only a day or two so that only some of the colouring matter is extracted from them. The wines are therefore low in tannin, so rosé should be drunk while it is young and fresh.

Recent years have seen the emergence of a new sort of wine that has the colour of the palest of rosés. These '*blancs de noirs*' are designed to satisfy demand for white wines in countries which have a glut of red wine grapes. They are made like white wine from black grapes and the slight colour results from the fact that it is difficult to do this without absorbing any of the colouring matter from the skins, as the Champenois know. In Champagne they have had much more practice at this than most California winemakers and are now able to produce limpid white wine from a blend of predominantly black-skinned grapes.

WHITE WINES Whereas skins are a vital element in red wine production since they give colour, they are not needed in the fermentation of white wines and the winemaker may well decide to eliminate them from the process as soon as possible. Accordingly, the grapes are destalked and crushed as soon as they arrive at the winery and the juice is then pressed out of the grapey mixture. There are many different sorts of wine press but the gentler the pressing action, the finer the quality of the juice and the less likelihood there is of crushing the pips to give a bitter taste to the must. The most basic presses now commonly used are like giant mincers, while in some of the most sophisticated presses the grapes are put into a cylinder in which is a large inflatable rubber bag. The bag is filled with air, sometimes computer-controlled, and the juice is gently pressed out and run off from the base. As with red wine, sulphur is added to stop oxidation, to kill unwanted bacteria and to stop fermentation starting straight away.

The juice at this stage is a thick, grapey-smelling mixture, an opaque greenish yellow not unlike pea soup to look at, and it is usual to clear the liquid of these solids – either by letting them fall to the bottom of a vat by leaving it overnight or, increasingly, by using a centrifuge, a machine that spins them out of the wine.

If the winemaker wants to give his white wines greater keeping potential, or extra aroma and flavour, he may decide to leave the must in contact with the grape skins for a while as this will increase the tannin and extract content of the resultant wine. In some areas the juice that is naturally run off the skins is kept separate from the coarser juice that is subsequently pressed out of them.

Fermentation of white wines is governed by the same factors as those already discussed for red wine, except that in many circumstances temperature is even more critical. White wines are usually fermented at lower temperatures, about 15°C (60°F), and for longer than red wines as this maximizes the amount of flavour extracted. In hotter areas it is at this point that extra acidity in the form of tartaric acid, some of which is present naturally in wine anyway, may be added. White wines are more prone to oxidation than red, so it is important to ensure that no oxygen enters the fermentation vat. This is often done by pumping an inert gas such as nitrogen into the vat before fermentation so that the wine pushes it out and allows air in. Or a 'blanket' of carbon dioxide may be left on top of the fermenting must. In hot climates, even the presses themselves are sometimes enveloped in carbon dioxide. To keep white wines fresh-tasting, the winemaker may try to keep some of this carbon dioxide in solution in the wine to give it a slight 'prickle', or he may try to prevent the malolactic fermentation happening by adding SO_2 so that the sharper malic acid is not softened to lactic.

The decision as to whether to stop the fermentation artificially is very much more important in whites than in reds. While in most reds all of the sugar is fermented out to alcohol, whites range from dry to sweet and one way of ensuring that a wine is sweet is to stop the fermentation before all the sugar is converted. Fermentation can be stopped by changing one of the factors to which it is sensitive. If the temperature drops below a certain point yeasts will be unable to work, so the wine can be refrigerated to stop fermentation, or carbon dioxide can be used to raise the pressure, or the yeasts are filtered out or, and this is the crudest method, sulphur dioxide may be added to stun the yeasts. The traditional way is to rack the wine frequently so that the yeast eventually runs out of nutrients on which to work. The winemaker has to judge very carefully how and when he stops the fermentation of his sweeter white wines.

After fermentation the wine is treated similarly to red wine, except that it is not usually aged in wood except in the case of the long-living Chardonnays and Sauternes. Most white wines are kept in stainless steel after being allowed to settle and clear and then bottled in the year after the vintage.

In Germany it is common to sweeten wines by adding what they call Süssreserve, 'sweet reserve', just before bottling. Each vintage about 10 per cent of Germany's grape must is prevented from fermenting, stabilized and concentrated to be used as Süssreserve. The law stipulates that the

Süssreserve must be of the same quality as the wine to which it is added, but it is felt by some winemakers outside Germany that this approach is just too far from nature and too close to the cookbook.

BLENDING AND BOTTLING Blending, one of the most important operations in the winery, often gets scant attention in guides to wine. Each vintage the winemaker will be presented with must from a wide variety of vineyards and perhaps from a wide variety of grape types. He has to decide which of these to vinify together, which to keep on one side as his special reserve of top quality wine, which to vinify separately for subsequent *assemblage*. Each fermentation vat then produces a slightly different wine that will continue to develop its individuality as it matures. Blending is not, as is sometimes suggested, a dirty word. When done carefully to maximize quality it is a skilled operation, essential for many of the world's great wines. 'Coupage' is the word often used in France for blending and a 'cuvée' is the end product.

Once the wine is ready for bottling, which in the case of many wines will be only six months or so after the vintage, it may be refrigerated for a short time so that it 'throws its tartrates', which means that the tartaric acid naturally present in the wine which is responsible for those harmless white crystals that form in wine bottles, are precipitated by the cold and fall to the bottom of the vat. This is done for cosmetic reasons.

Modern technology has also brought completely new techniques to the bottling of wine. The most important aspect is that the wine should not be exposed too long to air, otherwise it may oxidize, and everything should be free from any bacteria or agent that could cause the wine to go out of condition while it is in the bottle. This means particularly that there should be no possibility of yeast cells starting off a second fermentation while in the bottle.

Various techniques of bottling are used for wines of differing qualities, most of them involving high speed bottling lines in far from romantic surroundings. In sterile bottling the wine is passed through filter sheets and filled through a filling machine into sterilized bottles inside a little sterilized chamber. There is also pasteurization and hot bottling whereby the wine is heated up to kill any potentially harmful organisms. This is suitable only for low to medium quality wines which are not expected to develop in bottle as this tends to kill off any subtlety potential in the wine.

Then comes corking, capsuling and labelling, all done by sophisticated machines, and the wine might well be shipped out immediately. A low quality wine *could* be in the shops the next day.

6. The still, light wines of France

Bordeaux – Burgundy – Beaujolais – Rhône – Loire – Alsace – South-West France – Midi and Provence – Other wines of France

INTRODUCTION France produces the best wine in the world – and some of the worst. The classed growths of Bordeaux and the *grands crus* of the Côte d'Or make up only the tiniest fraction of her annual production of between 60 and 75 million hectolitres (one hectolitre = 100 litres = 22 imperial gallons) – and it is rare for more than a sixth of any vintage in France to qualify as Appellation Contrôlée wine at all.

The bulk of the rest is vin ordinaire, very ordinary wine indeed sold in litre returnable bottles in French supermarkets to be drunk at mealtimes with about as much ceremony as the British drink a mug of tea. Red wine outsells white in France by more than two to one and common or garden French red owes much to the vineyards of southern Italy for its strength and colour, Algerian vineyards performing the same function in the past. France is the biggest importer of Italian wine – she absorbs ten times as much as we do – but the wine is rarely put on the shelf as 'Produce of Italy'. It is blended with the lighter, less alcoholic wines that France produces herself in the vast vineyards of the Midi and sold as vin de table.

Another misunderstanding about wine in France is the assumption common among French and foreigners alike that the French are knowledgeable about wine. True, every Frenchman is a wine expert, just as every Frenchwoman is the one human being entrusted with the secret of the only correct way of making pot-au-feu. He will know a great deal about the wine he happens to buy: why it is better value than any other; why he gets a special price; why he and he alone is allowed the proprietor's special *cuvée*. But ask a Burgundian to name the four premiers grands crus of the Médoc, expect a Breton to tell you where Châteauneuf-du-Pape comes from, or ask a Parisian to name the grape that Beaujolais is made of and you will almost invariably be disappointed. Wines, like newspapers, are intensely regionalized in France and the breadth of knowledge that most British wine buyers are able to acquire is rarely encountered there.

BORDEAUX

Summary: Red bordeaux (claret) – light, dry, long livers, some of world's finest.
Sweet white bordeaux (sauternes) are also traditionally classics.
Bordeaux is by far France's most important quality wine producing region, each year responsible for about one in every four bottles of AC wine produced. The wonderful thing about the Gironde, the département that so neatly encompasses the vineyards of the Bordeaux region, is that it produces such a high proportion of good quality wine. And at the top end of the quality scale there are no wines finer than the finest bordeaux – though Burgundians, Germans and even Californians might claim that some of their wines can at least match this quality.

THE BORDEAUX REGION To an excited wine lover anxious to match physical reality with the names so familiar from saleroom catalogues and wine merchants' lists, the vineyards of the Médoc, the most classic area of this most classic region, can come as something of a disappointment – especially when he catches sight of the giant oil refinery by Pauillac. The land is flat, unremarkable and can in places look rather scrubby; many of the 'châteaux' hardly merit such a grand title, being little more than a set of farm buildings in some cases. The visitor has to cross the Garonne and Dordogne to the north to reach the pretty countryside of St Emilion before he can expect a treat from his sense of sight alone.

The structure of the Bordeaux wine business has changed

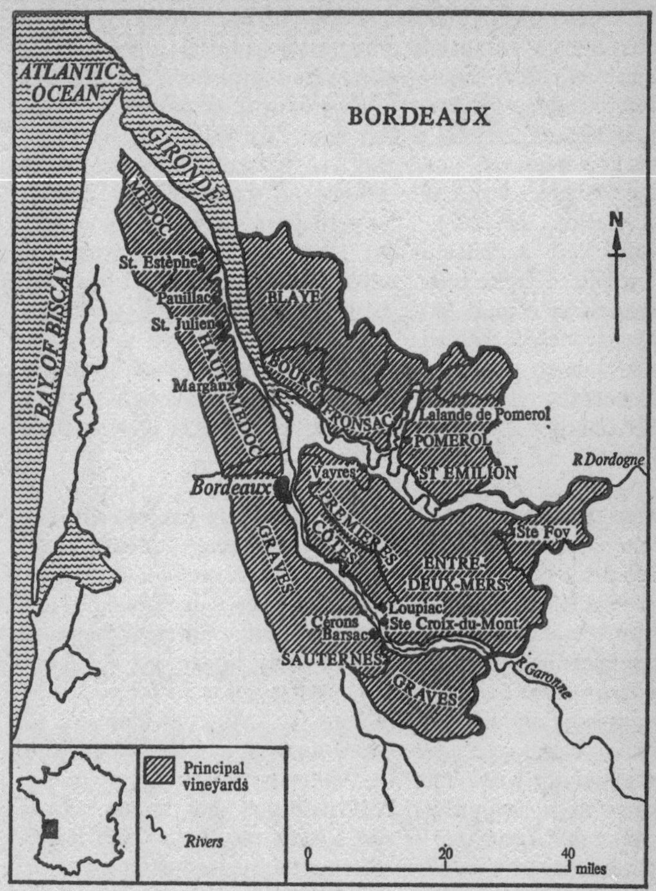

considerably since the time when each château was owned by a single proprietor who would live there with his family, make the wine and sell it to the *négociants*, the middlemen of Bordeaux whose job it was to find a market for the wine. Producing wine that needs to be matured before it is sold is an expensive business when interest rates are high and many properties are now owned by a consortium of investors or by public companies. Châteaux are sold, grouped and regrouped just like companies in any other sort of business, while the *négociants* are increasingly finding that some château owners can dispense with their services.

Bordeaux the city is very curate's egg-like, but its good parts are lovely – and there is that curious seaside light everywhere. Twinned with Bristol because they are so similar commercially, it has perhaps rather more in common with Bath architecturally: elegant *places* with rows of disciplined eighteenth century houses. In the old days the *négociants* would have their premises on the Quai des Chartrons so that wine casks could be rolled across the quayside to the ships. Today much wine leaves Bordeaux in containers, usually loaded in distinctly twentieth century surroundings, but the *négociants* continue to cherish their Quai des Chartrons addresses.

RED BORDEAUX A classic red bordeaux (we've called it 'claret' ever since the Middle Ages when Bordeaux, then ruled by our very own Henry II, sent us light red wines called *clairet*) is elegant and restrained – a dry wine, not too heavy in alcohol, one that reveals many different facets of its taste and texture as it expands in the glass. Claret doesn't come over and introduce itself, it waits for you to be impressed enough to take note. To many new converts to wine, claret can seem too austere, too self-sufficient, particularly when compared with the much more winning ways of the slightly richer traditional burgundies. Good claret is a taste that is not always easy to acquire but is impossible to lose. Even though the region produces more than half as much white wine as red, it is on red wine that Bordeaux's reputation now stands and these dry, often rather hard wines call out for food. The Bordelais would rarely drink their reds except at meals, preferring a sweet white wine as an aperitif.

BASIC BORDEAUX Bordeaux's most basic quality wine is sold as plain Appellation Bordeaux Contrôlée and the quality, even the style, of such wines can vary enormously.

They should carry at least the faintest stamp of the great claret style, being dry fruity wines with rather more tannin in them than, say, the average Côtes-du-Rhône.

There is also the Bordeaux Supérieur appellation but, as French speakers will know, *supérieur* means higher rather than better and in this case refers to alcoholic strength. The alcohol content of the wine is a minimum for red wines usually of 10° for plain bordeaux and 10.5° for bordeaux supérieur. But since most wine in a good vintage reaches 11 per cent anyway, the appearance of 'supérieur' on the label may indicate merely that the merchant thinks that the public will be impressed by it. Bordeaux Supérieur Côtes de Castillon has its own, much smaller appellation.

Such wines will probably be blends of many different wines from many different producers put together by *négociants*, though those which carry the name and often a drawing of a château have to come from one registered vineyard area. Unfortunately there is no simple way of telling which of these wines are likely to be better than any others other than by experimenting. The two most important clues are the name of the merchant and the vintage (if there is one). If not, the wine will either be a mixture of vintages, which is not necessarily a bad thing, or from a single unfashionable year. These lesser wines are being made to be drunk much earlier nowadays so that many of them can be attractive within a couple of years of the vintage, though they will vary considerably from year to year according to the characteristics of each vintage year.

OTHER GENERICS A 'generic wine' is one that carries the name of a geographical region, Médoc, Burgundy, Beaujolais, for example (as opposed to a 'varietal wine' named after a grape variety like Cabernet Sauvignon, Chardonnay, Gamay). Straightforward AC bordeaux and bordeaux supérieur are generic wines, and there is also a group of generics that are a cut above them because they come from a smaller geographical area. While ordinary AC bordeaux will probably come from the 'fringe' areas of Bordeaux, the lesser regions whose own names have not sufficient prestige to sell the wine (though it may be from a more central vineyard whose yield was too high for a better appellation), these other generics come from more specific areas within the Bordeaux region. Those commonly found in Britain are:

Médoc and Graves	*St Emilion and Pomerol*	*Bourg and Blaye*
Haut Médoc	St Emilion	Côtes de Bourg
Médoc	Pomerol	Premières Côtes de Blaye
Graves	Lalande de Pomerol	
	Fronsac	

These wines are divided into three groups according to the style of wine produced. The Médoc and Graves are the two most prestigious wine producing areas on the left bank of the river Garonne. The Haut Médoc, the higher, better part of the Médoc that is less of a drive for the wine producers from the city, is the home of the vast majority of the châteaux best known to wine lovers the world over while the flatter Bas Médoc leading to the Atlantic coast produces similar dry, light wines of less outstanding quality. It follows therefore that most of the wine carrying the Médoc appellation comes from the Bas Médoc, while any wine that can qualify as an Haut Médoc will probably be labelled as such. Very little white wine is made in the Médoc.

Graves, named after its gravelly soil, is the red and white wine producing region to the south of Bordeaux whose most prestigious properties are Châteaux Haut-Brion, La Mission Haut-Brion and Domaine de Chevalier. Red Graves are noticeably different from Médoc in their texture which is to some 'stoney', to others 'sandy', and when young they are perhaps less fruity than their counterparts from the Médoc.

The *encepagement*, the blend of grapes used in a typical Médoc or Graves vineyard, is 50 per cent Cabernet Sauvignon, 20 per cent Cabernet Franc, 20 per cent Merlot and perhaps 5 per cent each of Malbec and Petit Verdot, two local grape varieties that are known respectively for thei high yield and toughness. One of the most obvious difference between the wines of this group and those from the St Emilion and Pomerol on the right bank of the river is in the proportions of the grape varieties used. In a typical St Emilion property, Merlot would be the predominant grape comprising perhaps 60 per cent of the blend with Cabernet Franc accounting for another 30 per cent and Malbec making up 10 per cent. This produces much fuller, softer wines that mature earlier and are sometimes described as 'the burgundies of Bordeaux'.

Just north of St Emilion proper are its four satellite appellations, Montagne St Emilion, Puisseguin St Emilion, St Georges St Emilion and Lussac St Emilion, all of which sometimes appear on the shelves of British shops. Smaller appellations are Parsac and Sables.

Pomerols are rather more full-bodied versions of St Emilion, noted for their dark plummy colour and fullness of flavour with their superstar Château Pétrus fetching superstar prices at auction. Pomerol produces only about an eighth of the wine produced in St Emilion. Lalande de Pomerol produces similar but usually less concentrated wines, including those of Néac, while the wines of Fronsac and rarely-seen Canon Fronsac, may need time to soften but can be good value.

Bourg and Blaye wines rarely reach the heights of a good Haut Médoc, Graves, St Emilion or Pomerol but can provide good value lesser wines made typically from a blend of equal quantities of Merlot, Cabernet Franc and Malbec.

COMMUNE WINES The English word 'parish' most nearly corresponds to the French word *commune* and this is the most specific of any appellation in Bordeaux designating the vineyards surrounding just one tiny village. The name of the particular château is usually given in addition to the name of the commune, although it is occasionally possible to find generic commune wines carrying the name of the commune only, straight AC St Julien for example. In approximate descending order of prestige they are:

Pauillac: With three out of the top five châteaux of the

famous 1855 classification (given below) within its boundaries, the parish centred on this tiny seaside town clearly has something going for it. Very rich, long lasting wines.
Margaux: Château Margaux (not to be confused with straight AC Margaux commune wine) is its most famous property but there are many more producing very fine wines with great elegance and softness.
St Julien: Smaller than Pauillac, Margaux and St Estèphe, often thought of as the benchmark of the Médoc. Between Pauillac and Margaux in style, contains lots of the 'Ls', all the Léovilles for example, and both Ducrus.
St Estèphe: Harder wines, an acquired taste. Cos d'Estournel and the Ségurs are some of the best known.
Macau and Ludon: Small communes south of Margaux whose wines they resemble. Best known respectively for Châteaux Cantemerle and La Lagune which have to carry the appellation Haut Médoc since these communes do not have their own AC.
Moulis (en Médoc) and Listrac: Two useful ACs supplying middle quality slightly heavier-than-first-class wines.

Of all the châteaux producing wine in the Médoc there are a number that are acknowledged as producing consistently superior wines, the so-called 'classed growths' or *crus classés*. The classification referred to in the case of the Médoc is that drawn up for 1855 for the Paris exhibition which put the top châteaux into five divisions as shown below:

THE 1855 OFFICIAL CLASSIFICATION OF THE WINES OF THE GIRONDE

RED WINES

	Château	**Appellation Contrôlée**
Premiers Crus	Ch. Lafite	*Pauillac*
	Ch. Latour	*Pauillac*
	Ch. Margaux	*Margaux*
	Ch. Haut-Brion	*Graves*

	Château	Appellation Contrôlée
	Ch. Mouton-Rothschild (elevated to Premier Cru by Presidential decree 1973)	*Pauillac*
Seconds Crus	Ch. Brane-Cantenac	*Margaux*
	Ch. Cos d'Estournel	*St Estèphe*
	Ch. Ducru-Beaucaillou	*St Julien*
	Ch. Durfort-Vivens	*Margaux*
	Ch. Gruaud-Larose	*St Julien*
	Ch. Lascombes	*Margaux*
	Ch. Léoville-Barton	*St Julien*
	Ch. Léoville-Las-Cases	*St Julien*
	Ch. Léoville-Poyferré	*St Julien*
	Ch. Montrose	*St Estèphe*
	Ch. Pichon-Longueville	*Pauillac*
	Ch. Pichon-Longueville-Lalande	*Pauillac*
	Ch. Rauzan-Gassies	*Margaux*
	Ch. Rausan-Ségla	*Margaux*
Troisièmes Crus	Ch. Boyd-Cantenac	*Margaux*
	Ch. Calon-Ségur	*St Estèphe*
	Ch. Cantenac-Brown	*Margaux*
	Ch. Desmirail	*Margaux*
	Ch. Ferrière	*Margaux*
	Ch. Giscours	*Margaux*
	Ch. d'Issan	*Margaux*
	Ch. Kirwan	*Margaux*
	Ch. Lagrange	*St Julien*
	Ch. Langoa	*St Julien*
	Ch. La Lagune	*Haut-Médoc*
	Ch. Malescot-St-Exupéry	*Margaux*
	Ch. Marquis d'Alesme-Becker	*Margaux*
	Ch. Palmer	*Margaux*
Quatrièmes Crus	Ch. Beychevelle	*St Julien*
	Ch. Branaire-Ducru	*St Julien*

	Château	**Appellation Contrôlée**
	Ch. Duhart-Milon	*Pauillac*
	Ch. Lafon-Rochet	*St Estèphe*
	Ch. La Tour-Carnet	*Haut-Médoc*
	Ch. Marquis-de-Terme	*Margaux*
	Ch. Pouget	*Margaux*
	Ch. Prieuré-Lichine	*Margaux*
	Ch. St-Pierre-Bontemps	*St Julien*
	Ch. St-Pierre-Sevaistre	*St Julien*
	Ch. Talbot	*St Julien*
Cinquièmes Crus	Ch. Batailley	*Pauillac*
	Ch. Belgrave	*Haut-Médoc*
	Ch. Camensac	*Haut-Médoc*
	Ch. Cantemerle	*Haut-Médoc*
	Ch. Clerc-Milon	*Pauillac*
	Ch. Cos Labory	*St Estèphe*
	Ch. Croizet-Bages	*Pauillac*
	Ch. Dauzac	*Margaux*
	Ch. du Tertre	*Margaux*
	Ch. Grand-Puy-Ducasse	*Pauillac*
	Ch. Grand-Puy-Lacoste	*Pauillac*
	Ch. Haut-Bages-Libéral	*Pauillac*
	Ch. Haut-Batailley	*Pauillac*
	Ch. Lynch-Bages	*Pauillac*
	Ch. Lynch-Moussas	*Pauillac*
	Ch. Mouton-Baronne-Philippe	*Pauillac*
	Ch. Pédesclaux	*Pauillac*
	Ch. Pontet-Canet	*Pauillac*

A more sensitive guide today might be to look closely at prices fetched at auction but this 1855 classification is still surprisingly accurate.

Although there have been changes of ownership of various parcels of land which may have affected individual vineyards, and there may have been times when a new owner allowed his wines' reputation to suffer, or even rise above its 1855 station, the only official change to the classification in well over a century was made, as one would expect, by someone with a great deal of drive and not a little muscle. In 1973 Baron Philippe de Rothschild managed to get his Château Mouton-Rothschild promoted from second to first growth so that it now ranks equal with his cousin Eric's Lafite-Rothschild.

Below the ranks of the 1855 classification there are about 120 *crus bourgeois*, useful, well made, faster maturing wines from the Médoc of which half were designated *grand bourgeois* in 1978.

The wines of St Emilion had to wait a century for any similarly recognized classification. Even today these fiercely independent producers allow themselves the luxury of updating the classification constantly. This was the original 1955 St Emilion classification and there have not been any major demotions from the top ranks since then:

ST EMILION 1955 OFFICIAL CLASSIFICATION

Appellation St Emilion Premier Grand Cru Classé A Contrôlée	Ch. Ausone Ch. Cheval Blanc
Appellation St Emilion Premier Grand Cru Classé B Contrôlée	Ch. Beauséjour Ch. Belair Ch. Canon Ch. Figeac *Clos* Fourtet Ch. La Gaffelière Ch. Magdelaine Ch. Pavie Ch. Trottevieille
Appellation St Emilion Grand Cru Classé Contrôlée	Ch. l'Angélus Ch. l'Arrosée Ch. Baleau Ch. Balestard-la-Tonnelle Ch. Bellevue Ch. Bergat Ch. Cadet-Bon

Ch. Cadet-Piola
Ch. Canon-La Gaffelière
Ch. Cap-de-Mourlin
Ch. Chapelle-Madeleine
Ch. Chauvin
Ch. Corbin
Ch. Corbin-Michotte
Ch. Coutet
Couvent des Jacobins
Ch. Curé Bon
Ch. Dassault
Clos des Jacobins
Ch. Fonplégade
Ch. Fonroque
Ch. Franc-Mayne
Ch. Grand-Barrail-Lamarzelle-Figeac
Ch. Grand-Corbin-Despagne
Ch. Grand-Corbin-Pécresse
Ch. Grand-Mayne
Ch. Grand-Pontet
Ch. Grandes-Murailles
Ch. Guadet-St-Julien
Ch. Haut Corbin
Ch. Haut Sarpe
Ch. Jean-Faure
Ch. La Carte
Ch. La Clotte
Ch. La Cluzière
Ch. La Couspade
Ch. La Dominique
Clos La Madeleine
Ch. Larcis-Ducasse
Ch. Lamarzelle
Ch. Lamiote
Ch. Larmande
Ch. Laroze

Ch. Lasserre
Ch. La-Tour-Figeac
Ch. La-Tour-du-Pin-Figeac
Ch. Le Châtelet
Ch. Le Couvent
Ch. Le Prieuré
Ch. Matras
Ch. Mauvezin
Ch. Moulin-du-Cadet
Clos de l'Oratoire
Ch. Pavie-Decesse
Ch. Pavie-Macquin
Ch. Pavillon-Cadet
Ch. Petit-Faurie-de-Souchard
Ch. Petit-Faurie-de-Soutard
Ch. Ripeau
Ch. Sansonnet
Ch. St-Georges-Côte-Pavie
Clos St-Martin
Ch. Soutard
Ch. Tertre-Daugay
Ch. Trimoulet
Ch. Trois Moulins
Ch. Troplong-Mondot
Ch. Villemaurine
Ch. Yon-Figeac

Pomerol has no official classification though Château Pétrus prices regularly beat all comers and other highly regarded wines are Châteaux La Conseillante, Gazin, Lafleur, Lafleur-Pétrus, Petit-Village, Trotanoy and Vieux-Château-Certan.

Graves was officially classified in 1959 and here are the top red wine properties:

GRAVES 1959 OFFICIAL CLASSIFICATION

RED WINES

Appellation Graves Contrôlée

Ch. Bouscaut
Ch. Carbonnieux
Domaine de Chevalier
Ch. Fieuzal
Ch. Haut-Bailly
Ch. Haut-Brion
Ch. La Mission-Haut-Brion
Ch. La Tour-Haut-Brion
Ch. La Tour-Martillac
Ch. Malartic-Lagravière
Ch. Olivier
Ch. Pape-Clément
Ch. Smith-Haut-Lafitte

For more information about these properties and about many others consult Edmund Penning-Rowsell's *The Wines of Bordeaux*, or the French Bordeaux bible, Cocks & Feret.

WHITE BORDEAUX About a third of all the wine produced in the Gironde is white, but white bordeaux poses problems for producer and consumer alike. The problem for the consumer is that a white wine labelled straight AC bordeaux can vary from bone dry to sauternes-sweet, and yet there is often no indication on the label as to which of these two extremes is closer to the style of the wine (though dry wines should be in green bottles and sweet wines in clear glass). The problem for the producer has been that to make the wonderful sweet white wines that in the past have done so much for the reputation of Bordeaux is no longer economical. It requires careful selection of grapes and meticulous vinification that has not been rewarded in the prices people have recently been prepared to pay for such wines.

There has been a steady improvement, however, in the quality of the dry white wine produced in Bordeaux and now some of these Sauvignon-based wines can present a good-value alternative for those who had found that wine produced from the same grape in Sancerre and Pouilly Fumé is now out of their price range. The following are the dry white wines to look out for: Straight AC bordeaux; generic wines with the appellation Entre-deux-Mers (meaning between two seas, 'seas' being the rivers Garonne and Dordogne), all of which are dry; Graves whose wines can vary from dry to medium sweet, Blaye, Côtes de Blaye and Côtes de Bourg. The very best dry white bordeaux comes from the Graves region and can be heaven, full-bodied, dry wines that are capable of ageing and of standing up to rich food. The best are listed in this 1959 classification of white Graves:

WHITE WINES

Appellation Graves Contrôlée	Ch. Bouscaut
	Ch. Carbonnieux
	Domaine de Chevalier
	Ch. Couhins
	Ch. La Tour-Martillac
	Ch. Laville-Haut-Brion
	Ch. Malartic-Lagravière
	Ch. Olivier

The sweet wines of Bordeaux vary enormously in quality, from the cheapest of AC Sauternes with nothing but an overdose of sugar and sulphur dioxide to commend them, to the world-famous Château d'Yquem which the classifiers of 1855 elevated to a special rank, *grand premier cru*, above the four best red wine châteaux which were merely *premiers crus*.

The cheaper wines may be sweet just as a result of mechanical methods of stopping fermentation and a lot of SO_2, but the process of making a really top class sauternes is very time- and franc-consuming. In suitable misty autumn weather a certain sort of rot, *botrytis cinerea* (*pourriture noble* in French, 'noble rot' in English, and *Edelfäule* in German) forms on the grapes to cover them with a furry grey substance, shrivelling them so that their sugar content becomes very concentrated indeed. They look repulsive but will make wine that is mind-blowingly luscious. This works slowly through each bunch so that specially trained pickers have to go through each vineyard up to five or six times in order to pick each grape at its best. The grapes are then sorted carefully and are often put straight into small casks where their extraordinarily high sugar content means that fermentation is slow and gentle and will go on for several months before stopping naturally leaving a residual sugar content that is still high. The wines may then be aged in wood for a year or two so that they acquire keeping qualities, and are at least 13° – sometimes much higher – in alcohol.

Commonly encountered generic appellations for sweet white wines are Sauternes and its sub-region Barsac, Cérons, St Croix du Mont, Loupiac, and Premières Côtes de Bordeaux with Bordeaux and Graves Supérieur also producing sweeter wines. But the greatest sweet whites of Bordeaux are among the châteaux listed in this 1855 classification:

1855 CLASSIFICATION OF SAUTERNES

WHITE WINES

Premier Grand Cru	Ch. d'Yquem	*Sauternes*
Premiers Crus	Ch. Climens	*Barsac & Sauternes*
	Ch. Coutet	*Barsac & Sauternes*
	Ch. de Rayne-Vigneau	*Sauternes*
	Ch. de Suduiraut	*Sauternes*
	Ch. Guiraud	*Sauternes*
	Clos Haut-Peyraguey	*Sauternes*
	Ch. Lafaurie-Peyraguey	*Sauternes*
	Ch. La Tour-Blanche	*Sauternes*
	Ch. Rabaud-Promis	*Sauternes*
	Ch. Rieussec	*Sauternes*
	Ch. Sigalas-Rabaud	*Sauternes*

Seconds Crus	Ch. Broustet	*Barsac & Sauternes*
	Ch. Caillou	*Barsac & Sauternes*
	Ch. d'Arche	*Sauternes*
	Ch. de Malle	*Sauternes*
	Ch. de Myrat	*Barsac & Sauternes*
	Ch. Doisy-Daëne	*Barsac & Sauternes*
	Ch. Doisy-Védrines	*Barsac & Sauternes*
	Ch. Filhot	*Sauternes*
	Ch. Lamothe	*Sauternes*
	Ch. Nairac	*Barsac & Sauternes*
	Ch. Romer	*Sauternes*
	Ch. Suau	*Barsac & Sauternes*

Some of the *premiers crus* are particularly good value.

BORDEAUX ROSÉ A small amount of bordeaux rosé or *clairet* is made but is rarely seen outside Bordeaux.

BURGUNDY

Summary:
Reds – very variable, best are elegant, supple, sweeter than claret.
Whites – full, dry, great ageing potential, world's best dry whites?
Côte d'Or produces all the great wines, in small quantities.

Burgundy is France's other great wine region but is different in almost every way imaginable from Bordeaux. While Bordeaux is elegant and restrained, Burgundy is unashamedly gutsy, a difference in attitude that is reflected in the style of their great red wines. A claret reveals itself cautiously, but a good red burgundy has much more immediate charm. The wines tend to be higher in alcohol and rather sweeter than their counterparts on the other side of the Massif Central. They are shorter lived and even some of Burgundy's finest wines are at their best when only four or five years old.

There is another difference between Bordeaux and

Burgundy that is of great significance to the wine buyer – the Côte d'Or, the 'golden slope' between Dijon and Chagny that is the site of all the very best burgundy, produces less than a tenth of the amount of Appellation Contrôlée wine made in Bordeaux. This is an important part of the reason why fine burgundy is relatively more expensive than fine bordeaux, although a contributory factor recently has been the tightening up of controls on production in the region.

THE BURGUNDY REGION

It is often thought that Burgundy is one homogeneous wine producing region whereas it is in fact a term used to describe four (five if Beaujolais is included) different zones connected by more than 150 miles of the famous N6 Paris-Lyon autoroute, from the isolated pocket of vineyards round the town of Chablis in the north, via the classic Côte d'Or, then the tiny sprinkling of vineyards that comprise the Côte Chalonnaise or Région de Mercurey, to the much bigger area of Mâcon vineyards making Burgundy's least expensive red standbys and some useful cheapish whites. Further south than this are the rolling hills that constitute the Beaujolais region which the French, quite rightly, consider separately from mainstream Burgundy.

Considering its latitude, it is quite remarkable that Chablis produces any wine at all and, as Hugh Johnson points out in his *Atlas*, even more amazing that the name of this quiet little village should be known the world over as synonymous with white wine (though regrettably seldom with the sort of wine actually produced there).

One of the Côte d'Or's most exciting features for the tourist is the signposts, all those famous names following on in such concentration. The vineyards themselves are on a pathetically narrow strip of south east hillside leading down to the whizzing Citroëns and Renaults of Route Nationale 74. In the hinterland are the Hautes Côtes de Nuits and Beaune where the topography is more variable. There is undoubtedly a feeling of going towards the sun,

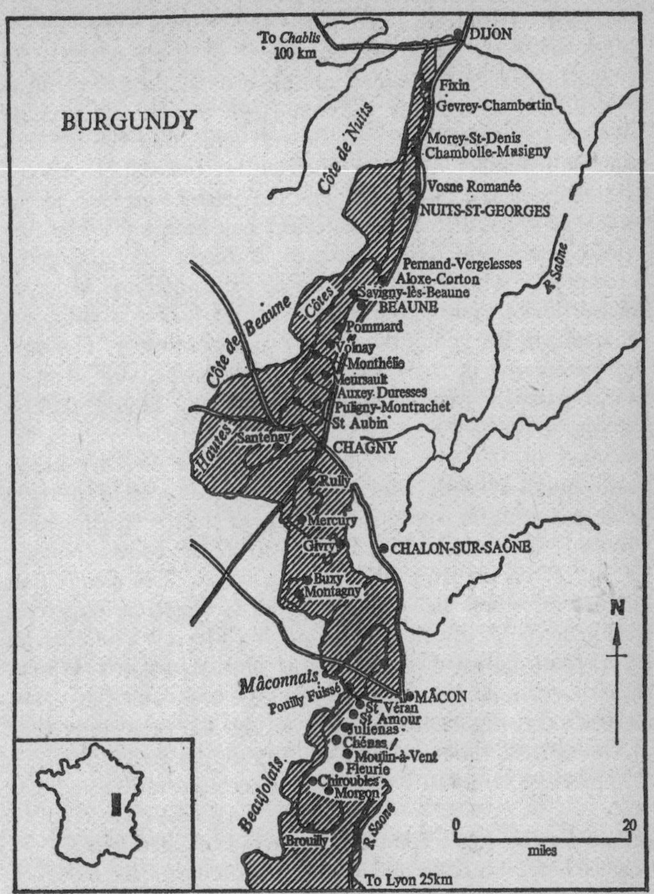

of the Côte's being well exposed to light and sunshine and protected from the severities of wind and cold from the north and west – no wonder this slope can produce such wonderful wines.

Then the Côte Chalonnaise and Mâconnais area becomes a little hillier. Throughout the region there are no great signs of obvious opulence. Few Bordeaux-style piles of grandeur, just a succession of prosperous large farmhouses.

The reason for this is simple – there are a very few big landowners in Burgundy and most of the vineyards (or *climats*, as they are called there), even if they are only a few acres, have many different owners. This is because of how the church's vineyards were split after the Revolution and, further, because inherited land was split between members of the family rather than passing *en bloc* to the eldest son, so that every vineyard has been split into tiny plots, each tended in a slightly different way, often by growers for whom this is but a spare time activity. Whereas in Bordeaux there is the solid benchmark of a well-known château, in Burgundy there is no such continuity. The only consistency is in the occasional grower who vinifies, ages and bottles his own wine – and sells it at a high price as a 'domaine bottled' gem.

Most of the wine produced is sold to the *négociants* who blend it with wines of the same appellation from different growers to produce a wine of their own particular house style in quantities sufficient to fill the orders they are likely to receive from all over the world. This means that there can often be greater similarity between a certain *négociant*'s Morey St Denis and his Gevrey Chambertin, say, than between his and another *négociant*'s Gevrey Chambertin. All very confusing, so the best course of action is to find a *négociant* whose style you like, and only then to investigate the intricacies of Burgundian geography.

Here are some of the top Burgundy *négociants*:

Louis Latour – full, long-lived, much-acclaimed wines.
Louis Jadot – a respected shipper, particularly for reds.
Prosper Maufoux – particularly good for whites. Marcel Amance is an associated company.
Remoissenet – good reputation traditionally.
Bouchard Père & Fils – some very good vineyards around Beaune. French-bottled wines noticeably better than London bottlings.
J. Faiveley – extensive holdings around Nuits.
Chanson – Beaune shipper producing lighter than average wines.

Doudet Naudin – soupy 'méthode ancienne' prolonged fermentation, wines.
Joseph Drouhin – prestigious shipper settling down after a difficult patch.
Leroy – fine wine but expensive, a distributor of the wines of the famous Domaine de la Romanée Conti.
Domaine de la Romanée Conti – thought of as the top-notch Burgundy estate, though usually by those who can't afford to taste their wines.

RED BURGUNDY Ask for an Englishman's idea of a typical red burgundy and he'll probably think of a rich, rather syrupy wine that gives the same sort of satisfaction as a bowl of soup. Ask a Frenchman and he'll talk about 'un bouquet très delicat, vins fins et elegants'. The tightening up of controls over the burgundy sold in this country in 1974 has been followed by confusion, inflation and even litigation.

At its best, genuine mature red burgundy is a warm, velvety wine, softer, more full bodied and less dry than a fine claret. There was a time when it was possible for *négociants* in Burgundy to emulate this style in even the lesser-known names by mixing in a generous dose of heavy red wine from somewhere like the Rhône, the Midi, southern Italy or even Algeria, then a French colony. This practice continued and Britons came to expect their burgundies to have a certain heaviness. Some were disappointed by the lighter burgundies they would be served in Parisian restaurants – the reds having a much higher degree of acidity than they were accustomed to consider 'proper'.

From the 1973 vintage onwards we, as good members of the European Economic Community in which France was busy tightening up her Appellation Contrôlée laws, could accept and sell as 'Nuits-St-Georges', say, only such wine as had documents to prove that all of it really was Nuits-St-Georges. And these documents are being handed out more and more tight-fistedly. No longer can a producer sell off his production of single vineyard wine that is surplus to the maximum yield allowed under AC laws as a wine with a lower appellation. He certainly is not allowed to sell as burgundy any wine that has in it even a drop that was not produced in the Burgundy region.

The net result has been that all burgundy has rocketed in price, not least because the Americans, the Dutch, the Belgians and the Swiss are so keen on it; no class restaurant in any of these countries can expect to get by without a Beaune or two on their list. We can also expect to find our burgundies much lighter than perhaps we have been used to. There is much to recommend in the delicacy of these 'French style' burgundies. They are more subtle and fragrant, though perhaps more volatile. There are still wines on the market, particularly from older vintages, and particularly English-bottled wines, that can provide the robust 'British burgundy' style, however. Look out for wines that do not carry the magic words 'Appellation Contrôlée', or whose labels carry the name of a fancy vineyard followed by the straightforward Appellation Bourgogne Contrôlée'. These will probably be pre-1973 examples of wines designed for the British market whose provenance is not always guaranteed but which can provide a lot of pleasure.

If you still hanker after the richness of traditional burgundy and find it difficult to afford the bottles in which this is certain to be found, try some of the Australian reds, or even an older rioja.

Burgundy's present AC system is based on geography and yield. A grower in a good *climat* can decide on the basis of how much wine he is going to produce from his grapes; whether to produce a limited amount of high appellation wine, rather more medium quality wine perhaps with just the commune appellation, or a lot of straightforward AC burgundy. Thus there should never be offered for sale, as for vintages before 1973 when growers were allowed to sell off surplus wine under a lower appellation, wine that 'is really exactly the same as wine sold as Chambertin Clos de Bèze' sold only with the burgundy appellation, so-called 'declassified burgundy'.

The most ordinary burgundy appellation (though beware the non-burgundy 'burgundy table wines' described in

Chapter Two) is the rather more than ordinary-sounding Bourgogne Grand Ordinaire. 'BGO' is not produced in great quantity but some pleasant enough light reds find their way to Britain. Bourgogne Passe-tout-grains is next step up, an interesting wine that is made up of Gamay and at least half as much Pinot Noir. The longer it is kept, the more predominant will become the superior Pinot Noir characteristics. Plain old AC bourgogne (burgundy) is a relatively high appellation, surprisingly enough, as it must be made of Pinot Noir in the mainstream areas of Burgundy, perhaps from the vineyards on lower side of the RN 74 downhill from the 'golden slope' proper. Bourgogne Hautes Côtes de Beaune and Bourgogne Hautes Côtes de Nuits are two further appellations of generic wines from the Côte d'Or from the hillier land behind the 'golden slope'. They can be good value, particularly in good years when the vineyards were not at too great a disadvantage compared with their relatives over the hill. There are new plantings all the time and this region is expected to become more important. Usually a good way below these generic appellations in quality is red Mâcon, predominantly Gamay. These wines are often the nearest a shipper can get to Burgundy and still present wines that do not seem prohibitive in price.

There are also Côtes de Beaune Villages and Côtes de Nuits Villages, wines that come respectively from the Côte de Nuits, the northern half of the Côte d'Or centred on Nuits-St-Georges and the Côte de Beaune, the southern half around the town of Beaune. These will usually be superior in quality to any other non-commune wine.

Sixteen villages on the fringes of the Côte de Beaune are allowed to blend their wines and sell them under this appellation, which they often do if their village has a name like Dezizes-lès-Maranges which does not yet trip off the tongue of the average wine buyer. Blending will usually be carried out by one of the big *négociants*. Côtes de Nuits Villages comes from one of seven villages scattered along the Côte de Nuits but, unlike Côte de Beaune Villages, the wine cannot be sold under the village name instead and does not have to be blended with wine from another village. All of which perhaps illustrates that Burgundian wine law is less a function of logic, more of parish politics.

Next up the scale are commune wines, wine that carries the appellation of a single village. Some of the best value in Burgundy now that Côte d'Or wines have become so expensive is to be found in the commune wines of the Côte Chalonnaise, a few patches of vineyards just south of Chalon and centred on Mercurey. Names to look out for in red wines are Givry and Mercurey.

This category includes all the famous names like Nuits-St-Georges, Chambolle Musigny, Aloxe Corton etc. Here are a few alternatives to the better known names:

Alternative	*Close to*
Auxey Duresses	Volnay
Fixin	Gevrey Chambertin
Monthélie	Volnay
Morey St Denis	Gevrey Chambertin and Chambolle Musigny
Pernand Vergelesses	Aloxe Corton
St Aubin	Chassagne Montrachet
Santenay	Beaune
Savigny-lès-Beaune	Beaune

At the very top of the Burgundy tree, for those who can afford to climb that high, are the single vineyard wines, usually identified by the name of the commune followed by the name of the vineyard, as in Chambolle Musigny Les Amoureuses or Vosne Romanée Suchots. The exceptions to this are some of the very best vineyards which, rather like those Scottish noblemen who are called The Tulloch of Glen Tulloch or the Loon of McDoon, are called simply 'Le Corton', or 'Le Musigny'. You can spot them by the price. See the list of *grands crus* at the end of this section.

WHITE BURGUNDY White burgundy has mercifully been much freer of the trickery that occasionally smudged red burgundy in the past. The wines have had to rely locally on establishing themselves as crisp but full, dry whites – a *dosage* of wine from southern Italy might help along a red burgundy but would be unlikely to help the blender of white burgundy. Recent vintages have been more fortuitous for whites than reds too, and the chances of a bottle of white burgundy's being a disappointment are less than those of a red.

The hierarchy of white wine appellations in Burgundy is exactly the same as for red, except that the appellation Bourgogne Aligoté replaces Bourgogne Passe-tout-grains. Aligoté is the distinctly more ordinary of the two widely planted white grape varieties in Burgundy. It produces thin, light wines high in acidity compared to the noble richness of the Chardonnay.

Chablis has its own sub-system of appellations. The best of these crisp, very dry wines can have a lovely clean freshness, though they can be expensive. There are seven *Grand Cru* vineyards whose wines can age and develop for up to ten years, under which in quality terms is Chablis *Premier Cru*, specific vineyards producing wines of superior quality, now down to scarcely more than ten of any note. Straight AC Chablis is the most commonly encountered wine and is of medium quality white. Petit Chablis comes from the fringes of the vineyard area and is usually very light.

The great white burgundies, rich dry wines that will mature for a decade and more, are to be found in the *grands crus* of the Côte d'Or (see the classification at the end of this section), but the Mâconnais and Côte Chalonnaise are more helpful for whites than red wines in providing lighter-weight alternatives. All good are the wines of Montagny, Rully and Buxy on the Côte Chalonnaise and the rather rounder, better whites of the Mâconnais further south. These include St Véran, Beaujolais Blanc (which two appellations are sometimes used interchangeably), Mâcon Villages or Mâcon-Lugny, Mâcon-Clessé, Mâcon-Prissé, Mâcon-Viré or other of the forty villages allowed to tag their names on to the end of Mâcon, a Mâcon Villages blend. Pouilly Fuissé (which has no connection with

Pouilly Fumé from Pouilly-sur-Loire) is now prohibitively expensive and a good example of any of the wines listed should be able to give as much pleasure. Even a straightforward AC Mâcon blanc is usually very much better than its red counterpart, being made of the noble Chardonnay grape rather than the verging-on-ignoble Gamay which may be used for AC Mâcon rouge. The appellation Pinot Chardonnay Mâcon sometimes seen is another Burgundian oddity since it is not necessarily superior to straight Mâcon, just a name that reflects the sometime confusion about the relationship between Pinot Blanc and Chardonnay. It may be made from either.

The classic communes for white wines further north are Meursault, whose wines have a distinctive butteriness, Puligny Montrachet and Chassagne Montrachet, firm wines with great ageing potential. Auxey Duresses, Pernand-Vergelesses and St Aubin all produce good quality white burgundy without a fine name and price to match.

BURGUNDY ROSÉ Rosé is produced in quantity only in the village of Marsannay right at the north end of the Côte d'Or.

BURGUNDY GRANDS CRUS

Côte de Nuits	*Gevrey-Chambertin*
	Chambertin
	Chambertin-Clos-de-Bèze
	Chapelle-Chambertin
	Charmes-Chambertin
	Griotte-Chambertin
	Latricières-Chambertin
	Mazis-Chambertin
	Mazoyères-Chambertin
	Ruchottes-Chambertin
	Morey-St-Denis
	Bonnes-Mares (also in Chambolle-Musigny)

	Clos-de-la-Roche
	Clos-de-Tart (also in Chambolle-Musigny)
	Clos-St-Denis
	Chambolle-Musigny
	Bonnes-Mares (also in Morey-St-Denis)
	Clos-de-Tart (also in Morey-St-Denis)
	Musigny (including a little white wine)
	Vougeot
	Clos-de-Vougeot
	Vosne-Romanée
	Echézeaux
	Grands-Echézeaux
	La Tâche
	Richebourg
	Romanée-Conti
	Romanée-St-Vivant
Côte de Beaune	*Aloxe-Corton*
	Charlemagne
	Corton (red wine and some white)
	Corton-Charlemagne (white wine only)
	Puligny-Montrachet & Chassagne-Montrachet (white wines only)
	Bâtard-Montrachet
	Bienvenues-Bâtard-Montrachet
	Chevalier-Montrachet
	Criots-Bâtard-Montrachet
	Montrachet

BEAUJOLAIS

Summary: Fresh fruity reds made to be drunk young and cool.

If ever there was a wine that did warrant that curious description 'a real *drinking* wine', it is beaujolais. True beaujolais is above all a fruity refreshing drink, for any time of day, with or without food, in hearty draughts as it is drunk in its native region just north of Lyon. The pretty rolling hills of Beaujolais, Clochemerle country, produce refreshment for this gastronomic capital of France.

A little beaujolais blanc is produced in the north on the borders with the Mâconnais but it is the reds that are important.

The vineyards of the Beaujolais seem to bring out just the right amount of juicy roundness from the Gamay grape which further north produces Burgundy's less distinguished reds. The grapes are usually vinified fast, by throwing whole bunches into the fermentation vat in a version of carbonic maceration as described earlier. The wines are bottled early and most are meant to be drunk young. No wonder beaujolais is so popular – it has all the refreshing acidity of a white wine, with the depth of flavour beloved by red wine drinkers. It's a good compromise wine, and a delicious one when drunk slightly cool, the sort of temperature at which most shops keep their wines.

Beaujolais Villages is a cut above this in quality, really mouth-watering wine coming from one or more of the forty-odd villages in the better northern half of the region. They may alternatively add the name of the village to sell their wine as Beaujolais with the name of the village, though few of the villages has as yet achieved great fame – other than Vaux-en-Beaujolais, supposedly the original model for Clochemerle.

In the top rank of Beaujolais are nine communes, the 'crus beaujolais', in the north which have earned their own appellations and are capable of producing wines that can be kept more than a couple of years;

Fleurie: So prettily named and often the lightest of the crus – or is it just the name?
Chiroubles: Similar and close to Fleurie.
St Amour: Another lighter cru, and another pretty name.
Chénas: Between Juliénas and Fleurie.
Juliénas: Firmer and richer.
Brouilly: Largest of the crus, wines slightly earthier than average.
Côte de Brouilly: Heartland of the Brouilly area on the slopes of Mont Brouilly.
Morgon: As one wine list said, 'not a Welsh rugby player, but a good fruity beaujolais'. Weightier than average nevertheless.
Moulin-à-Vent: This 'windmill' wine is the beaujolais with the greatest keeping qualities. After about six years these wines become more and more like good red burgundy from much further north.

Beaujolais primeur is a wine which usually warrants about one per cent of the fuss that is made of it. This is beaujolais that has been hurriedly vinified, heavily dosed to stabilize it, bottled and shipped out to the expectant world just a few weeks after the vintage. There is much discussion about the difference between beaujolais nouveau and beaujolais primeur. The generally accepted rule, for what it's worth, is that primeur is released for sale on 15 November (at a fraction of a second past midnight) whereas nouveau is not put on to the market until 15 December, by which time it stands a better chance of lasting till after February. No cru wine may be released before 15 December. The wine itself is purplish, thin and usually very high in acidity. Only in very ripe or very early years is primeur more than an overpriced fad, but then in late November wine drinkers in northern Europe need all the excitement they can get out of life – even if it is only a bottle of badly shaken crimson ink that was just a bunch of grapes a month before.

RHÔNE

Summary: Deep, slow maturing, good value reds from the north (Hermitage country); easier, softer wines from the south (Châteauneuf country).

The Rhône valley, known to many British motorists only as an escape route to the Mediterranean, has been more famous as a wine region than it is now. Hermitage and Châteauneuf-du-Pape have in their time been acclaimed as the kings of wine (Pope, in the case of Châteauneuf?) but now, with British wine buyers at least, the area is often overlooked, which makes many of them good value.

There are great differences between the northern and southern parts of the valley. In the north the valley is narrow, with room only for the river, the autoroute and a few steeply terraced vineyards on the valley sides. The climate is not unlike that of Beaujolais just a few kilometres to the north. In the south there is a sharp change to a Mediterranean climate, the valley widens, the houses need shutters, olive trees dot the landscape. The cherry orchards give way to melon fields edged with cypresses to protect them from the capricious *mistral*, the strange wind that persists in Provence and allows men to murder their wives while affected by its malevolence.

RED RHÔNE Côtes-du-Rhône is the catch-all appellation of the Rhône valley and most comes from the south. The wines are light, straightforward examples of the warm, spicey wines of the area and about three-quarters of all the wine made here is sold under this appellation. Popular with the French when market variations make it a better buy than bordeaux or beaujolais.

Côtes-du-Rhône Villages is a firmer, longer lasting version of this and must have at least 12.5 per cent alcohol, while ordinary Côtes-du-Rhône need have only 11°. Up in the hills north-east of Châteauneuf are the villages allowed to use this appellation, sometimes adding the name

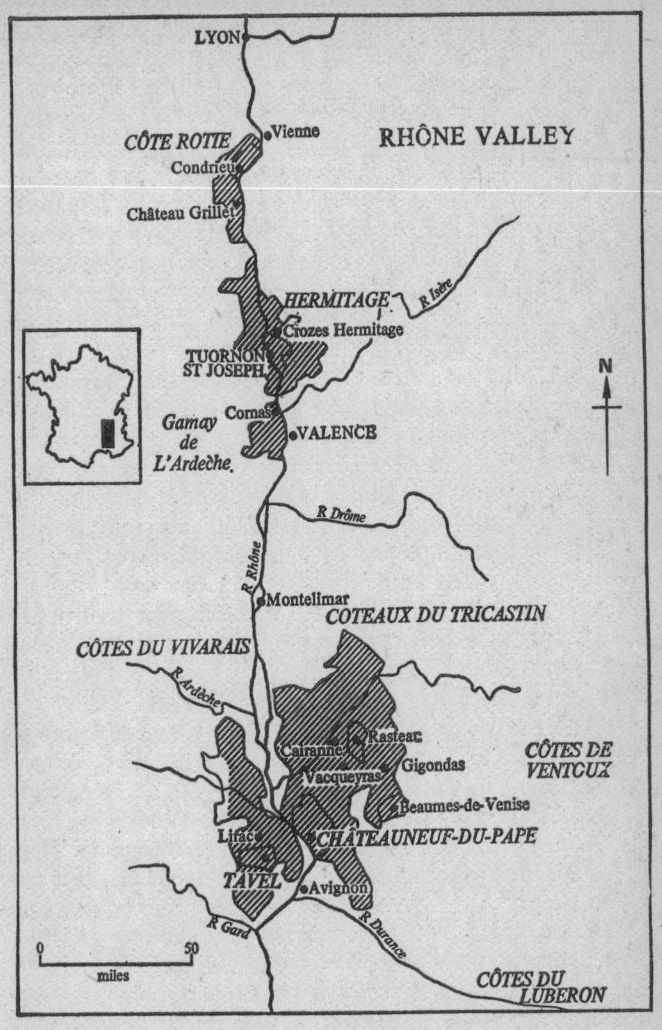
RHÔNE VALLEY
LYON
Vienne
CÔTE ROTIE
Condrieu
Château Grillet
HERMITAGE
R Isère
Crozes Hermitage
TUORNON
ST JOSEPH
N
Cornas
Gamay
de
L'Ardeche.
VALENCE
R Drôme
R Rhône
Montelimar
COTEAUX DU TRICASTIN
CÔTES DU VIVARAIS
R Ardèche
Rasteau
Cairanne
Gigondas
Vacqueyras
CÔTES DE
VENTOUX
Beaumes-de-Venise
Lirac
CHÂTEAUNEUF-DU-PAPE
TAVEL
Avignon
R Gard
R Durance
0
50
miles
CÔTES DU
LUBERON

of the village itself. Commonly seen in Britain are Beaunes-de-Venise (better known for its Muscat fortified wine), Cairanne, Chusclan, Vacqueyras, Vinsobres, Visan and Gigondas, whose meatier wines are allowed an appellation all of their own.

The model on which these southern wines are based is Châteauneuf-du-Pape, whose name and vineyards date from the fourteenth century when the Popes decamped from Rome and ruled at the Palais des Papes in Avignon. Châteauneuf was also the birthplace of the Appellation Contrôlée system under Baron Le Roy in the twenties. Its wines vary enormously in style, for up to thirteen different grape varieties are used with Grenache, Cinsaut, Syrah and Mourvèdre being most common, and there are any number of different winemaking methods. The growers who use a high proportion of Grenache make wines for early consumption, those who add up to 50 per cent of other varieties, including the long-lived Syrah from the north Rhône, and vinify slowly, make wines that will improve for up to eight years. They are big peppery wines with at least 12.5 per cent alcohol, often much more. Some of the best of these traditional estates are Château Fortia and the Domaines de Beaucastel and Mont Redon.

Other southern Rhône reds of this style and quality are made on the fringes of the area with the Côtes de Ventoux and Coteaux du Tricastin appellations, with VDQS Côtes du Vivarais and Côtes du Lubéron being fainter shadows.

The reds of the northern Rhône make good value buys for those who hanker after the style of rich burgundy. They are made from the intense, Syrah grape that can last for up to twenty years and takes at least six or seven years to develop to the stage where it is worth uncorking a bottle. The Syrah is often softened by the addition of up to 10 per cent white grapes, as is done in Chianti.

Hermitage is the classic north Rhône wine. It is capable of lasting up to twenty years and has a very deep mulberry colour. Côte Rotie is another very fine wine, rather more delicate than Hermitage and more difficult to find since even smaller quantities are made. Cornas, sheltered from the *mistral*, is capable of producing wines to match Hermitage while Crozes Hermitage, the easiest north Rhône wine to find in this country, is a rather paler version, now often made by carbonic maceration. St Joseph is a slightly fuller all-Syrah wine. Also worth looking at are two wines from the St Joseph area, Syrah and Gamay de l'Ardèche. The Syrah is made from vines too young to earn the St Joseph appellation, while the Gamay is a good example of what the Gamay can do outside Beaujolais.

WHITE RHÔNE Only about 5 per cent of all the wine produced in the Rhône valley is white. There are now some attractively made white Côtes-du-Rhônes, mainly from the south, with a good balance between grapiness and acidity, and in the north white wine is made in Crozes Hermitage and Hermitage (where it can reach a sort of nuttiness with age) from the Roussanne and Marsanne grapes.

The most famous, and most expensive, of the Rhône whites come from two small areas in the far north. Condrieu and Château Grillet – indeed Ch. Grillet with less than four acres is the smallest AC area in France to be awarded its own appellation, and is priced accordingly. Made from the pernickety Viognier grape on steeply terraced vineyards that are difficult to work, the wines have a very distinctive aroma not unlike apricots. Ch. Grillet is given some wood ageing and may be kept longer than Condrieu whose freshness can be appealing while it is still very young.

RHÔNE ROSÉ It is in the southern Rhône that rosés start to come into their own. Many of the villages in the south east of the valley make good rosé versions of their red wines, and across the river from Châteauneuf-du-Pape are two areas particularly famous for their rosé, Tavel and Lirac. Tavel is France's most classic rosé, often a staggering (quite literally) 14 per cent in alcohol and really more of a pale dryish red. Nearby Lirac also produces a similar rosé and increasingly good red wine.

LOIRE

Summary: Wide range of light appetizing wines produced. Best known for Muscadet, Rosé d'Anjou, Saumur, Vouvray, Sancerre and Pouilly Fumé.

After Bordeaux, the Greater Burgundy area, which includes the Beaujolais/Mâconnais, and then the Rhône Valley, the Loire is France's biggest source of Appellation Contrôlée wine. The Loire river, 600 miles long, with its great sweep north then west across France links a number of distinct wine-producing regions, each with its own specialities. At its mouth is the busy port of Nantes, all shellfish and Atlantic breezes. Its middle stretch, land of Anjou, Saumur, Vouvray and the other wines of Touraine, is the picture-postcard Loire, valley of castles, châteaux, gardens and tourists. Sancerre and Pouilly, small towns facing each other across the river much further east, are the twin stars of the Central Vineyards.

The Loire marks the northernmost limit of wine production in France. North of the westernmost more exposed part of the Loire, the thirsty traveller has only the apple orchards of Normandy to supply him with refreshment and stimulation. The valley produces dry, sweet and sparkling whites, rosés and light reds which will be looked at separately while travelling upstream.

LOIRE REDS Though not a great red wine producing region, the Loire is responsible for Chinon and Bourgueil, two interesting examples of what the Cabernet Franc can do if left to its own devices. The wines are light in alcohol, dry with a curious texture and flavour reminiscent of wood shavings and raspberries. Most should be drunk young and fresh though some St Nicolas de Bourgueil, a sub region of Bourgueil with its own appellation, can improve with a few years' bottle age. These wines should be drunk cooler than is normal for red wines.

Similar though often lighter wines may be produced with the appellation Anjou, Touraine and Saumur Champigny.

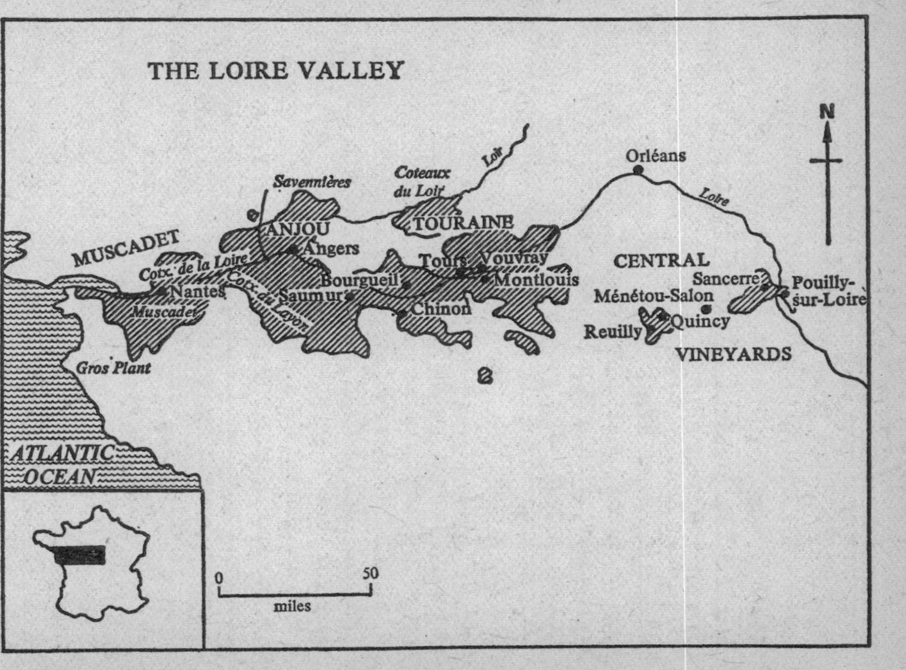
THE LOIRE VALLEY
N
Orléans
Loire
Loir
Coteaux
du Loir
Savennières
ANJOU
Angers
TOURAINE
MUSCADET
Cotx. de la Loire
Cotx. du Layon
Nantes
Muscadet
Saumur
Bourgueil
Chinon
Tours
Vouvray
Montlouis
CENTRAL
Sancerre
Pouilly-
sur-Loire
Ménétou-Salon
Quincy
Reuilly
VINEYARDS
Gros Plant
ATLANTIC
OCEAN
0
50
miles

There have also been extensive plantings of the Gamay grape of Beaujolais fame in the Loire and Gamay de Touraine is trying hard to fill the gap left by rising beaujolais prices.

DRY WHITE LOIRE Gros Plant Nantais is a thin, acid wine, said to taste more generous if sipped with oysters on the quayside at Nantes. Muscadet, called after the grape of the same name (not connected with Muscat), has the same high acidity as Gros Plant, but more body to balance it. Muscadet is meant to be a simple wine, a background wine without too much character. Muscadet de Sèvre-et-Maine, named after two tributaries of the Loire, has more prestige, as does the little-seen Muscadet des Coteaux de la Loire. The words 'sur lie' on the label mean that the wine was bottled straight off the lees and should therefore have more flavour and freshness than average. A muscadet made in a particularly ripe year can have almost as much body as a southern white burgundy. Muscadet is the only AC to specify a maximum alcohol content, 12°.

Anjou and Saumur both produce some dry white wine under these appellations, from the Chenin Blanc grape, but the district between Angers and Saumur is better known for rosés, sparkling and sweeter white wines. The best, Savennières, has its own AC and lives long, with a curious flowery flavour. Vouvray makes a similar wine in rather greater quantity but the character of the Chenin Blanc seems particularly well suited to sweeter wines. Around the town of Tours the Sauvignon grape, can produce some fresh lively wines that can sometimes lift Sauvignon de Touraine up to the quality level of Sancerre and Pouilly Fumé at half the price. These twin villages produce very similar wines from the Sauvignon grape, whose clean refreshing qualities, and hint of blackcurrants in the smell, have become very popular in recent years. Similar, though often thinner wines are to be found in nearby Quincy, Reuilly and Ménétou-Salon. All these dry white Loires should be drunk as young as possible and can be disappointingly stale within three or four years of the vintage.

A word of warning – straight Pouilly-sur-Loire without the word Fumé on the label (Pouilly Fuissé being something quite different from southern Burgundy) is a very commonplace wine made from the very commonplace Chasselas grape.

SWEETER WHITE LOIRE The Chenin Blanc grape, the predominant white wine grape of the middle Loire, is capable of producing sweet wines that can rival anything produced in Sauternes or Germany, though its honeyed floweriness is not in high fashion at the moment. It may seem extraordinary that great dessert wines are produced so far north, but the Coteaux du Layon is a sheltered pocket of vineyards just south of Angers whose very best wines carry the appellations Bonnezeaux and Quarts de Chaume. These wines are particularly good value. Further up river, Vouvray and Montlouis across the river are noted for their medium sweet wines which have the same honeyed quality from the Chenin Blanc grape if not allowed to ferment out to often less exciting dry wines. The best of these can last for more than fifty years, though the cheapest should be drunk while still fresh. Good for drinking without food, outside when the sun is shining.

LOIRE ROSÉS The Loire is one of the few wine regions in which rosés are important. In Anjou they represent more than half total production. Rosé d'Anjou, perhaps the most famous rosé in the world but for Mateus, is at its best a refreshingly fruity middle-of-the-road wine, at worst a sickly concoction. Better than this straight Rosé d'Anjou made from a mixture of Groslot and Gamay grapes is Cabernet d'Anjou rosé. This wine is made from Cabernets Sauvignon and Franc, and these classic claret grapes make rosés of great character here, usually quite dry with enough sweetness to bring out the Cabernet perfume. Scented wines to be savoured not sniffed at. A rosé de Touraine will probably be similar in style to rosé d'Anjou.

ALSACE

Summary: Mainly white wines made from German grapes in French style. Full bodied, perfumed, dry.

Of all the French wine producing regions, Alsace is the least French, which is hardly surprising since the region's geography is so clearly German and its chequered history has had it under German rule for almost half the last century. Instead of wondering whether he is in fact French or German, the Alsatian gets on with the business of being Alsatian, and this applies as much to his winemaking techniques as anything else.

It is said about the winemakers of Alsace that they make Germanic wines in the French style. Whereas the Germans are looking for sweetness and tend to produce fragrant, flowery wines relatively low in alcohol, their counterparts across the Rhine in Alsace, which is after all as far south as Baden, ferment out all the sugar in the grapes to produce bone dry wines that are deceptively high in alcohol – often half as strong again as their German equivalents. What makes Alsace wines different from those made in the rest of France is that the grapes grown are the fragrant German ones, rather than the more steely and austere Chardonnay of Burgundy and Sauvignon of the Loire and Bordeaux. All of which produces wines that have that attractive combination of a heady, fragrant smell and a taste that reveals itself as both dry and relatively high in acidity.

Alsace is also good value because the general quality level of the wines exported is markedly high, perhaps because Alsace was one of the first regions to insist on bottling at source, and because winemakers there are fanatical about minimizing the use of chemicals, disdaining techniques which may have become standard practice elsewhere.

Alsace wines can be recognized by their tall green *flûte* bottles, a sort of tall, skinny Moselle bottle, and their labels which carry an often confusing mixture of French and German proper names on them. The best known houses,

Hugel (whose advertising copy line a few years back was 'Possibly the best wine you've *never* tasted'), the two Dopffs, Trimbach, Beyer, all sound German, as do the addresses – Riquewihr, Eguisheim and so on.

Once the Alsace labelling code has been cracked, however, identification should be a relatively easy matter. There is just one appellation for the region, AC Alsace, with Alsace Grand Cru for particularly good grape variety/vineyard combinations. The wines are differentiated only by grape variety and producer. Producers are still largely family concerns who own some of their own vineyards and buy in the rest on a scrupulously organized basis from the growers.

The region itself is charming, so charming that in the summer it is crammed with visitors. The medieval villages nestle in narrow valleys, criss-crossed by cobbled streets, dotted with half-timbered houses, courtyards, pretty window boxes, fountains and wine parlours. A perfect first pitch for an aspiring travel writer. It is a region of hearty food and the people of Alsace believe that their wines can stand up to the heartiest of their local specialities which include venison, quiche Lorraine (remember Alsace-Lorraine?), pâté de foie gras and Munster cheese – so much for the red wine doctrine.

ALSACE WHITES Edelzwicker is the most basic Alsace likely to be exported. Literally translated it means 'noble mixture' and some people still think that this means that wine sold as Edelzwicker may be made only of the noblest grape varieties – Riesling, Gewürztraminer, Muscat and Tokay. In fact wine producers are wily enough to see that such wines would sell much better under their own names and the distinction between Zwickers and Edelzwickers was abandoned back in 1972. Edelzwickers today are made up of mixtures of rather less noble grapes – the more prolific and less temperamental Sylvaner, Pinot Blanc and Chasselas (which is gradually being replaced by Pinot Blanc). Many of these basic blends are sold under a brand name such as Hugel's Flambeau d'Alsace or the Chevalier d'Alsace available from Peter Dominic. These wines will usually have the identifiable Alsace characteristics of perfume followed by a dry finish, but these will not be as pronounced as for one of the better grape varieties.

Pinot Blanc is increasingly sold as a named grape variety. Tends to lack acidity but is pleasant when young.
Sylvaner is another wine best drunk young, often with a slight prickle. Often rather sharper than the Pinot Blanc.
Pinot Gris, known as Tokay in Alsace (though nothing to do with the Hungarian wine of the same name), makes full, rich wines that are high in alcohol, sometimes up to 14° with lots of character.
Muscat is the Alsace cousin of the Muscat that is grown extensively all over the world. In Alsace it produces wines with the same intensely grapey perfume, but follows this up with a crisp, dry finish. Very good aperitif wines.
Gewürztraminer is the distinctive grape of Alsace. Devilishly difficult to spell and pronounce, angelically easy to recognize. This is the easiest introduction to Alsace. Gewürz means 'spicey' and the wines are characterized by their musky perfume reminiscent of tropical fruit. After this knockout richness on the nose the dryness of the wine in the mouth comes as a pleasant surprise. Perhaps too obvious a wine to drink often.
Riesling is seen as king in Alsace, just as in Germany. Elegant racy wines that are both fruity and dry in perfect balance. Rieslings from good years mature well.

In addition to grape variety, further hints at quality may be given (usually none too obviously) on the Alsace label. Vendange Tardive is the Alsace equivalent of Spätlese or Late Harvest. This signifies that the wine will be specially rich and concentrated. Réserve/Cuvée/Séléction Exceptionelle are other terms which may be added to grape variety. These wines repay keeping – at least six years and some can last more than twenty.

ALSACE (PALE) RED The Pinot Noir grape is grown in

Alsace where it produces some very light red wine, the colour of a Spanish rosé. More of a curiosity than a bargain and not much exported.

SOUTH-WEST FRANCE

Summary: Mainly red wines that will keep because they are made from Cabernet or its local relatives.

These are some of the more commonly encountered AC wines from this region stretching round Bordeaux to the western Pyrenees:

Côtes de Duras: Just west of Bordeaux making fruity reds and whites, some good value Sauvignons.
Cahors: Its 'black wine' was once famous for its keeping properties. Now it matures rather faster, not unlike soupier claret.
Gaillac: Red, white or sparkling white. Not exceptional.
Bergerac: Just to the east of Bordeaux whose (red and white) wines it resembles.
Côtes du Marmandais: Close to Bergerac, VDQS.
Pécharmant: Red wines whose best can resemble St Emilion.
Monbazillac: 'Poor man's Sauternes'.
Montravel: Dry white best drunk very young.
Côtes de Buzet: Bordeaux-like wines tied up by the local co-operative.
Jurançon: Rich white was once famous and still ages well. Now it produces a Brut version too.
Madiran: Local red with Bordeaux characteristics.
Tursan: VDQS whose reds resemble Madiran and whites Jurançon.
Irouléguy: Light rosé version of these Pyrenean foothill wines.

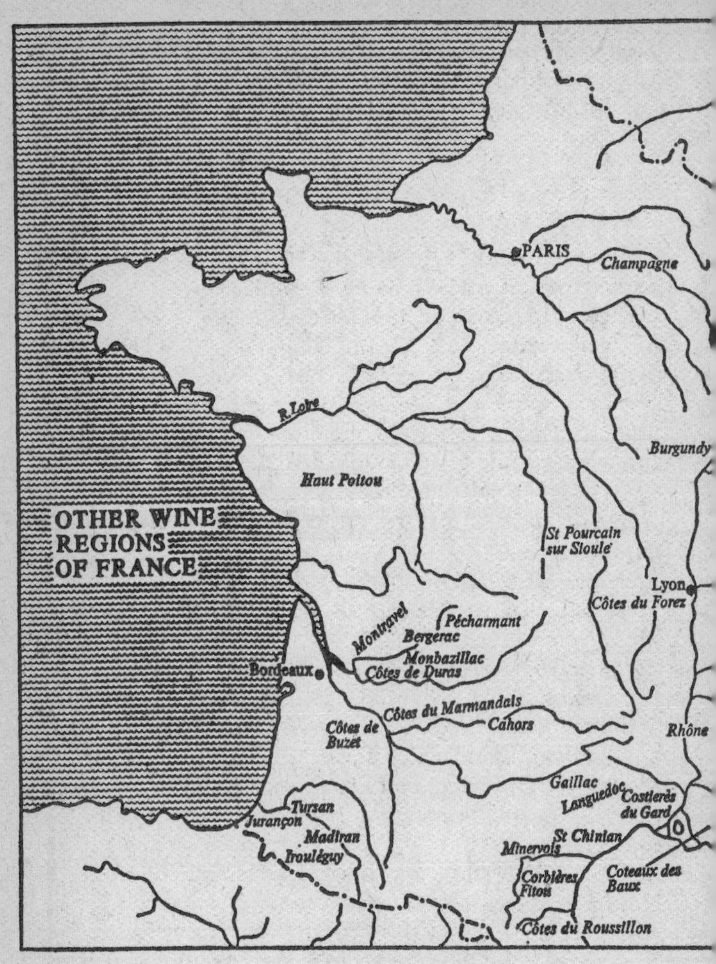
OTHER WINE
REGIONS
OF FRANCE
PARIS
Champagne
R. Loire
Burgundy
Haut Poitou
St Pourcain
sur Sioule
Lyon
Côtes du Forez
Montravel
Pécharmant
Bergerac
Monbazillac
Côtes de Duras
Bordeaux
Côtes du Marmandais
Cahors
Côtes de
Buzet
Rhône
Gaillac
Languedoc
Costières
du Gard
Tursan
Jurançon
Madiran
Irouléguy
St Chinian
Minervois
Corbières
Fitou
Coteaux des
Baux
Côtes du Roussillon

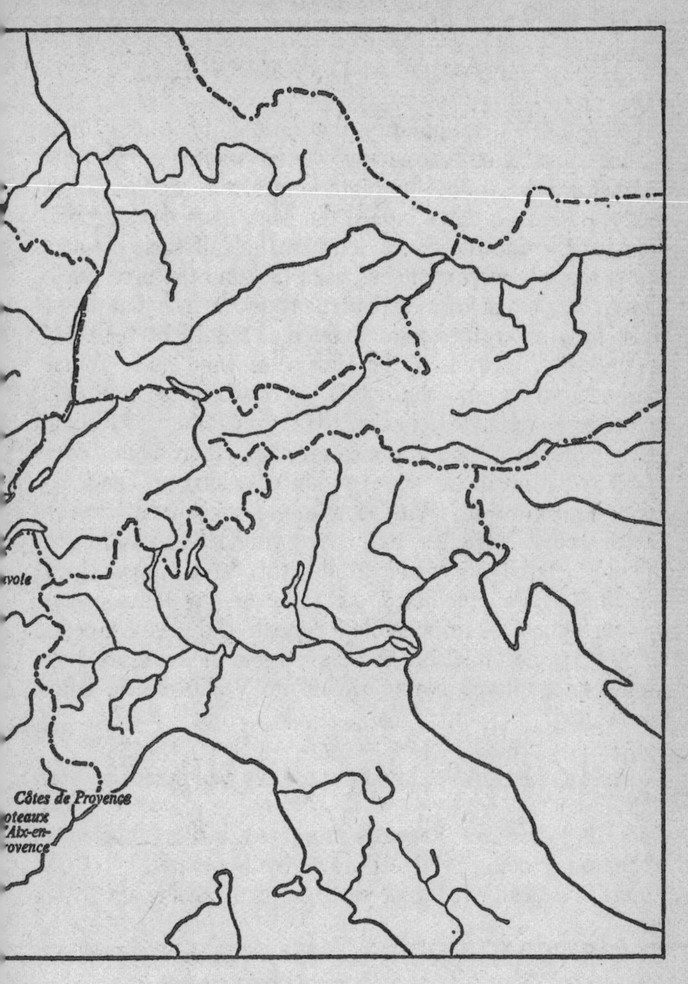

avoie
Côtes de Provence
oteaux
'Aix-en-
rovence

THE MIDI AND PROVENCE

Summary: High on quantity, low on quality. Mainly reds.

This vast wine producing region stretches from the Spanish border round the hinterland of the Mediterranean to the Italian border – indeed the Midi is used by Frenchmen to describe the entire southern half of their country. The French government has been tackling the problem of how to encourage growers here to produce wines that people want to drink rather than those that would be better off at the very bottom of the European wine lake. Widely planted is the high yielding Carignan which is 'improved' in better wines by Grenache, Syrah and others. Although many different grape varieties are used, there is not overmuch variation in the wines produced which are made for early consumption. With continuing experimentation in better grape varieties and new vinification techniques (including carbonic maceration) this area shows great potential as a source of good cheap everyday wines.

This is the area responsible for much of the wine labelled simply 'vin de table' but these are some of the more commonly encountered names which are VDQS unless otherwise stated.

Coteaux du Languedoc: Light but usually well made southern reds.

Côtes du Roussillon: Recently promoted to AC. Some wines of character being produced now, like hot claret.

Fitou: AC heady red that can be worth ageing up to six years.

Corbières: Often slightly looser than Côtes du Roussillon.

Minervois: Vigorous, sometimes peppery reds.

St Chinian: Softer reds.

Costières du Gard: Light wines in some of which the Grenache becomes pleasantly noticeable.

Coteaux des Baux: Too many expensive restaurants in the area to spare much for export.

Coteaux d'Aix-en-Provence: Another recent promotion to

AC. Some good rosés but one of the best properties, Château Vignelaure modelled on a Bordeaux château, is way above the rest in quality and price.
Côtes de Provence: Similar, some good rosés. AC too.

In addition to these there are the appellations Bandol (rich, well made reds), Palette (distinctly ordinary), Cassis (better than average whites, no connection with vin blanc cassis), Bellet (next to Nice) and the heavyweight wines of Corsica. Local demand is usually too heavy in these holiday areas to allow many of these to escape the region.

More often seen, and often good value, are the vins de pays described on page 62. Many small areas give their names to these (usually) carefully made country wines but important departements are, west to east, Aude, Hérault, Gard and Var to a lesser extent, the last two of which make some quite attractive white wine too.

OTHER FRENCH WINES

The Jura in the mountains between Burgundy and Switzerland is important to British wine buyers only as the birthplace of Louis Pasteur, who did so much research on wine chemistry, and as the source of Cendre de Novembre 'vin gris' dry rosé from Henri Maire, the producer who dominates the Jura and is now making his mark in Beaune too.

Savoie wines are hardly seen in Britain, apart from a little light Crépy white, unlike the wines from the Coopérative de Haut Poitou south of the Loire between Poitiers and Angers. Here some excellent wines, particularly white, from classic grape varieties are available at fair prices. Also available are good Gamays from the Côtes du Forez and Auvergne and the Loirish white from St Pourcain sur Sioule.

Oddities further north include the light red wine AC of Irancy made from Pinot Noir grown south west of Chablis and the crisp, dry Sauvignon de St Bris produced in the village of the same name just up the road. This can qualify only as a VDQS wine as Sauvignon is not a recognized grape variety for AC Burgundy and can be a cheaper alternative to Sancerre and Pouilly Fumé.

And in the Champagne region there are the expensive still wines bearing the appellation Coteaux Champenois, either often thinnish whites or the light Pinot Noir red, much of which bears the delightful name of Bouzy Rouge.

7. Still, light wines of the rest of the world

Germany – Italy – Spain – Portugal – Luxembourg – Switzerland – Austria – Hungary – Czechoslovakia – Romania – USSR – Bulgaria – Yugoslavia – Greece – Cyprus – Near East – Far East – North Africa – South Africa – Australia – New Zealand – North America – South America – England and Wales

GERMANY

Summary: Light, white medium dry wines. Land of moselle (green bottles, from the river of the same name) and hock (brown bottles from regions on the river Rhine). Her best wines, elegant, racy, sometimes very rich, are unrivalled.

If France traditionally supplied English (and Scottish) gentlemen with their finest red wines and Portugal their favourite dessert wines, then it was left to Germany to provide their white wine treats. And the nineteenth-century passion for hocks and moselles is echoed today by the enormous popularity of Germany's more ordinary wines, even with those who try nothing more exciting than a Liebfraumilch. These easy medium dry whites, low in alcohol and just high enough in sugar, are tailor-made for new wine drinkers.

A typical good German wine is white (only 10 per cent of Germany's vineyards are planted with red grape varieties), rarely more than 10 per cent alcohol, with an assertive, flowery fragrance and (this is the most important part) sugar and acidity in perfect balance. If a sweetish wine of this sort is to escape being cloying, and if it is to last for more than two or three years, it is vital that it is fairly high in natural acidity – though not so high that it has the thin tartness of wines made in poorer years.

Germany's driest wines are the new Trocken (dry) wines and the wines of the Saar and Ruwer tributaries of the Moselle are usually relatively low in sugar too. Then comes the bulk of Germany's more ordinary wines and some of her more northerly Spätlesen and Auslesen which are medium dry, moving up the scale of sweetness to the golden syrupy Beerenauslesen and Trockenbeerenauslesen.

Because these better quality wines are delicate they are made to be savoured, without distraction from food. The Germans themselves reserve their best wines for contemplative sipping after meals rather than using them as lubrication for their Sauerkraut and Leberwurst and this is easy to understand. Germany's richer wines can be very expensive indeed and certainly deserve maximum concentration. The Germans are robust wine drinkers, spurning the spittoon even at many official tastings, preferring to rely on the absorption properties of the contents of the omnipresent bread basket.

As wine producers the Germans have been notable in recent years for the stability of their prices and their scientific expertise; the first being a function of the second. They have worked hard not only at developing new and more suitable grape varieties, but they have also extended their scientific thoroughness to the winery where today they are able to use all manner of devices to combat the capriciousness of their climate and make wine production more economical. As explained in more detail in Chapter A of this reference section, it is common practice to chaptalize, to add sugar to the unfermented must in order to raise its eventual alcohol content (though this is forbidden for QmP wines); to add chemicals, usually chalk, to counteract high acidity in poor vintages; and to add concentrated grape juice, *Süssreserve*, after fermentation to make the wine sweeter.

As explained in Chapter Two, German wines are of these three ascending quality levels: Deutscher Tafelwein or table wine from German vineyards only; Qualitätswein bestimmter Anbaugebiete (QbA), quality wine from one of Germany's eleven quality wine regions; and Qualitätswein mit Prädikat (QmP), quality wine with one of the 'predicates' detailed below. This system relies not on geography as in France and Italy but on sugar levels in the must, which means that at the start of each vintage year every wine, in theory at least, has the chance of attaining QmP status, provided there is sufficient sun to ripen the grapes. It also means that the amount of wine produced in each of these categories varies considerably from year to year, depending on how sunny it has been. In the mean year of 1972, for instance, only 12 per cent of the wine produced managed must weights (sugar content) that pushed them into the QmP category, whereas the hot summer of 1976 resulted in an amazing 82 per cent of all German wines managing to qualify for a Prädikat.

The Germans are fond of pointing out that whereas about 70 per cent of all wine produced in Europe is only of table wine quality, the corresponding proportion in Germany rarely rises above 10 per cent. Some argue, however, that for all its precision, the German system may have set its bottom limits of what constitutes 'quality' too low.

The system is at least very easy to understand. Deutscher Tafelwein is basic wine and may be a blend from a wide area, while QbA wines have to come from one, specified, quality wine region – the Ahr, Mosel-Saar-Ruwer, Mittelrhein, Rheingau, Nahe, Rheinhessen, Palatinate (Rheinpfalz), Hessische Bergstrasse, Württemberg, Baden or Franconia (Franken) regions. Moselle is the general term used to describe wines from the second of these regions (the French spelling always seems rather unfair but is standard) and comes in tall, thin green bottles. 'Hock' is the term used to describe a Rhine wine from any of the next five regions and comes in a brown bottle. It was particularly popular in the last century and the word is thought to derive from the town of Hochheim. It still has a certain cachet; there are some merchants who sell the same wine, quite legally, as 'Hock' to gentlemen's clubs and 'Liebfraumilch' to restaurants.

Liebfraumilch (heaven presumably does know how it got its name) is defined as a QbA wine that has the characteristics of a Riesling/Müller-Thurgau/Silvaner wine. It comes mainly from the Rheinhessen, but may also come from the Palatinate, Nahe or Rheingau – though it is unlikely that a wine producer in the prestigious Rheingau region would want to sell his wine with such a lowly designation. At best Liebfraumilch is an innocuous medium dry wine and the quality of the biggest brands can usually be relied upon, even though heavy advertising may push up the price.

Wines with high enough must weights may qualify to be Qualitätswein mit Prädikat rather than QbA wines. These, in ascending order of required must weight, prestige and price, are the Prädikats:

Kabinett – Minimum must weights, which are carefully specified for each grape variety in each region for every Prädikat, are about 20 per cent higher than the minimum required for QbA wine, 70 Oechslé (measurement of sugar content) for Riesling in the Mosel-Saar-Ruwer, for instance, which would produce a wine of 9.4 per cent alcohol if all the sugar were fermented out.

Spätlese – Means literally 'late picked' and usually is. Should be made of 'fully ripe' bunches. Popular versatile wines that are not necessarily any sweeter than medium dry.

Auslese – 'Specially picked', it could be said that the reputation of Germany's wines rests on her fine Riesling Auslesen. The poorer grapes should be sorted out and if the grapes have ripened slowly they will still be sufficiently high in acidity to produce a beautifully balanced wine.

Beerenauslese – Means 'specially picked grapes'. These are prestige wines made either from over-ripe grapes or from grapes affected by Edelfäule, noble rot. Expensive and difficult to produce since yeasts are reluctant to tackle wines so high in sugar.

Trockenbeerenauslese – Means 'specially picked dried grapes'. Very rare, produced only in ideal conditions. A must weight of 150° Oechslé is required, so high that if it were possible for the wine to be fermented out it would be all of 21.5 per cent alcohol, about the same strength as port. As it is, these wines are usually very low in alcohol, only about 6 or 7 per cent, since such richness slows the yeasts to inactivity at about this level. These are the wines the Americans call 'TBAs'.

*

In addition to any of these Prädikats, usually Auslesen and above, a wine may also be an Eiswein, one produced by leaving the grapes on the vine into December - sometimes even to January so that wine carries the year of the next vintage - and picking them when the juice is concentrated and frozen.

While the quality designations are very straightforward, the Germans do not make life so easy for the wine buyer in terms of identifying how specific an area a wine comes from. Gebiet is 'region' of which there are eleven, described below. Bereich is a sub region or district. There are thirty of these, such as Bereich Bernkastel in the Moselle and Bereich Nierstein in the Rheinhessen.

Grosslagen means 'collective sites' and these were introduced with the new German Wine Law in 1971. These 150 Grosslagen are all part of the process of making the previous 20,000 named sites more comprehensible. They are collections of vineyards, not always contiguous, which have been put together and named after the best known vineyard in the collection. Zeller Schwarze Katz, for instance, is not one vineyard, but a collection of many. Einzellagen are individual sites that can be difficult to distinguish from the very much less distinguished Grosslagen, as the names look the same. Both have the same structure with the name of a vineyard following the name of a village suffixed by 'er'. Piesporter Michelsberg is a wine from anywhere in that Grosslagen while Piesporter Gunterslay is from one special Einzellage. There are 2500 of these Einzellagen and they produce Germany's greatest wines. The best way of identifying them is to study a copy of the paperback *German Wine Atlas*, just a fraction of the cost of a bottle of Auslese from most Einzellagen.

THE REGIONS Each of Germany's eleven wine regions produces wines of markedly different character as specified below.

Ahr: Germany's only red wine region, producing light, minerally reds from Portugieser and Blauburgunder (Pinot Noir). Not much exported.

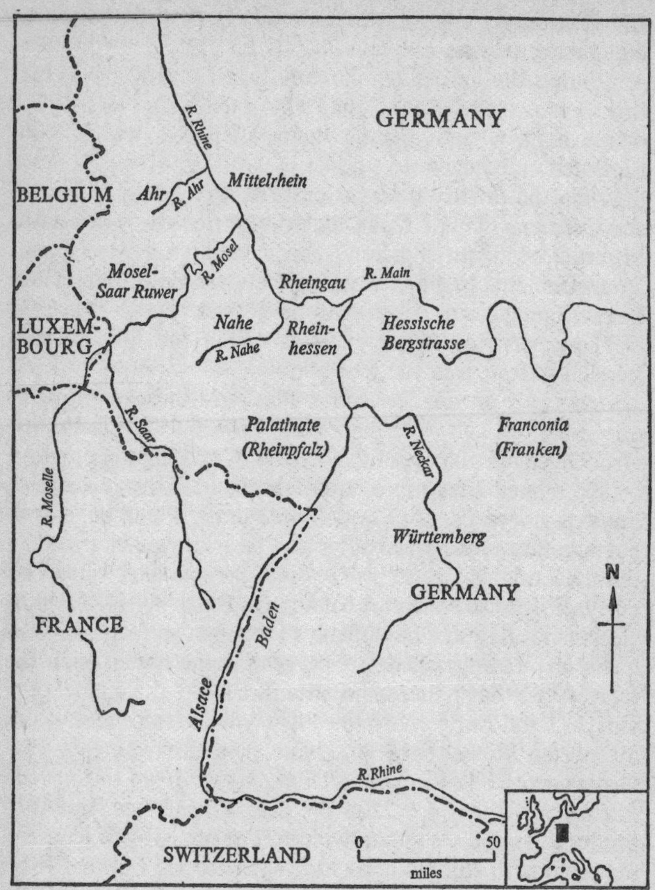

Mosel-Saar-Ruwer: One of the world's most distinctive wine regions producing light, dryish wines with refreshing tartness. Very pale colour often with a tinge of green, and sometimes a slight spritz on the tongue. Divided into Saar, Ruwer (tributaries of the Upper Moselle), Middle, Upper and Lower Moselle with Saar and Ruwer producing the sharpest wines, Middle Moselle the classics, The Riesling reigns supreme here, as in Germany's other classic area, the Rheingau. Best known villages: Saarburg, Ayl, Wiltingen, Scharzhof, Piesport, Wehlen, Graach, Bernkastel and Zell. Best known Grosslagen: Wiltinger Scharzberg, Klüsserather St Michael, Piesporter Michelsberg, Bernkasteler Badstube, Ürziger Schwarzlay, Kröver Nacktarsch (bare bottom), Zeller Schwarze Katz (black cat).

Mittelrhein: Fruity bouquet, robust wines not much exported.

Rheingau: The classic wine producing region. Great Rieslings in great years so 90 per cent of sites are planted with this aristocratic grape that can produce fragrant, elegant wines that can live for decades after good vintages. Concentration of famous individual sites, Einzellagen, and home of Geisenheim Research Station and Kloster Eberbach Academy and State Winery. Best known villages: Rüdesheim, Johannisberg, Winkel, Oestrich, Hattenheim, Hallgarten (nothing to do with the firm of the same name), Erbach, Eltville, Hochheim.

Nahe: The 'crackle' of the Moselle, the body and extract of the Rheingau, but not usually quite as distinguished as either. Equally divided between Silvaner, Müller-Thurgau and Riesling which can be very good. Best known village: Schlossböckelheim. Best known Grosslage: Rüdesheimer Rosengarten (nothing to do with the superior wines from Rüdesheim in the Rheingau).

Rheinhessen: Great provider of Liebfraumilch. Mellow wines made from a variety of grape varieties, mainly Müller-Thurgau and Silvaner. Best known villages: Lots of 'heims' and Nierstein. Best known Grosslagen: Niersteiner Gutes Domtal, Oppenheimer Krötenbrunnen.

Palatinate (*Rheinpfalz*): Wide variety of grape varieties producing full aromatic wines low in acidity. Best known villages: Deidesheim, Bad Dürkheim, Forst. Best known Grosslage: Förster Mariengarten.

Hessiche Bergstrasse: Germany's smallest wine region specializing in fruity Rieslings.

Württemberg: Farming area of hearty eaters with wines to match from Trollinger (reds) and Riesling (whites). Not

much exported.
Baden: Long strip of agricultural land in the south west of the country producing a wide variety of wines relatively low in acidity. The co-operative is important here and is becoming increasingly interested in exporting its good value wines.
Franconia: Fresh, lively, slightly earthy wines in the traditional Mateus-like Bocksbeutel.

ITALY

Summary: World's biggest wine producer, quality improving. Good value cheaper wines, best wines are red.

Each year France and Italy compete with each other to be the world's biggest wine producer. Italy wins more often than not and with an average annual production of more than 65 million hectolitres, both Italy and France are streets ahead of their nearest rivals, the Soviet Union, Spain and Argentina, who rarely manage to bring half as many grapes to their wineries. But although Italy produces wine in such quantity, most of the wine is not the stuff to which guide books are needed. The big volume producers in Sicily and Apulia, the heel of Italy, use the hot climate to produce strapping wines high in alcohol and colour, low in finesse, which are shipped to the vermouth producers of Turin, and blenders of table wine all over Europe.

The Italians must have the most relaxed attitude to wine in the world. There are few parts of Italy in which vines are not grown, but they are often mixed in with other crops in the charmingly named *cultivazione promiscua* for domestic consumption in much the same way as the British gardener sows a row or two of potatoes to keep his family supplied with an essential commodity. And the average Italian family pay no more attention to their wine than to their coffee, probably rather less. Wine is something to mix with water in large glass beakers, set down on oilcloth beside a bowl of pasta and then forget.

Partly as a result of this native insouciance, Italian wine

producers have become increasingly interested in exporting and in some areas have been very successful in tailor-making low-to-medium quality wines for wine drinkers more used to the wines of France. This is particularly true in the Veneto, source of the seemingly limitless Soave, Valpolicella and Bardolino, and in the far north east of the country where a number of good varietal (named after grape variety) wines are being produced.

There has been a notable improvement in the standard of the white wine exported from Italy. While more traditional areas may still be producing rather tired wines with a tendency to oxidation, by early picking and sometimes by chemical acidification, most Soave, Verdicchio, Frascati and Orvieto can now be depended upon to be fresh enough, even though they may be a bit short on character.

All the wines for which Italians would claim greatness are red, usually very dry and often very powerful. The area with the most prestige in Italy is Piedmont, region of truffles and motor cars in the far north west. It is here that the much-praised Barolo and Barbaresco are made, along with a wide range of slightly less weighty wines. These are made by keeping the wine in enormous casks often for more than three years. They are high in tannin and alcohol, needing at least a decade to soften to drinkability.

Perhaps more in tune with northern European tastes for lightish dry reds with some finesse are the better wines of Tuscany, Italy's second fine wine producing region. This is the land of Chianti, made in its own special way to produce a wine that is softer and faster maturing than its counterparts in Piedmont. The main, rather hard Sangiovese black grape is blended with between 10 and 30 per cent of white grapes, Trebbiano and Malvasia, to make the wine fruitier and more attractive. Also widely practised is the *governo* system of adding dried grapes after fermentation is over to provoke a second fermentation and hence a little prickle in the wine. This is particularly suitable for chianti that is to be consumed young. Much more than the wines of Piedmont, chianti varies in quality, however, and it is important to realize that some producers have used the rule that they are allowed to mix in a certain proportion of wine from the south to bad effect. The worst chianti is a sweetened up wine with no character, the best, usually from the Chianti Classico heartland of the region, a wine with a distinct vegetabley perfume that is well balanced and can improve with four years or more in bottle.

The most commonly encountered wines red (R) and white (W) are listed alphabetically below:

1 *Aglianico del Vulture* R: One of the few interesting reds to come from the deep south. Strong and rich, needs a few years in bottle.
2 *Alto Adige* R W: Usually well made wines in the style of the Austrian Tyrol to which many of them are exported. S Maddalena, Casteller, Caldaro (Kalterer) are best known.
3 *Amarone* R: Literally means 'bitter'. *See Recioto.*
4 *Barbaresco* R: With Barolo, of which it is a slightly lighter version, the first wine to be promoted to DOCG. Built to last from the Nebbiolo grape.
5 *Barbera* R: Another intensely flavoured grape, much more widely planted in Piedmont than Nebbiolo, producing dark purple wines with taste to match. Barbera d'Asti is one of the best and Barbera d'Alba can mature sooner.
6 *Bardolino* R: One of the Holy Three of the Veneto. Very similar to Valpolicella but rather lighter and higher in acidity.
7 *Barolo* R: The Italians' 'king of wines'. Made from the very dark, concentrated Nebbiolo grape, often gets too long in wood and too short a time in bottle. DOCG.
8 *Brunello di Montalcino* R: Very highly priced, very long lived wine made only from the Sangiovese grape, for which Brunello is another name, in the south of the Chianti region. DOCG.
9 *Cabernet* R: The claret grape produces some attractive wines in Fruili-Venezia-Giulia in the north east of Italy.
10 *Canonau* R: One of Sardinia's better wines.
11 *Carema* R: Version of Barolo made softer by fast vinification.
12 *Chianti* R: See above for vinification method. Made

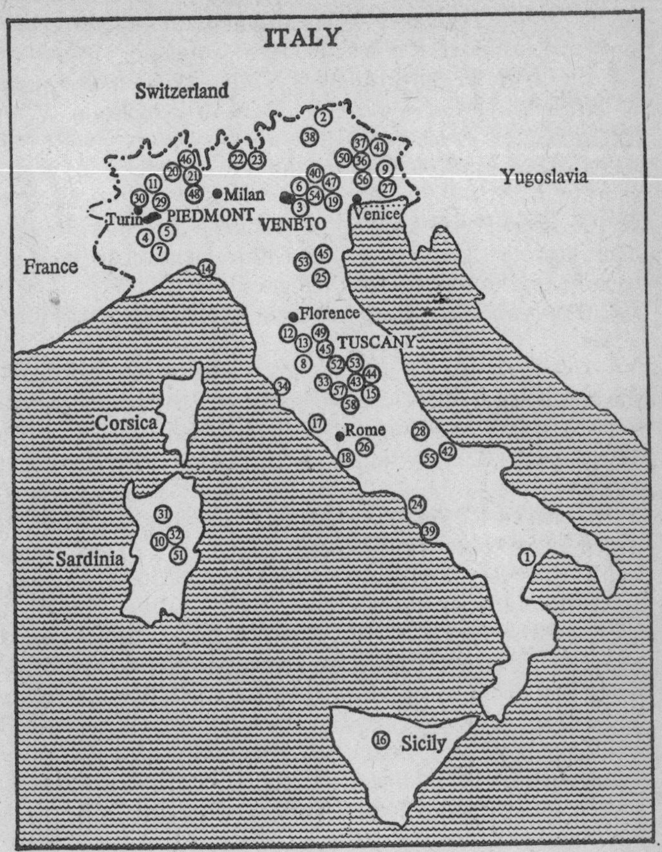

from a mixture of red and white grapes to produce a wide range of perfumed, medium bodied, dry wines.

13 *Chianti Classico* R: The best and most central region in Chianti with its quality control imposed and promotion organized by its own Consorzio. Recognizable by a black cockerel seal round the neck of the bottle.

14 *Cinqueterre* W: Little-exported variable whites made on the Italian Riviera.

15 *Colli del Trasimeno* R W: Count Lamborghini major producer in this region near Rubesco Torgiano.
16 *Corvo* R W: Surprisingly good quality from vineyards as far south as Sicily made by Duca di Salaparuta. Very alcoholic.
17 *Est!Est!!Est!!!* W: Name is more famous than the wine, rightly so.
18 *Frascati* W: Grapey white from the hills near Rome. More flavour than most Italian whites because the must is usually kept in contact with the grape skins.
19 *Gambellara* W: Very close to Soave, making similar wines.
20 *Gattinara* R: Made round Gattinara in northern Piedmont from the Nebbiolo grape which is here called Spanna. Often more approachable than Barolo.
21 *Ghemme* R: Very similar, close in style and geography to Gattinara.
22 *Grumello* R: Another Nebbiolo wine made just south of the Swiss border in Valtellina.
23 *Inferno* R: Close and similar to Grumello. Tastes less hellish than it sounds.
24 *Lacrima Christi* R W: Another set of wines better known for their name than their quality. With no DOC the name has come to be taken as a generic name for sweet and white.
25 *Lambrusco* R: Sparkling red oddity from Emilia Romagna in the mid west of Italy. Has had enormous success in the United States. Varies from a dry, rather acid wine that can be a good foil for rich food to sickly-sweet grape juice.
26 *Marino* W: Some well made whites similar to those from nearby Frascati.
27 *Merlot* R: The St Emilion grape does well in the north east of Italy where it produces soft, appealing wines to be drunk fairly young.
28 *Montepulciano d'Abruzzo* R: A full, slightly bitter red from an area halfway down the Adriatic coast, not otherwise noted for its wines.
29 *Moscato* W: Italian version of the Muscat grape,

mostly used for sparkling wines.

30 *Nebbiolo* R: This is the classic red wine grape of Piedmont responsible for all its most prestigious wines. In addition to those wines sold as Barolo, Barbaresco etc., there are also wines sold as straight Nebbiolo, perhaps because the yield was too high or the alcoholic strength too low to qualify for a more specific Denominazione. Can be good value.

31 *Nuraghe* and 32 *Nuragus* W: Sardinian whites with enough acidity to keep them fresh.

33 *Orvieto* W: Mainly from Trebbiano grapes, the wine varies from dry to various shades of sweetness. Secco is dry, Amabile or Abboccato sweet. In the past there was a tendency to produce heavy wines, but vinification techniques have improved considerably.

34 *Parrina* R W: Light but well made red and white from the Tuscan coast.

35 *Passito* W: Often rather stale sweet heavy wine made from dried grapes.

36 *Pinot Bianco* W: Probably the Pinot Blanc, makes straightforward whites in the north east of Italy.

37 *Pinot Grigio* W: Probably the same as Pinot Gris, makes fairly full-flavoured wines in the north east. Collio Goriziano is a particularly successful version.

38 *Pinot Nero* R: Pinot Noir. The Burgundy grape is most successful in the Trentino.

39 *Ravello* R W: Lovely labels from this non DOC wine, 'Vino Gran Caruso' made on the clifftops south of the Bay of Naples.

40 *Recioto* R W: A sort of Italian Auslese in which specially selected grapes are dried and then fermented to produce wines up to 16° in alcohol. Particularly popular in the Veneto where Recioto di Soave is a sweet white wine. Recioto della Valpolicella is a strong, rather sweet red and Recioto Amarone della Valpolicella is a dry version of it, verging on bitterness. Sometimes listed simply as 'Amarone'.

41 *Riesling* W: Lesser Italian version of the Riesling grape producing medium dry wines.

42 *Rosso Conero* R: Red sister to Verdicchio, made

similarly near Ancona. A fruity wine from the Montepulciano grape, governo sometimes used.

43 *Rubesco Torgiano* R: Excellent rather fuller version of chianti made by the enterprising Dr Lungarotti in the Umbrian hills. The white version is not often seen.

44 *Sassicaia* R: A highly-regarded curiosity of a wine produced from 100 per cent Cabernet Sauvignon grapes in Tuscany. Good for claret lovers, needs ageing.

45 *Sangiovese* R: The predominant red wine grape of Tuscany and much of the rest of central Italy. Sangiovese di Romagna can be good value.

46 *Sizzano* R: Another softer version of a Piedmont Nebbiolo near Gattinara.

47 *Soave* W: Almost synonymous with Italian white wine. At its best can be almost almondy, usually a none-too-flavourful crisp dry white made from Garganega and some Trebbiano. Drink as young as possible.

48 *Spanna* R: Local name for the Nebbiolo grape in the area of Gattinara north east of the classic Barolo area. Some good reds sold under this name.

49 *Tignanello* R: A very special claret style red produced only in exceptional years by the Antinori family in Tuscany from Chianti grapes aged in small Bordeaux barrels.

50 *Tocai* W: White grape grown in north-eastern Italy, similar to Pinot Grigio.

51 *Torbato* W: Unattractively named dry white from Sardinia.

52 *Toscano Bianco* W: The white wines of Tuscany, usually average quality Trebbiano. Takes up any spare white wine production not wanted by the Chianti producers. 'Fantasy names' used by individual producers. Bianco Vergine and Bianco di Pitigliano come from the south east and the far south-west respectively.

53 *Trebbiano* W: Common white grape of central Italy. Trebbiano di Romagna can be good value, white sister to Sangiovese di Romagna.

54 *Valpolicella* R: What Soave is to white, Valpol is to red. Light, slightly bitter wines from a mixture of local grapes in vineyards between Verona and Lake Garda.

Often a hint of cherry-like acidity in the flavour. Drink young.

55 *Verdicchio* W: A usually reliable fresh white from the grape of same name packaged traditionally in a special amphora-shaped bottle from vineyards just south of Ancona on the Adriatic coast. Verdicchio dei Castelli Jesi is best known.

56 *Verduzzo*: Robust dry white from the Colli Orientali del Fruili in the north east.

57 *Vernaccia* W: A highly flavoured grape that really is a bit reminiscent of varnish. Should be drunk young. Can make stale wines. Vernaccia di San Gimignano is not as beautiful as its provenance.

58 *Vino Nobile di Montepulciano* R: Well-balanced Tuscan red that has earned the promise of a DOCG along with Brunello di Montalcino, but is much better value. Doesn't need so many decades of patience.

SPAIN

Summary: Source of cheap blending wines; but her better quality wines, especially rioja, can be very good value.

Spain sends almost as much light wine to Britain as Italy does but until recently it was only her prize fortified wine, sherry, that had made any impact on connoisseurs. It is still the case that the majority of wine exported from Spain is sold in bulk for cheap blends, but the proportion of wines exported in bottle (which is the closest possible definition of better quality Spanish wine) is increasing as more and more wine lovers are realizing what good value they can be.

Rioja, Spain's Bordeaux and Burgundy rolled into one, is her biggest and best quality wine region but there are producers in the Penedes in Catalonia, in Navarre and even in the more workmanlike La Mancha region who are exporting carefully made wines worthy of attention from any open-minded wine lover. Even though a disastrously small vintage in 1977 sent prices soaring, Spanish quality wines are still good value compared with wines of similar character from France, and EEC entry should make prices even more attractive.

Although she is only fourth in the world wine production league, Spain has more land under vine than any other country. The reason for this apparent anomaly may be partly semantic, but it is also true that her vineyards have not yet been developed to a state of efficiency in terms of the general state in which they are kept and the grape varieties used. Set the superbreeders of Geisenheim loose on the vineyards of Spain and her annual production could overtake that of Italy and France – a prospect that fills the French and Italians with terror.

Being wines that are not exactly austere, the better Spaniards are easy to appreciate right from the very first sniff, for their warmth and obvious wood ageing can be very appealing. In general the reds are more attractive than the whites. The combination of a hot climate and the widespread practice of leaving all wines in cask much longer than is usual in northern Europe makes for some seductively powerful reds but can produce whites that just don't seem crisp enough to British palates. Efforts to produce light whites with enough acidity are increasing, however, and Spain is now exporting some good value cheaper wines of this sort. A carefully-nurtured old white rioja can be delicious too, becoming very Meursault-like with age, but too many whites are either too oxidized or too 'baked' to appeal overmuch to those north of the Pyrenees.

There are also reds that are left too long in cask and some of the riojas on sale that are already in their twenties can taste too much of wood and too little of fruit. Many good quality wines reach an optimum of quality in their seventh or eighth year, having had three or four years in cask. Since Spain has a fairly dependable climate, there is not as much variation between vintages as is common further north. It is also thought that many winemakers have been none too punctilious in their application of vintage years so it is best to rely on the year stated only as an indication of the average age of the wine. Some labels also indicate how long the wine was kept in wood. '4° año' indicates, for example, that the wine was put into bottle in the fourth year after the vintage. For years the producers would keep even their lesser wines in wood almost until they received an order and only then bottle it prior to shipping it out immediately. There is now a trend towards establishing a shorter period of wood ageing, and then giving the wine the benefit of subtler bottle age.

The wines are extremely robust and last for ages, not just in the mouth after they have been swallowed, but also in the bottle once they have been opened. Some of the wines taste better on the day after the bottle is opened and the wine left in a recorked bottle should last for up to a week.

Specific grape varieties do not yet play an important part in Spanish winemaking, though Miguel Torres is experimenting successfully with imports from France and Germany in the Penedes. Wines tend to be made from a great mixture of local grape varieties which are all vinified together; wood rather than grapes tends to determine flavour. Common red wine varieties are Garnacha (Grenache), Tempranillo, Graciano, Mazuelo, Sumoll. White wine grapes include Malvasia, white Garnacha, Moscatel, Monastrel, Macabeo.

Since 1970 Spain has been setting up a quality designation system modelled on France's Appellation Contrôlée designating Denominacion de Origen areas. But, like Italy's DOC, the stamp of the Consejo Regulador (organizing authority) of one of these Denominacions does not necessarily guarantee great quality for the Denominacions include, in addition to better quality regions, the vineyards that are responsible for the nondescript heavy wines shipped in bulk to be sold as cheap blends and brands. Of these areas those nearer the coast such as Tarragona, Valencia and Alicante, tend to produce the coarsest wines.

These are the Denominacion areas in approximate descending order of quality:

Rioja: Of the better quality wine regions of Spain, rioja is by far the best known and most widely available in this country. Funny word, some lovely wines. Pronounced something like a Highlander would say 'Ree-ocker'. Every bottle of wine from one of the bigger bodegas carries a small deckled edged stamp on the label which signifies a guarantee of authenticity from the Consejo Regulador. Often with very ornate names and labels (a lot of Marques's about in Rioja) and fancy bottles, some of them swathed in wine netting.

The hallmark of a real rioja is its warm vanilla nose that comes from the American oak barrels in which the wines are matured – usually for a minimum of two years to gain the Consejo's stamp in a bodega specializing in ageing wines, often many more if it's a Reserva. There are signs, however, that rioja producers are starting to see the importance of bottle ageing and are bottling their wines earlier than they used to. Some bodegas are even exporting one and two year old wines now but these are too young to have the characteristics of a typical rioja, even though they may carry the Consejo's stamp.

Rioja is a mountainous region in northern Spain which is divided into Rioja Alta (high), Rioja Baja (low) and Rioja Alavesa (in the province of Alava). Rioja Baja has a reputation for producing coarser, heavier wines but there is no need to ignore producers who are based there as the exact location of a producer's bodega (winery) may not necessarily indicate the source of all his wines. Most bodegas are in Rioja Alta either at Haro or Logroño.

Most producers buy in their grapes from Spanish farmers – sometimes, it is rumoured, not even from Rioja farmers, though this should not make as much difference here as in most wine areas since it is the careful ageing rather than the grape and the soil types of Rioja that give most of the wine's character. Many bodegas attempt to produce a 'bordeaux style' wine and a fuller, richer version in the style of burgundy, each put into appropriately-shaped bottles, straight sided for bordeaux and sloping shouldered for burgundy. These wines are usually labelled 'tinto' (red) but there are also 'claretes' which are light weight reds between tinto and roasado (rosé) in colour.

Vinification methods here are based on traditional Bordeaux techniques since a hundred years ago Rioja enjoyed an influx of Bordeaux winemakers who were fleeing the dread phylloxera. The bodegas of Rioja are stacked high with pyramids of Bordeaux style casks, *barriques*, softening in flavour and lightening in colour the wine they contain.

Federico Paternina has a vast new bodega just outside Haro and produces a wide range of wines including Spain's best-selling though not exciting Banda Azul and the excellent Gran Reserva. Franco-Españolas is also owned by the Rumasa conglomerate and their best wine is Royal Reserva. Marques de Riscal is one of the most respected producers, as is Marques de Murrieta who produce Castillo Ygay and a white rioja that is really worth ageing. CUNE's (Compania Vinicola del Norte de España) Imperial is a very good older wine and all their wines have more elegance than most. Marques de Cacares still has strong connections with Bordeaux and there is conscientious experimentation here. Muga, Riojanas, La Rioja Alta and Lopez de Heredia all have good reputations.

Penedes: This is the Catalan name for Panades, a small region in the hills behind the Costa Brava. Best known for its sparkling whites described later, this region is also capable of producing excellent still wines of all hues. Many of the better wines of Penedes are distinguished by a paper seal reminiscent of Gauloises over the top of the bottle which is usually of a rounded burgundy shape. The big name here is Torres, a dynamic family firm which is experimenting with classic grape varieties and sophisticated vinification methods – they even produce a Spanish Gewürztraminer. Their Santa Digna is made from Burgundy's Pinot Noir grape and Gran Coronas Black Label is their deeply satisfying Cabernet Sauvignon Reserva.

Other producers whose wines are seen abroad include Freixedas (nothing to do with sparkling wine producer neighbours Freixenet) whose basic brand is Santa Marta; family firm Marques de Monistrol whose operation keeps a whole village in employment; and Masia Bach, noted for its sweet white Extrisimo.

Navarre: Just to the north of Rioja, its wines are similar in style and can sometimes match them.

Carinena: Range of more ordinary wines in Aragon.

Ribeiro and Valdeorras: In Galicia, the north-western tip of the country, these two Denominacions are just across the border from Vinho Verde country in Portugal and make similar red and white wines made to have slight refreshing pétillance.

Alella: Small white wine region near Barcelona.

Mentrida and Valdepeñas/La Mancha: Valdepeñas is the town often giving its name to any wine from the rolling La Mancha Don Quixote country. This vast vineyard area produces ordinary table wine of which little is exported. Can be reasonably made everyday wine.

Jumilla, Yecla, Utiel Requena, Valencia, Manchuela, Cheste, Almansa, Alicante, Tarragona, Priorato: All producers of heavy wines that rarely have enough 'zip' to lift them out of the ordinary. Can be as strong as 16 per cent alcohol and sometimes even more.

Other notable wines include the odd bottled Sangria wine and lemonade mix, the country wines of Leon in the north west which can provide good value and Vega Sicilia, a connoisseur's wine that is in such short supply that it has almost developed a cult following. It is made by one Don Jesus Anadon near Valladolid in Old Castile from claret grapes by careful slow maturation over a minimum of ten years. Laymont & Shaw of Truro import limited quantities.

PORTUGAL

Summary: Land of Vinho Verde prickly whites, Dão reds and Mateus rosé.

The average British wine drinker may well know only two wines from Portugal – her lifeblood port, the drink the British virtually created, and Mateus rosé, the archetypal medium wine. Mateus is a brilliant piece of marketing, but is by no means typical of the interesting light wines that Portugal has to offer.

Wine is very important to the Portuguese; their per capita wine consumption has now overtaken that of the French and the Italians and most estimates put it at more than 170 bottles a year a head. This statistic may not surprise those who have been to Portugal and discovered that the quality even of ordinary table wines is more inspiring than in almost any other country in Europe. Many of these wines are sold under the producer's or a brand name rather than by specifying which region they come from.

The Portuguese government are only just starting to see the advantages of exporting their better quality wines and have not yet knocked their quality designation system into shape. At the moment only white Vinho Verde, the prickly 'green' wines from the north, and her earthy reds from the Dão region are exported to any extent. Wines from the other, obscurer designated regions are rarely seen outside Portugal itself, although rare old vintages occasionally come up for auction when some old cellar is being sold off to pay death duties. The other demarcated areas are Carcavelos, Colares, Bucelas and Moscatel de Setubal, all tiny areas around Lisbon that are no longer as important as they once were. They are distinguishable by their paper *Selo de Origem*, the seal of origin over the top of the bottle.

Areas producing big volumes of good light wines that have not yet been officially recognized are the Estremadura, a large region between the river Tagus (Ribatego) and the Atlantic, most of the Douro (famous for port which takes up a third of its wines) and Bairrada and Lafoes south of the Douro. Atlantic breezes moderate the climate in all these areas so that the wines of Portugal often have more finesse than those from Spain on the headier side of the Iberian Peninsula.

Tinto and *branco* are red and white while *maduro* means that a wine is meant to be aged as opposed to a vinho verde.

These are the designated wine regions and most commonly encountered or most prestigious brands:

Bucelas: Fresh dry white from the Arinto grape, not often exported.

Carcavelos: Sweet amber wine from vineyards now almost swamped by the swimming pools of Estoril.

Colares: Another dwindling demarcated zone from the phylloxera-free sandy coast, this time just north of Lisbon. Rambling, ungrafted vines produce dark tannic wines.

Dão: Dão (pronounced 'dow') is to Portugal what rioja is to Spain. As for rioja, perhaps the wood is sometimes overdone and its reds are better than the often overweight whites. Slow fermentation produces complex wines with lots of body. High glycerine and alcohol content. These wines, made from the Tourigo and various other red grapes and sometimes the Arinto white grape, deserve ageing. Grão Vasco from Sogrape of Mateus fame is the most commonly exported brand.

Ferreirinha: Much in demand with the port shippers in Oporto. Excellent well-balanced Douro red made in limited quantities by the port firm Ferreira. Look out for their Barca Velha.

Lancers: Rosé similar to Mateus but in a simulated stone jar. Popular in the United States.

Mateus: Artificially carbonated rosé made by Sogrape at Vila Real just north of the Douro valley. Mateus exports are more than total port exports.

Moscatel de Setubal: The fourth historical denominated zone, actually a fortified wine similar to the Muscats of southern France.

Perequita: Good vigorous red made by J. M. da Fonseca.

Serradayres: Reliable blended red and white from Carvalho, Ribeiro & Ferreira. Popular with TAP, the national airline.

Vinho Verde: Only whites are exported, often specially sweetened up, although twice as much red wine is produced as white. One is tempted to see a hint of green in them, but *verde* (green) refers not to their colour but their age. These northerly vines often trailed high on pergolas are picked early and bottled young so that the carbon dioxide given off by the second fermentation is retained in the bottle to give the wines some prickle. The Portuguese like their vinho verde bone dry and relatively high in acidity. Aveleda from Sogrape of Mateus fame is the most commonly exported brand. Monção is the best area for Alvarinho, the predominant white Vinho Verde grape.

LUXEMBOURG

The EEC's fourth wine producer. (England comes last but not least in this guide.) Very light wines high in acidity because of the latitude of the vineyards. The fact that Luxembourg's wine industry, which supplies three in every four bottles of wine drunk by the Luxembourgeois, actually exists, seems less surprising when one considers that the town of Remich in the heart of Luxembourg's vineyard district is only a few miles across the hills from the well known wine village of Ayl in the Mosel-Saar-Ruwer.

She produces wines that are lighter and drier in style than their German counterparts, and are often all but colourless. Of the vines cultivated, all white, the ungenerous Elbling that in the German Moselle valley is sold as base wine for *sekt*, is the most common, though other German varieties are grown too. Perlewein is a local speciality, just slightly sparkling and, like all Luxembourg wines, low in alcohol – a good party wine.

SWITZERLAND

The Swiss themselves are too keen on keeping their wines to themselves to make Swiss wines anything other than overpriced curiosities abroad. The Swiss are also keen blenders and the cheaper wines in Switzerland itself usually contain a hefty dollop of imported Italian. Most vineyards are on the south-facing side of the Upper Rhône valley (Valais) and the lake of Geneva (Vaud). The Chasselas grape which in France and Germany is usually treated with disdain is widely planted as they are keen on maintaining high yields in the land of milk and money.

Aigle: Dry white Vaud, sometimes with more character than par for the Swiss course.

Beauvalais: Valais version of beaujolais nouveau. A heavily sweetened young red released just a few crafty days before the beaujolais.
Dôle: Sweet, often thin red from Pinot Noir and/or Gamay grown in the Valais.
Dorin: Thin white from Chasselas grown in the Vaud. At best crisp and clean.
Fendant: Valais version of Dorin.
Johannisberg: Valais name for Sylvaner which here produces dry whites with more character than the Chasselas.
Merlot: St Emilion grape produces good round reds in Ticino in the south.
Salvagnin: Vaud equivalent of the type of light red wine called Dôle in the Valais.

AUSTRIA

Rather gutsier versions of German wines, many with more than a hint of spiciness and almost all clean and assertive. Although the average Briton knows few wines other than the unfortunately named Schluck, it would pay him to seek out Austria's better quality wines as they can offer very good value, particularly her luscious white dessert wines which are not all that popular with the Austrians. The natives are more fascinated by Tyrolean reds from Austria and Italy.

The wines are carefully controlled with a system very similar to the German one with better quality wines ranging from Kabinett to Trockenbeerenauslese and the equivalents of QbA wines identifiable by the red, white and gold Weingutesiegel, Austrian Wine Seal, round the neck. Alcohol levels are all higher than those required in Germany with quality wines reaching a minimum of 10.5°.

Her rich dessert wines, while they lack the finesse of their German equivalents, can be good value, as are her ordinary quality wines from varieties such as the predominant Grüner Veltliner, fruity yet zippy. The Rheinriesling (the proper Riesling of Germany as opposed to simple 'Riesling' which is the inferior Welschriesling) produces particularly good wines in the Wachau region.

The Gumpoldskirchen vine specialities Rotgipfler and Zierfandler (or Spätrot) produce headier wines which can improve after several years' bottle age. Even the 'open wine', brand new wine served at the charming Heurigen, simple cafés and the suburbs of Vienna, is of reliable liveliness.

Chief red wine grapes are the Blaufrankish (Gamay) and the Portugieser which is also grown in Germany. Other white wine grapes not commonly grown outside Austria are Bouvier and Neuburger, both of which produce unexceptional soft wines. Also grown are Müller-Thurgau, Pinot Blanc and Muscat.

The main wine regions whose wines are seen outside Austria are within easy driving distance of Vienna – Burgenland to the south east, Wachau to the west and the Weinviertel (wine quarter) to the north west. Burgenland is famous for its sweet wines with Ruster Ausbruch being wine between a Beerenauslese and a TBA in sweetness from the wine centre of Rust. Oggau is another important wine centre in Burgenland. Krems is the main town of Wachau where the grapes for Schluck are grown. Good for Austria's native Grüner Veltliner is the Weinviertel whose wine centre is Retz.

Those who export wine from Austria include Lenz Moser, the business started by the man who developed the special wide and high grape cultivation method named after him; Alois Morandell of Vienna; Klosterneuberg, Austria's answer to Germany's Kloster Eberbach. Better known names are Schluck, a rather spicier sister product Blue Danube and Schloss Grafenegg from Krems.

HUNGARY

Hungary has a noble wine history and produces a wide range of robust wines. In olden days Hungary's best known wine was the semi-legendary Tokay with its reputed lifegiving properties, though now this position may be occupied by the hearty red Bull's Blood, 'wine with horns' as the admen put it.

But it is undoubtedly Tokay, pronounced 'To*koy*', that made Hungary's vinological reputation. Tokay Aszu is a rich dessert wine, produced in the far north-east corner of Hungary close to the Russian border, from mainly Furmint grapes many of which have been attacked by the same noble rot responsible for Sauternes and the finest German wines. It is sold in distinctive squat half litre bottles in ascending order of 'Puttonyos', the measures of the Aszu paste of crushed concentrated grapes which have been added to the wine. The more Puttonyos, up to a maximum of five, the sweeter the wine and the higher the price. Tokay Szamorodni Sweet is a paler version. The wine has more than a hint of the oxidized quality of sherry in it and when sold as Tokay Szamorodni Dry with none of the Aszu to add richness this comes to the fore. Drink the dry version as an aperitif. Tokay Furmint is a straightforward light white from the Furmint grape. Tokay Essencia is supposed to be an even more concentrated form of Tokay Aszu which was reputed to have prolonged the life of many a Tsar, but only those very close to Hungarian officialdom are allowed to taste the much reduced stocks that remain in the State cellars.

The more common or garden wines of Hungary include the heady red Bull's Blood, or Egri Bikaver, to give it its Hungarian name. This wine, made north-east of Budapest in Eger mainly from the Kadarka, Hungary's best known red wine grape, is said to improve immensely with a few years' cellage age, though it rarely gets the chance. A Hungarian-bottled version is superior to the wine exported in bulk.

Hungary's bread and butter white grape is the Olasz Riesling, her version of the Welsch or Italian Riesling, not the elegant Riesling of the Rhine and Moselle. It produces pleasant ordinary medium dry wine with Pecs being one of the best known, a Hungarian answer to Yugoslavia's Lutomer Riesling. Lake Balaton produces some of Hungary's most interesting whites, including the spicey wines from Hungarian grapes Furmint, Keknyelu and the Szurkebarat from Badacsony.

Sopron on the Austrian border makes Kekfrankos (Gamay) red and Somlo between Sopron and Balaton is capable of doing good things with Furmint and Riesling.

CZECHOSLOVAKIA

Not a great exporter of wine – though the occasional full bodied, slightly spicey white has been sighted in Britain – Czechoslovakia is well placed to produce wines similar in style to the best of her close neighbours Austria and Hungary. She concentrates on white wines made from typical Hapsburg varieties. *Poland* to the north produces about as much wine as Czechoslovakia and it is presumably similar in style but even less is exported. *East Germany* is also a wine producer.

ROMANIA

After a brief flirtation with the owners of the Solitaire branded wine, Romanian wine producers have been ignored by British wine buyers for some years, though not by Americans. They have been increasing their vineyard acreage rapidly and, unlike Hungary and Bulgaria, Romania has a wine industry that is still largely in private hands. It may well be that Romania will be exporting some interesting wines before long for her climate and topography are auspicious. She produces more wine than any Eastern European country other than the Soviet Union and a wide variety of classic western European grape varieties are planted in addition to Balkan vines. Whites, which make up 60 per cent of production, are thought to be best with common varieties including the Romanian version of the Italian Riesling and a fruity local variety called Feteasca, along with Hungary's Furmint, Muscat, Pinot Gris and Sauvignon. Red varieties include Hungary's Kadarka plus Pinot Noir, Merlot and Cabernet Sauvignon.

Cotnari is Romania's less intense version of the dessert wine of Tokay in Hungary. The Tirnave vineyards in the centre of the country provide a Transylvanian Traminer which surely couldn't fail to be a great commercial success if labelled as such?

USSR

As far as statisticians can make out the Soviet Union, never over-generous with figures, is now the world's third biggest wine producer making more than 30 million hectolitres of wine, about half as much as France or Italy, annually. The government has been planting vines rapidly in an effort to wean the Russians off vodka and on to wine. As visitors to the Soviet Union will know, the wines have a tendency to oxidation and heavy sweetness and there are considerably more whites than reds. They also produce sparkling and fortified wines in great quantities, naming them shamelessly after their originals in the West. The vineyards are all around the northern coast of the Black Sea from Moldavia in the west to Armenia in the south east. While the quality of everyday wine may not be such as to inspire westerners it is rumoured that the State research institutes are producing superlative wines modelled on western European classics. There is not much chance of seeing them or any Soviet wines other than the occasional sweet 'shampanskoe' fizz outside the USSR though, since despite her extensive vineyards, she still needs to import vast quantities to satisfy domestic demand.

BULGARIA

Bulgaria on the other hand, is one of the world's top wine exporters sending 80 per cent of her wines to the Soviet Union, Germany and beyond. There is now delightfully incontrovertible evidence of how well Bulgaria, after many years of Muslim rule, can grow classic European grape varieties. Some excellent Chardonnays and Cabernet Sauvignons which are concentrated and should be aged. Most wine production is efficiently controlled by the State. There are some lovely local names such as Misket (Muscat), Mavrud (a Cabernet-like grape), Melnik, and Pamud (their everyday red wine grape).

YUGOSLAVIA

Yugoslavia is the world's tenth biggest wine producer, between Romania and Hungary. Her most successful export is Laski Riesling. This medium dry slightly spicy white is made not from the proper Rhine Riesling but from the Yugoslavian version of the lesser Italian Riesling. Slovenia in the north produces the country's best and most exported wines, though Croatia and Serbia further south make bigger quantities. On the much-disputed border between Slovenia and Italy the wines produced are, not surprisingly, very similar to the Merlots, the Pinots and the Cabernets of north-eastern Italy, while the wines produced in the far north-eastern corner of Yugoslavia close to Hungary's Lake Balaton area are predictably similar in their slightly pungent flavoursome style. Slovenia produces some very good value varietals, Sauvignon, Traminer, Sipon (Hungary's Furmint), Sylvaner, Rajinski Riesling (proper Riesling), Cabernet, Merlot and Pinot Noir. The chief towns of Slovenia are Lutomer, Ormoz, Maribor and Radgona famous for its sweet white 'Tiger Milk'. Most Yugoslavian wines are excellent value for the government seems anxious to keep prices competitive.

GREECE

The traveller in Greece who finds it impossible to acquire a taste for Retsina has a tough time, for half of all Greek wine is given this strange pine resinating treatment resulting in an unmaskable aroma of furniture polish. Like it or love it, the Greeks must love it for they have been resinating their wines for centuries – not, as Hugh Johnson points out, to preserve them (for Retsina does not age well) but presumably because they like the flavour. Most Retsina is white, though some *kokkineli* (rosé) is resinated.

Other wines that may be seen in Greek restaurants around the world are the prettily labelled Demestica, a red and white table wine blended by the biggest wine company Achaia Clauss who are based in the Peloponnese where much Greek wine is produced. There is also Mavrodaphne, a strong red usually sweet and the sweet Muscat from Samos, both of which have been more popular than now. Naoussa strong dry red has a milder version in Castel Danielis. The town of Monemvasia is thought to be the home of the Malvasia grape which is widely planted throughout Europe and is responsible for Malmsey on Madeira. Most wines, red and white, are fairly hefty but Verdea Comutos and Robola dry white from the island of Cephalonia are more lissome. Most prestigious property is Chateau Carras, the wine of the man of the ships, modelled strictly on Bordeaux.

CYPRUS

Another country whose wines most regularly appear in restaurants run by emigrés. Cypriot light wines are very similar to those of Greece though she has also built up a good reputation for her own version of the Jerez fortified wine, sherry. Othello made by Keo is Cyprus's equivalent of Demestica from Greece and is similarly a full, earthy red. Olympus is a lighter, drier red. Of the whites Aphrodite is fuller and sweeter than Arsinoe.

NEAR EAST

Turkey grows grapes in enormous quantities but they are more often encountered in plum pudding than in the plummy wines they are capable of producing. Total production is about 350,000 hectolitres each year and little is exported. *Lebanon* produces a little wine (some good fresh rosé) but not on a big commercial scale and *Israeli* vineyards, planted with common Midi varieties, make more wine than Turkey does to satisfy international demand for kosher wine.

FAR EAST

Only *Japan* with her commercial zeal is producing wine in any quantity. She does her best to make wine in the style of Bordeaux, often blending in the real stuff to increase verisimilitude. Rarely seen outside Japan.

NORTH AFRICA

Algeria, in the days of French rule, was an important producer of hearty wines used often for blending and there can be few Britons who were buying wine at the end of the War who do not think of Algeria as synonymous with plonk. Things have changed for Algerian wine producers now though. They have lost their most important export market and most of the native population do not drink alcohol so they are having to restructure their wine industry. There is accordingly a trend away from quantity to quality and the better hillsides rather than the high yielding plains are being planted. Although her total wine production is declining, Algeria could well be exporting some good rich wines, particularly reds, not unlike the wines that were sold as Volnay and Pommard in the fifties.

Morocco is also capable of making some good quality wine and is noted for her rosés which are much drier and lighter than might be expected. Sidi Larbi produces strapping reds, but the best area is between Meknes and Fez north west of the Atlas Mountains.

Tunisia is also uprooting her vineyards to some extent, although she still produces slightly more wine than Morocco (though considerably less than Algeria). Her strong, sturdy wines are rarely very exciting.

SOUTH AFRICA

There has been a great deal of experimentation and improvement inside the wineries of South Africa's beautiful wine country on the Cape. Now it is the turn of the vineyards for there is still work to be done to improve resistance to disease and match varieties to micro-climates.

Almost half of the wine produced each year is absorbed into the Government-run distilling industry but there is increasing encouragement to produce good quality wines for consumption in South Africa and abroad. The general level of quality of South African table wine is hearteningly high, with concentrated reds that can sometimes be rather heavy and syrupy, and whites that are refreshingly crisp, often thanks to chemical acidification. Some of these are being exported and can be excellent value.

The South Africans have a carefully-devised quality control system which designates quality wines as 'Wines of Origin'. A seal around the neck of the bottle shows that the wine comes from one of the fourteen designated areas with a blue band, that it is a single vintage wine with a red band, and that the wine contains at least 80 per cent of the named grape variety (called cultivar in South Africa) stated on the label with a green band. The meaning of 'estate wine' has also been carefully defined and there is now some incentive for the forty-odd designated estates to produce wines of particularly good quality. Many of these have Afrikaans names that foreigners find difficult, but estate wines will all have the word 'estate' on the neck label above the blue band.

The most common red wine grape is a South African speciality. Pinotage is a cross between Cinsaut (also called Hermitage) and Pinot Noir and here makes strongly flavoured wines in good quantity.

Cinsaut is also grown on its own and is sometimes blended with Cabernet Sauvignon, the classic grape of the Médoc, which can produce good full-bodied claret style wines on one of the better estates. Another Rhône grape,

Shiraz (Syrah) makes attractive, rather spicey wines on the Cape and the winemakers are still experimenting with other cultivars such as Pinot Noir and even the California Zinfandel.

Of the widely planted white cultivars, the sherry grape Palomino (called 'French grape' here) goes mainly for distillation and Steen is the most successful. There is discussion as to the relative merits of Steen, Stein and Chenin Blanc here but it seems likely that Steen is a clone of the Chenin Blanc of the Middle Loire and that Stein, if it exists as a separate entity at all, does so only in the eyes of the marketing men. The wines are full but crisp and have a shadow of floweriness reminiscent of Vouvray and Saumur. The South African Riesling is also widely planted and is a little less substantial. Rhine Riesling is planted on some estates, notably at Nederburg where very creditable Late Harvest wines are made in classic German style sold under the name of Edelkeur. Also grown are Colombard (the French Colombard of California) and Gewürztraminer. There is great experimentation with other white European cultivars, including some of the newer ones developed in Germany.

AUSTRALIA

When intrepid venturers set off from Europe, the cradle of the world's wine production, to explore the wines of the New World, it is about Australia that they usually rave most on their return. Perhaps it is because the Californians have blown their own trumpets rather more successfully than the Australians that Europeans are so surprised to find wines that are as good in the Antipodes. The Australians have been producing wine for nearly 200 years and therefore have more tradition to fall back on than the Californians, but the great advance in Australian winemaking has come very recently with a sudden upsurge of interest in wine in Australia. As in California, winemakers are extremely knowledgeable and innovative – typically a winemaker would be someone highly intelligent who has already proved themselves in another field, notably medicine. The hint of tonic wine taste in Australian wines may not be entirely coincidental. The trouble is that very little high quality Australian wine is exported. Her old export trade was in fortified wines which have now largely priced themselves out of world markets and there is no well-established trade in light wines to take their place. Transport costs add considerably to the eventual selling price and the Australians themselves are avid buyers of wine, particularly whites of which at the time of writing there is a serious shortage.

The Australian wine industry was built on producing 'hock' that wasn't, 'riesling' that wasn't, claret, hermitage, burgundies and sauternes which weren't either, all of which could make label-reading a hazardous experience for non-Australians. The increasing acreage now planted with classic European grape varieties has led to an increase in varietal labelling, however. The standard Australian white grape is the Semillon which is responsible for sauternes in Bordeaux but perversely is often labelled 'Riesling' in Australia. Its red counterpart is Shiraz, the Syrah of the northern Rhône, often labelled rather more logically Hermitage. Now Cabernet Sauvignon the claret grape, Pinot Noir the red burgundy grape and proper Rhine Riesling are becoming increasingly common and there is also experimentation with the white burgundy grape Chardonnay. It is common practice for one property to produce a wide variety of different styles of wine, not just different sorts of light wine, but sometimes fortified wines too.

South Australia produces more wine than any other state with the wine production traditionally centred on Adelaide. Southern Vales, Clare/Watervale and the Barossa Valley are all important good quality wine producing areas in South Australia. New South Wales makes less than half the amount of wine produced in South Australia but includes the famous Hunter Valley with its wine dynasties and new area Riverina. The state of Victoria also has a flourishing wine industry, notably at Coonewarra and Tahbilk. Queensland, Western Australia and Tasmania are not major wine producers, yet. Some of the better known names are d'Arenberg, Château Tahbilk, Hardy's, Kaiserstuhl, Lindeman, McWilliams, Orlando, Penfolds, Seppelt's, Stonyfell, The Rothbury Estate and Tyrell.

The Australian Wine Centre at 25 Frith Street, London W1 offers good tasting facilities for those seriously interested in Australian wine.

NEW ZEALAND

There have been considerable improvements in the types of vines grown in the north of New Zealand though little wine is exported. Hybrids predominate but Pinotage, Cabernet Sauvignon and Müller-Thurgau are the most common European grape varieties.

NORTH AMERICA

With Australia, California is the most exciting wine region in the world at the moment. Enthusiastic experimentation is backed by a very high standard of knowledge in skilful winemakers and fascinated wine lovers queuing up to buy California's best wines from her 'boutique' wineries. So far exports have been limited but it is now possible to buy wines of most levels of quality in Britain. It is only reasonable to suppose that more and more California wine will be shipped across the Atlantic, if only to satisfy the curiosity of those who read about comparative tastings between them and the great French wines. California wines, all made from European vinestock, unlike New York State wines (see below), can be very good indeed though they deserve to be sold on their own qualities rather than on their resemblance to French classics.

There is considerable variation in climate even within the small strip of northern California that provides such a beautiful setting for the best vineyards.

The classic fine wine producing region (if 'classics' can exist in a wine area so young) is the Napa Valley, a fertile stretch of land north of San Francisco that happens to have a particularly temperate micro-climate housing most of California's most prestigious wineries. Sonoma to the north is rather hotter as is Mendocino even further north but the Alexander Valley just north of Napa shows great promise. The much hotter San Joaquin valley in the interior is the source of most of California's more ordinary 'jug wines' and houses the world's biggest winery, Gallo, which comprises a complete operation, including a glass furnace for the bottles, stopping only at a grove of *Quercus Suber* for the corks. There is also considerable new planting all down the Central Coast south of San Francisco.

Grape varieties play an important part in the labelling of California wine and wine buyers are very conscious of the distinction between varietals and generics. The generic Chablis has almost become American for standard white wine just as Burgundy has become the catch-all appellation for any everyday red. Variations on this theme are Gallo's Hearty Burgundy and there's even Pink Chablis. The ordinary table wines of California are noticeably more acceptable than their counterparts in France, both red and white having a distinctive slightly sherbety sweetness. Because prestige is attached to wines carrying the names of grape variety (which now means that it contains 75 per cent of that variety), a number of varietals are sometimes made of grapes that the European winemaker might want to keep quiet about, but there is no shortage of information for the wine buyer in California. There was even a suggestion at one time that all the 'ingredients', the components of every wine should be listed on the label, until someone pointed out that labels didn't come big enough.

The most successful red wine grape has been Cabernet Sauvignon which is responsible for some wonderfully complex, dry wines, often fuller than their Bordeaux equivalents. Ruby Cabernet, a cross between Cabernet and the much higher yielding Carignane (US spelling of Carignan) has also been very successful here. Pinot Noir imported from Burgundy is still searching for its ideal spot in California but the native Zinfandel has established itself as a producer of versatile fruity wines that can be very interesting.

Gamay Beaujolais is *not* the Gamay used to make beaujolais – it is a flighty relative of Pinot Noir – whereas Napa Gamay is proper Gamay. If a wine is labelled simply Gamay it is probably Napa Gamay. Another confusion is that Petite Syrah is not related to the great Syrah of the northern Rhône, and produces much less substantial wines. Grenache is widely planted and makes particularly good rosés.

Chardonnay is the grape most in demand currently and this white burgundy grape has had tremendous success at California wineries where they have treated it as in Burgundy but not overdone the wood ageing. The white Sauvignon of Bordeaux, Sancerre and Pouilly Fumé has also produced good results, with steely dry whites often called Fumé Blanc or Blanc Fumé. The Johannisberg Riesling is the name Californians give to the real Rhine Riesling and can produce late picked wines of considerable quality. Emerald Riesling is a much lesser variety but can make fresh, fruity whites. Gewurztraminer can sometimes reach the quality of the Alsace original too, and Chenin Blanc, Semillon and French Colombard are all used to make perfectly acceptable whites, often labelled with the name of the grape variety. Rosés are popular and so are the blancs de noirs described earlier.

Large wineries which export on a considerable scale are Christian Brothers, who alone produce the Pinot St George, a heftier Pinot Noir, and Château La Salle, a lovely grapey sweet white; Almaden with a representative range of varietals; and Paul Masson who has done much to popularize Emerald Riesling. Robert Mondavi is a more prestigious winemaker who is making serious attempts to sell California wine abroad. Most of California's top wines come from considerably smaller enterprises too numerous to list in this guide.

The state, not the urban jungle of Manhattan, is responsible for *New York*'s wines, made 'upstate' round the Finger

Lakes from American grape varieties or American/European hybrids. Most of them have the characteristic 'foxiness' which can be offputting for those brought up on European varieties of *vitis vinifera*. The most widely planted grape is Concord which makes a pretty good grape jelly. These wines are rarely seen outside the US even less than California wines.

Similar wines are made in *Ohio* and in *Ontario* across the border in Canada where Chardonnay and Gamay are planted in addition to American vines. There are few states in the US now that do not harbour at least one winemaker, usually experimenting with American grape varieties. Some producers, notably Tualatin, have had considerable success with *vitis vinifera* varieties north of California in Oregon, thought to have great potential as a wine producing region.

SOUTH AMERICA

Chile has been producing good wine for some time now and Chilean Cabernets are no strangers to British wine merchants' lists. She has so far been less successful in making white wines with any freshness but the red Reserva Antigua of Cousiño Macul has delighted Europeans in the past. There are signs however that the wine industry has suffered as a result of recent political upheavals. Phylloxera has never struck the Chilean vineyards, centred on Santiago, so no grafting of vines is necessary.

Argentina produces almost as much wine as the Soviet Union most years, which makes her the world's fourth biggest wine producer and, after Portugal, Italy and France, she is also fourth in terms of per capita wine consumption. Argentina is now starting to think in terms of quality as well as quantity and is making conscious efforts to export her wines. British wine buyers have been looking to Argentina as a source of reliable, if rather beefy, table wines as prices in Europe shoot up. Better quality wines include a Cabernet from Toso, a Riesling from Furlotti and Vino Particular. Most of the vineyards are in the province of Mendoza, overlooked by the snow-capped Andes.

Mexico, Venezuela, Peru and Paraguay all produce wine in a small way (though Mexico's way is getting bigger all the time) but Brazil and Uruguay both have large scale wine industries, so far confined to satisfying the domestic market. The vineyards are concentrated on the Atlantic coast north of Buenos Aires and both American and European vines are grown. Moët & Chandon, are also developing a winery in Brazil producing still and sparkling wines.

ENGLAND AND WALES

The two successive heatwave summers of 1975 and 1976 set Britons planting vines furiously and now the English Vineyards Association has more than 650 members from Cornwall to Leicester, from Pembroke to Norwich. England had a flourishing winemaking tradition throughout the Middle Ages until the acquisition of Bordeaux in 1153 brought a new and trustier source of good wine. Only the monasteries soldiered on trying to defy latitude until their Dissolution under Henry VIII.

English (and Welsh) wine is still necessarily expensive because it is made on a small scale and the Government imposes the same taxes on it as on imported wine, but some quite acceptable wine is now produced in Britain. It is almost all white (although the Austrian red Zweigelt grape shows promise) and the varieties which perform best are, as one might expect, Germanic. Müller-Thurgau, Scheurebe and Schönberger have all produced wines of some distinction with a good bouquet, so long as they are drunk while young and fresh and the Seyval Blanc American/European hybrid that has no pronounced 'foxiness' has shown itself to be remarkably hardy. Chaptalization is usually necessary. Vineyards which have won acclaim include Hambledon (a pioneer), Adgestone on the Isle of Wight, Felstar in Essex, Biddenden and Lamberhurst Priory in Kent, Kelsale in Suffolk and Pilton Manor in Somerset.

8. Sparkling wines

Sparkling wines, the rather ponderous term for some very vivacious wines, are worthy of a book to themselves but this is a brief guide to how they are made and the best known of them. These wines, in which bubbles are produced by gas in solution in them, are the perfect celebration wines. The bubbles are always bubbles of carbon dioxide, but there is great variation in the subtlety of the various methods of getting these bubbles into the base wine, just as there is tremendous variation in the quality of the base wine itself. This accounts for the wide price differential between the cheapest of sparkling wines and the best champagnes.

Any drink called 'champagne' in most countries must come from the Champagne region in north-east France and be produced by the method laid down by the Champenois. They fight very hard to preserve the right to the name champagne, and have won in all of western Europe but have still to convince the North Americans to give up their use of the word champagne for domestically produced sparkling wines.

Carbonation: This is the simplest and crudest way of putting bubbles into a still wine and the so-called 'bicycle pump process' is used only for the cheapest wines. It involves nothing more sophisticated than the injection of carbon dioxide gas into tankfuls of still wine in much the same way as Tizer and Coca Cola manufacturers ensure that their drinks are fizzy. The wine is then bottled while still under pressure. The bubbles resulting from this treatment are large and will collapse after the wine has been in the glass for only a few minutes, even though the bottle probably opened with an unrivalledly showy explosion.

Tank method: (Cuve close, Bulk fermentation, Charmat process) As explained on page 133, fermentation is the action of yeast on sugar to form alcohol and carbon dioxide. It is by capitalizing on this simple chemical equation that every other method of making sparkling wine is based. In the tank method the base wine, having been produced by one fermentation already, is pumped into a huge sealed tank (the French for which is *cuve close*). A second alcoholic fermentation is then provoked by adding sugar and specially cultivated yeasts. The carbon dioxide given off cannot escape the sealed tank and therefore remains dissolved in the wine only to reappear as bubbles when the bottle is eventually opened and the wine is released to the atmosphere. The dead yeast cells, the resultant sediment, are then taken out by a filtering process conducted under pressure and the wine is bottled, still under pressure.

This process, developed by a Bordeaux-based scientist called Charmat, is the most common method of making non-champagne sparkling wines. It produces bubbles that are more long-lived than those in an artificially carbonated wine but is not regarded as sophisticated enough by the French to allow it for the making of any Appellation Contrôlée sparkling wine.

Transfer method: This is halfway between the tank method and the *mèthode champenoise* and was devised in recognition of the fact that a sparkling wine gains character and maturity by coming into contact with the sediment that forms as a result of the second fermentation. This less common method should produce less common wine, for the second fermentation takes place in bottle and the wine is allowed to rest in bottle in contact with the sediment for long enough to improve the final quality of the wine, though not usually for nearly as long as champagne is matured. The wine is cleared of sediment by sucking the wine out of each bottle under pressure, filtering it and then re-filling it still under pressure, into clean bottles before recorking.

Méthode champenoise: This is the finest, the longest, the most labour intensive and undoubtedly the most expensive way of putting bubbles into wine. As its name suggests the method originated in the Champagne region but it has now been adopted by good quality sparkling wine producers not only in France but all over the world. There are producers throughout France (notably in the Loire and Burgundy), in northern Spain and Italy, in the United States, Australia and even in England who are trying out this meticulous method of producing wines that have a persistent stream of bubbles, or 'bead', so that the sparkle remains long after the bottle has been opened.

The best detailed description of the champagne method is given in Patrick Forbes' classic book *Champagne* published by Gollancz, but these are the vital elements in the production of a good champagne.

A blend of cuvée is carefully assembled from a collection of still base wines and specially developed yeasts together with some sugar are added to the wine which is then bottled and sealed immediately, usually with a simple crown cork. The bottles are then laid on their sides in cold, dark cellars for about three years. During this time another alcoholic fermentation takes place leaving a sediment on the bottom of the bottle and giving off carbon dioxide which remains in solution in the wine which gradually gains flavour and maturity through its period of resting on the sediment that forms on the underside of the bottle.

The bottles now contain what can be very delicious dry champagne, but the difficult part, that of removing the sediment from each bottle without losing the gas, is still to come. The solution is ingenious but devilishly tortuous. The bottles are put into hinged boards, *pûpitres*, studded with bottleneck-sized holes, so that over a period of several weeks, the bottles can be gradually moved from nearly horizontal to nearly vertical but upside down. The sediment is gradually manoeuvred on to the cork by dint of some dextrous work on the part of highly skilled men called *remueurs*, literally 'shakers'. They whizz along the rows of upended bottles shaking and tilting them in pairs at the rate of up to 40,000 bottles a day. Each bottle is manipulated thus about 150 times with the sediment each time being persuaded to get a little nearer to the cork until it finally all settles in a clump just between the cork and the wine. The bottles can then be stacked upside down (this is the origin of the 'punt' or indentation in the bottom of them) for as long as necessary until the *degorgement*, 'disgorging'. The bottles, still inverted, are put into a very cold bath of calcium chloride to freeze the necks so that the sediment is expelled as a pellet of ice when the bottles are opened. The bottle is then quickly topped up with more wine into which the required *dosage*, the sweetening, is dissolved according to the style of champagne required. The bottle is then stoppered with a proper, necessarily very strong, champagne cork. Most champagnes, however dry, are given a little *dosage* since the wines of Champagne are naturally very dry indeed. Brut, Extra Sec, Sec, Demi Sec and Rich are, in ascending order of sweetness the most common styles of champagne, though there the exact dosage given each style varies considerably from firm to firm. Bollinger, for instance, have always called their driest wine Extra Dry, but it is in fact less sweet than many other champagnes described as Brut.

FRANCE These are the best known AC wines, all made by the *méthode champenoise*. Most regions produce some sparkling wine, from Gaillac in the south west to Alsace in the north east.

Champagne: The king of wines and wine of kings made in the Champagne region centred on Rheims and Epernay. There is an enormous variation in price and quality, from 'grocers' champagne' hurriedly made and sold in French supermarkets for a fraction of the price of one of the best wines from one of the 'grande marque' houses.

The basic wine is usually a mixture predominantly of black grapes, Pinot Noir and Pinot Meunier, with Chardonnay. Careful pressing keeps the colour of the black skins out of the wine, except for the small quantity of rosé champagne that is made. Blanc de blancs are popular now and are made from white grapes only. The basic champagne is a non-vintage wine and the big houses will go to great lengths to maintain a consistent house style from year to year. Then in exceptional years a vintage wine is made, to combine the characteristics of the house with those of that particular vintage year. The year will be stated on the label.

Then there are, yet more expensive, 'de luxe' champagnes. These are made from only the first pressing of the finest grapes, and matured so that they are just *à point*. Pioneer of these was Moët & Chandon's Dom Perignon but there are now many more, including Roederer Cristal that comes in a clear glass bottle with no punt, Taittinger's Comtes de Champagnes which is a blanc de blancs as is Dom Ruinart, and Heidsieck Monopole Cuvée Diamant Bleu.

Saumur: Some of France's best non-champagne vins mousseux. Made in the Loire from Chenin Blanc grapes. As in Champagne, the wine is matured in underground caves hewn out of chalk.

Anjou and Vouvray: The sparkling wines of these middle Loire regions are less well known than sparkling Saumur. A little more flowery and less steely.

Burgundy: Sparkling burgundy is made in all shades of colour and sweetness though they have been more of a good buy in the past.

St Péray: Full-bodied sparkling white from the Marsanne grape grown just south of Cornas in the northern Rhône valley.

Clairette de Die: Another Rhône sparkling wine from the valley of the Drôme tributary. The Brut is made from Clairette and is clean enough, while the Tradition has varying proportions of Muscat mixed in to make it grapier.

Blanquette de Limoux: A surprisingly elegant wine from the middle of the Midi.

Brands: These blends are usually made by the cuve close method with Veuve du Vernay being one of the best known. The more expensive Kriter is made in Beaune by a version of the transfer method.

SPAIN The Spanish are enthusiastic consumers of sparkling wine, most of it sweet, but some excellent value dry whites are now being exported from the Penedes sparkling wine centre of San Sadurni de Noya in Catalonia. These wines are made from a mixture of local grapes and by the *méthode champenoise*, sometimes using large crates on pivots instead of *remueurs*. They do not have the finesse of a good champagne and have a very distinctive 'nose' but are good buys. Codorniu are the biggest producers and both their and Freixenet's wines are of good quality and exported. Jean Perico, Castellblanch and Castillo la Torre (which is not *méthode champenoise*) are all building up a following in Britain.

ITALY Italy's most famous sparkling wine is of course Asti Spumante, now being replaced by the less rigidly controlled Moscato Spumante. These light grapey wines made from the Muscat grape whose sweetness is retained by stopping fermentation halfway through by refrigeration. They are only about 8 per cent alcohol, whereas champagne is often 13. Italy also makes some dry sparkling wines of which Ferrari brut, made by the *méthode champenoise*, has won most admiration. Also good is Riccadonna's President Brut. Prosecco is a fruity sparkling wine that can be a bit stale on the nose.

GERMANY Germany makes a great deal of wine sparkling though does not make all that much sparkling wine. That is to say, she is an enthusiastic importer of wines which she then turns into sparkling wine or *sekt*, usually by the tank method or some modified version of it. The highest standard of sparkling wine made in Germany is QbA sekt and which need contain only 60 per cent German wine. The best of them can be very pleasantly flowery, combining the characteristics of Riesling type grapes with the refreshing quality of a sparkle. Henkell Trocken and Deinhard Lila are well known brands.

BRITAIN English winemakers at Pilton Manor in Somerset and Felstar in Essex are experimenting with the *méthode champenoise*. There are also sparkling wines made from imported grape concentrate. These include the low-strength Concorde, Tiffany and Britain's best-selling sparkling wine Moussec.

Sparkling wines: the rest of the world

Sparkling wines are made in most wine producing regions with varying degrees of success. The *Russians* are indefatigable shampanskoe-makers, *Australia*'s best known is Great Western, *South Africa*'s is called 'vonkelwyn', and *California* has attracted interest at Domaine Chandon from the owners of Moët & Chandon, no less.

9. Fortified wines

Fortified wines are all wines that have been fortified or strengthened by the addition of alcohol, usually white spirit made from distilled wine. They include sherry, port, vermouth, madeira, marsala, a host of old-fashioned dessert wines and a number of newer aperitif concoctions from countries like France and Italy.

The EEC term for what we used to call table wines, i.e. wines that we would drink with a meal rather than before or after it, is light wines. Light wines vary between about 8 per cent for some lightweight German whites and 16 per cent for some heavyweight Italian reds, fortified wines vary between about 15 per cent for some paler versions of sherry to about 21 per cent for port.

SHERRY Sherry gets its name from Jerez, pronounced 'Hereth', the Andalusian town that was the birthplace of the sherry making process (now copied in bodegas as far apart as Australia and Kingston-upon-Thames). Only the true Jerez product may be called simply 'sherry'. All the rest must be labelled as 'Cyprus sherry', 'South African sherry', and so on. We British drink more sherry than any other nation, ten times more than is drunk in its native land, Spain.

Sherry comes in an enormous range of styles and qualities but the thing that characterizes it is that flat, rather stale smell that would be so unattractive in a light wine but is essential for true mouth-watering sherry. Sherry is made up of a blend of different white wines grown mainly from the Palomino grape in the chalky vineyards around Jerez. After being blended into suitable mixes for different qualities of wine, the wine is stored in wooden casks and classified into *finos* which are destined to become light, dry sherries and *olorosos* which will age to produce heavier, more perfumed wines and then fortified. They are then put into a corresponding solera system, groups of casks arranged so that when a bit of wine is taken from the last cask for final blending and shipment, it is topped up with wine from the penultimate cask and so on with the 'first' cask being topped up with the new blend of wine. This has the result that each cask should, in theory at least, contain a little bit of wine, however small, from the batch with which that solera's casks were originally filled, perhaps decades earlier. This explains why sherry is not vintage dated; it is a blended wine in every sense.

On the top of a cask of *fino* sherry a very strange culture forms. *Flor* looks like soggy Mother's Pride and lies in a thick layer on top of the wine in the cask protecting it from the air and giving it that distinctive tang. *Olorosos* are encouraged to oxidize.

Wine taken from the last cask in the solera system for shipment is usually then coloured and sweetened with special concentrated colouring and sweetening wines and further blended according to which of the following most common types of sherry is required. The more expensive and traditional the style of sherry, the less of this late stage alchemy is involved.

Fino: Very dry, pale and light in alcohol. The Spaniards drink fino from half bottles that can be downed at a sitting without the sherry's losing any of its freshness. The fino's shipped to this country can be as delicate as light wines; drink them chilled and quickly. Very good as an aperitif wine that can be drunk through the first course too.

Manzanilla: Very similar to fino except that it is matured in Sanlucar de Barrameda, another Atlantic port just north of Jerez, where it is supposed to acquire a slightly salty tang. The wine is kept in a slightly different sort of solera system which keeps the wine young and fresh.

Amontillado: A true amontillado is a *fino* that through age acquires a lovely dry richness, a great wine for keeping out the cold on winter mornings. Most amontillados sold today, however, and certainly all the less expensive ones, are just sweetened-up blends, and the word has come to describe a style of sherry that is 'medium' in almost every respect.

Oloroso: This should be a well-aged, nutty, dark golden sherry, but again has come to describe a style of sherry, between an amontillado and a cream.
Cream: This is the sweetest and darkest style of sherry that is widely available, made of *oloroso*-classified sherries sweetened and coloured according to the desired blend. These dark, rich wines are often put into casks that are left outside in the merciless Andalusian sun to speed up the concentration and enriching process. These are the wines for those who feel wicked when drinking alcohol in any other form.
Pale cream: This perverse product of the marketing men is like a cream with the colour removed rather than accentuated.

MONTILLA Poor little Montilla-Moriles, a fortified wine producing region not far from Jerez and even closer to Cordoba, produces wines that are very similar to sherry and can reach higher strengths without having to rely on fortification. The word 'amontillado' means 'like a Montilla', but the sherry producers are so powerful that they have managed to prevent the Montilla producers from using any terms more exciting than dry, medium and cream for their wines. These Montillas can be good value, but should usually be drunk up within a few days of opening the bottle.

OTHER SORTS OF SHERRY There are sherry imitators in Australia, South Africa, Cyprus, and in many other wine regions around the world. Sherry-like wines are also produced in the Rhône valley (Rasteau) and the Jura (vin jaune) in France. The techniques used are usually very similar to those used in Jerez and special *flor* yeasts are often employed. South African sherries can be excellent value and difficult to distinguish from The Real Thing. Cyprus sherry is best when light and dry.

PORT This is the classic after-dinner wine, made in a completely different way from sherry. While sherry is fortified after the grapes have been fermented out, port is made by stopping fermentation of the grapes by adding alcohol so that the wine is both strong and sweet. Port comes from northern Portugal, from vines grown on the impossibly rugged-looking slopes of the Douro valley, via casks held in the port shippers' lodges in Oporto ('*O porto*' meaning 'the port'), the city at the mouth of the river.

Each shipper has his wine making centre up the Douro valley where the grapes are half-fermented so that they still have a lot of sugar in them and then spirit is added, as the point of port is that it should be sweet and strong. But red port, if it is to live for some time, should also be very red as it is essential to extract as much colour as possible from the grape skins. Until quite recently the colour was 'trodden' out, all done by Portuguese feet, but a less romantic process called autovinification is now very much more common whereby the juice and skins are constantly churned about rather as in a washing machine.

The new wine, deep purplish-red, fiery because of the spirit and very fruity from the partially fermented grapes, is then stored 'up the Douro' until the spring following the vintage when it is brought down to the lodges in Oporto for assessment. It is then decided for which of the styles of port described below it is most suitable and the all-important maturation process begins.

All red port starts life as a young ruby and, as it is kept in cask, it softens, takes on a tawny colour and throws its sediment. In bottle, a good port will also mature, but very much more slowly and more subtly, thereby gradually concentrating its flavour rather than smoothing it out. It is crucial, therefore, how much wood age is given to a port before it is put in bottle.

White port: Made from white grapes grown in the Douro valley, either in the same way as red port to produce a medium sweet style or fermented out before fortification as in the sherry making process to make a full-bodied dry white aperitif wine much drunk in Portugal but relatively difficult to find in Britain.

Ruby and tawny: These are the cheapest ports in any shipper's range. They will usually be young 'wood ports', wines that have been aged in wood for only a very few years. The tawny version is just a blend of young ruby and white ports to give a colour and style reminiscent of the lovely genuine old tawnies that rubies become after being kept in wood for a decade or more.

Old tawny: These are the wines most commonly drunk by the port trade in Oporto, blends of wines that have been kept in cask for ten to forty years and have become paler, a lovely opalescent amber with a smooth, mellow taste to match. Note that if a port is described as being twenty years old on the label this refers to the average, not the minimum age.

Vintage port: Only about three times in a decade do the port shippers 'declare a vintage' by deciding that a particular vintage year is good enough to produce long-lasting wines capable of developing in bottle for well over twenty years, sometimes for sixty or seventy. Vintage port is usually bottled when it has spent only a couple of years in wood (it will at that stage be a very tannic young ruby still) and it is expected to do most of the maturing in bottle. Vintage port is quite different in character to an old tawny. It is deep in colour, amazingly concentrated in flavour and once open can continue to improve for many hours. This is the wine for decanters and ceremony, for guessing games about shippers and years.

Late bottled vintage and vintage character: 'The modern man's vintage port' is how Hugh Johnson describes this style. These are wines, from a single year if there's a date on the label, a blend if not, that are not quite up to vintage port quality but are not far behind. They are allowed to mature fast in wood for between four and a half and six years before being bottled so that they share the characteristics of a much older vintage port, though without as much subtlety and depth. Most wines of this sort are not intended to mature in bottle and may be drunk immediately without decanting as it is only after long development in bottle that a port throws a sediment.

MADEIRA Portugal's 'other fortified wine' from a beautiful

volcanic island jutting out into the Atlantic well off the coast of Portugal but still a Portuguese possession. Madeira has been more popular in the past than now, but its distinction is that it is a fortified wine that during vinification is 'cooked', heated up under strict controls to give it a characteristic burnt flavour – and its amazing constitution. Madeira is one of the world's longest-lasting wines and even a bottle left open for weeks can keep without spoilage of any sort. A high proportion of hybrids are planted, even though the different styles continue to be named after the traditional European grape varieties used originally.

Sercial: The 'fino' madeira named after the sort of grape that traditionally produced this dry, aperitif wine.
Verdelho: Another grape and wine name combination. Slightly sweeter than Sercial and less often exported.
Bual: A rich dessert wine.
Malmsey: The sweetest, plummiest madeira made traditionally from the Malvasia grape.

VERMOUTH The vermouth-making process is considerably more commercial than any described so far. The vermouth-making centre of the world is in Turin in northern Italy, well placed for the Alpine herbs that traditionally flavoured the aperitifs. Base wines are shipped up to Turin, often from the vineyards of Sicily and Apulia in the south. They are then denuded of taste, colour and most distinguishing characteristics and then fortified and aromatized by various mechanical means. The word vermouth comes from *vermut* or wormwood which was traditionally one of the chief ingredients in the herby flavouring compounds. Most vermouth producers make an Italian vermouth that is red and sweet, a French vermouth that is white and dryish, a bianco that is white and medium sweet and sometimes a rosé that can vary considerably in its sugar content. All are flavoured fortified wines. The French also make vermouth of which the most delicate are made in Chambéry.

MARSALA Italy's second best known fortified wine. Marsala

is made in the west of Sicily, a rich, dark dessert wine that is useful in cooking and invaluable in the eggy pudding Zabaglione.

MALAGA Another dark, rich fortified wine, beginning with 'M' that has known better days in terms of its popularity. This town on the southern Spanish coast is now better known for its golf courses than for its Christmas-cakey dessert wine.

VINS DOUX NATURELS These honey-coloured fruity wines, often made from the Muscat grape, are a speciality of southern France. The wine is only part-fermented so as to retain some of the sugar, as in port, and then laced with grape spirit. Try Muscats de Beaumes-de-Venise, Lunel, Frontignan and many others from the Languedoc-Roussillon region.

BRITISH WINES These are made 'in the style of' various nobler fortified wines from fermented imported grape-juice concentrate.

Endpiece – the lees

Carrying the wine analogy perhaps painfully far, I should at this stage distil what remains of this book, the lees, to make some mind-blowing concoction that will sustain the reader during his search for good value wines and ways in which to enjoy them at their best.

Instead I will end with the simple wish that this book has helped the reader, in however small a way, to enjoy wine a tenth as much as I do. I can't claim to remember my first taste of wine – it was less of a Pauline revelation, probably more a glass of mediocre amontillado – but I do remember how my interest developed. At my very first job in an Italian hotel I was delighted at the easy relish with which my workmates swigged their *mezzogiorno rosso*. I remember trying to improve my knowledge of wine at Oxford, pressing my nose against the glass of G. T. Jones' front window with the mantra 'green for moselle, brown for hock'. And then I spent a year in Provence where I saw the fascinating mechanics of producing wine for a living. When I got back to Blighty I just had to get a job that involved wine, never dreaming I'd be lucky enough to find one that allowed to me to learn so much about it, and it's been downhill all the way ever since, learning more and more every day.

But I am acutely aware that no matter how willing the wine drinker is to learn, it can be a daunting subject at first. All those unpronounceable names, unexplained rules, snooty wine waiters and wine snobs combine to make wine seem a strangely frightening subject. I hope that this book at least makes wine seem approachable and puts it in its proper context, in your glass to be enjoyed.

Bibliography

These are the books I have found invaluable and would recommend on any particular subject:

GENERAL

Wine, *World Atlas of Wine* and *Pocket Wine Book* by Hugh Johnson, Mitchell Beazley.

Encyclopedia of Wines and Spirits by Alexis Lichine, Cassell.

The Wine Trade Student's Companion by David Burroughs and Norman Bezzant, Collins.

Teach Yourself Wine by Robin Don MW, Hodder & Stoughton.

The Plain Man's Guide to Wine by Raymond Postgate, Michael Joseph.

TECHNICAL

Basic Viticulture and Basic Oenology by Anton Massel, Heidelberg Publishers Ltd.

WINE TASTING

Wine Tasting by Michael Broadbent MW, Christie's Wine Publications.

BORDEAUX

The Wines of Bordeaux by Edmund Penning-Rowsell, Penguin.

Guide to the Wines of Bordeaux by Pamela Vandyke Price, Pitman.

Bordeaux et ses Vins, Cocks et Feret.

BURGUNDY

Burgundy Vines and Wines by John Arlott and Christopher Fielden, Davis Poynter and Quartet.

Guide to the Wines of Burgundy by Graham Chidgey, Pitman.

CHAMPAGNE

Champagne by Patrick Forbes, Gollancz.

Guide to the Wines of Champagne by Pamela Vandyke Price, Pitman.

GERMANY

German Wine Atlas, Davis Poynter and Mitchell Beazley.

SPAIN AND PORTUGAL

Sherry by Julian Jeffs, Faber.

Port by George Robertson, Faber.

Guide to the Wines of Spain and Portugal by Jan Read, Pitman and Faber.

NORTH AMERICA

The Wines of America by Leon Adams, McGraw Hill.

AUSTRALIA

Australian Complete Book of Wines by Len Evans, Hamlyn.

PERIODICALS

Decanter, 16 Black Friars Lane, London EC4.
A glossy monthly magazine on wine with particularly useful vintage assessments by well known wine tasters.

Drinker's Digest, PO Box 63, London N1.
An independent monthly guide of practical help in buying wine. Specific recommendations and up-to-date news.

Appendix

A PRONUNCIATION GUIDE

Here are some of the trickier tongue-twisters that may be encountered by the wine lover:

FRENCH

Appellation Contrôlée	apple-assian kontrol-ay
Ay	eye
Blaye	bligh
Bourgueil	boor-goy (to rhyme with Brummy 'hey')
Bourgogne	boor-goyne
Chx Gruaud Larose	grew-oh la-rose
Montrose	monrose
Rieussec	rear-sec
Suduiraut	sood-er-oh
Yquem	ee-kem
climat	klee-ma
Clos de Tart	klo de tar
Hérault	eh-row
marc	ma
Montlouis	mon-louis
Montrachet	mon-rash-ay
Muscat	moos-ka
Pauillac	poyak
Pouilly Fuissé	pwee fwee-say
Quincy	can-see
Tokay	tok-eye

GERMAN

German names are easy to pronounce if the following rules are observed:

Where 'e' and 'i' appear in combination, pronounce the second one – 'ie' rhymes with 'be', 'ei' rhymes with 'bye'. Hence Riesling is 'reece-ling'.

Umlauts are the dotty pairs above some vowels with the

following (approximate) effects:

ä is pronounced 'eh', ö is pronounced 'ugh', ü is pronounced 'oo' through very tightly pursed lips.

'ch' is pronounced as in Scottish 'loch'.

ITALIAN

As in German, pronunciation is pretty logical.

'Ch' is 'k', 'Gh' is 'g' as in 'goat' not 'large'.

'C' or 'cc' is pronounced 'ch' before 'e' and 'i'.

'Zz' is pronounced 'ts'.

SPANISH

Bodega	bod-aygar
cosecha	ko-secker
Jerez	hereth
Jumilla	hoomilla
Rioja	ree-ocker

PORTUGUESE

This is a fiendish language for the foreigner. They say that so long as you pronounce every word as though you were chewing a toffee you should get by.

The two most commonly exported wines are difficult enough.

Dão (sort of) sounds like 'dow'. Vinho verde sounds like 'vinge verd' in Portugal.

Index